THE UNIVERSITY OF MICHIGAN
CENTER FOR CHINESE STUDIES

MICHIGAN MONOGRAPHS IN CHINESE STUDIES
NO. 51

CAREER PATTERNS IN THE CH'ING DYNASTY

The Office of Governor-general

Raymond W. Chu
William G. Saywell

Ann Arbor
Center for Chinese Studies
The University of Michigan
1984

Library of Congress Cataloging in Publication Data

Chu, Raymond W., 1936–
     Career patterns in the Ch'ing dynasty.

     (Michigan monographs in Chinese studies ; no. 51)
     Bibliography: p. 135
     1. China—Governors—History. 2. China—Governors—
Biography. 3. China—Politics and government—1644–1912.
I. Saywell, William G., 1936–
III. Series.
JQ1519.A598C535 1984   354.5103'16'09   84–29310
ISBN 0-89264-055-3
ISBN 0-89264-056-1

Printed in the United States of America
cover design by Janis Michael

For "C. C."
Professor Shih Ching-ch'eng
Scholar, Teacher, Colleague, Friend
with great respect and affection.

Contents

List of Tables		viii
Acknowledgments		ix
Introduction		xi
List of Abbreviations		xvii
Chapter I:	Historical Survey and Powers of Office	1
Chapter II:	Ethnic Composition and Dynastic Control	27
Chapter III:	Career Patterns	49
Chapter IV:	Professional Mobility: Determinants of Success and Failure	71
Conclusions		87
Appendix 1:	Percentage of Complete Data by Subject and Ethnic Group	91
Appendix 2:	Memorials by Lin Tse-hsü and T'ao Chu	93
Appendix 3:	Official income of Governors-general	97
Appendix 4:	Examples of Regulations and Penalties for the Conduct of Governors and Governors-general	99
Notes		111
Glossary		131
Bibliography		135

List of Tables

2.1 Number of Governor-generalships by Period and Political-ethnic Group, 1644-1911   43

2.2 Number and Duration of Governor-generalships Held by Political-ethnic Group, 1644-1911   45

3.1 Governors-general with the *Chin-shih* Degree   53

3.2 Ch'ing Local Officials Who Began Their Careers with Inherited Positions (by ethnic group)   57

3.3 Local Officials by Ethnic Group, 1796-1908   66

4.1 Average Age at Attainment of *Chin-shih*   74

4.2 Average Age at First Appointment as Governor-general   75

4.3 Length of Tenure in Provincial Posts   76

4.4 Percentage of Governor-general Tenures Ending in Demotion or Dismissal (general averages, and by political-ethnic group)   77

4.5 Percentage of Governor-general Tenures Ending in Demotion or Dismissal (by region)   79

4.6 Number of Governor-general Tenures Ending in Demotion or Dismissal (by period)   80

Acknowledgments

We are most grateful to Professor Evelyn Sakakida Rawski, who read the manuscript at an early stage and offered a number of extremely useful suggestions. Ms. Nancy Evans offered editorial assistance throughout the preparation of the original manuscript. Ms. Patricia Saywell helped in the preparation of the final editorial changes. Mrs. Ruth Maloney of the University of Toronto and Mrs. Joan Pearson at Simon Fraser University offered graciously of their time and talent in much of the typing of the manuscript.

We gratefully acknowledge the financial assistance of the University of Toronto in the research for the book and in its preparation for publication.

Finally we should like to claim that our editors, Ms. Janis Michael and Ms. Janet M. Opdyke, must be paragons of patience and good spirit.

Introduction

The office of governor-general *(tsung-tu)* was the highest provincial post throughout the Ch'ing dynasty. As such, it was a vital link in the control of a vast empire by a very small and alien ruling elite. This is primarily a biographical and statistical analysis of the incumbents of that office. By analyzing the biographical data of those who held the position of governor-general, much may be learned about the nature of the office itself. However, the main objective of the study is to provide information on career patterns, that is, the variety of different posts held from the first official appointment to that of governor-general, of an important cross section of successful Ch'ing bureaucrats. By plotting and analyzing the different patterns their official careers took, we should be able to determine what kind of men reached the top of China's provincial and national administration during the final centuries of China's imperial history; the qualifications that were required; the factors which prompted rapid promotion or sudden disgrace. We should also be able to determine the extent to which these and other factors varied markedly among Manchu, Mongol, Chinese Bannerman, and Han incumbents and whether changes throughout the dynasty can be detected in policies concerning the office or in the career patterns of its personnel. If such detection is possible, this study may lend support to the view that late imperial China was not static, but a society undergoing significant change.

A number of important studies in Japanese, Chinese, and Western languages have appeared that are either devoted to a number of the problems with which we are concerned, or that contain important insights on these issues. While some of these are more exhaustive in their analysis of certain issues, none, to the best of our knowledge, concentrate specifically on the office of governor-general or study it with as broad a sweep of interests as is attempted in this analysis. A good deal of general information on the office itself is available in such studies as Ch'ü T'ung-tsu's *Local Government in China under the Ch'ing,* and the earlier work of Hsieh Pao-chao.[1] No study of Ch'ing government is possible without frequent use of Thomas Metzger's indispensable book *The Internal Organization of Ch'ing Bureaucracy.*

Important early works such as John King Fairbank's study on the Manchu-Chinese dyarchy have analyzed, at least for short time periods, the problems faced by the alien Manchu rulers in controlling the large, ethnically distinct, indigenous population of Han Chinese and in implementing a dyarchy, problems of particular importance to the office of governor-general.[2] Valuable insights into the office and some of its better-known incumbents, especially those of the nineteenth century, are available in such studies as Franz Michael's work on the Taiping Rebellion and Ssu-yü Teng's study of the Nien Rebellion.[3] Also of great value are: J. Y. Wong, *Yeh Ming-ch'en: Viceroy of Liang Kuang, 1852-58*; Liu Kwang-ching, "Li Hung-chang in Chihli: The Emergence of a Policy, 1870-1875," in Albert Feuerwerker, et al., eds., *Approaches to Modern Chinese History*; Daniel Bays' article in *Modern Asian Studies*, "The Nature of Provincial Authority in Late Ch'ing Times: Chang Chih-tung in Canton 1884-1889," as well as his book-length study of Chang, *China Enters the Twentieth Century: Chang Chih-tung and the Issues of a New Age, 1895-1909*; and S. A. M. Adshead's work in *Papers on Far Eastern History* (The Australian National University), "Vice-regal Government in Szechwan in the Kuang-hsü Period (1875-1909)." On many questions related to career patterns or factors encouraging or impeding social mobility, there is an enormous amount of literature already in existence, including a study by R. M. Marsh and the seminal works of Ho Ping-ti.[4]

More specific studies on the office of the governor-general and its incumbents throughout the Ch'ing dynasty normally have included the office of the governor (*hsün-fu*) as well and have tended to limit their range of interest to matters related to the ethnic identity of those who held the posts (collectively known as *tu-fu*). Although, as we shall describe briefly below, the distinctions between the offices of governor-general and governor were few and generally unclear, we have not included governors in this study for several reasons. Our work is primarily a case study of career patterns. If its main purpose was a thorough analysis of the office of governor-general, more attention to the role of governors would have been required to elucidate as fully as possible those elements that distinguished the governor-generalship from the governorship. However, for a study of career patterns, we believe the governors-general alone offer a sufficiently large sample to make the data statistically significant and our interpretation of them reliable. They offer a sample, moreover, for which biographical data is a good deal more complete than for the much larger group of governors. Therefore, in most areas of our statistical analysis we have greater confidence in the reliability of our data on the governors-general, and the extrapolations we make from them than we do in the comparable data for governors. Finally, while the responsibilities of the two offices were deliberately overlapped to provide a system of checks and balances, the governors-general were in rank and status at the top of the provincial hierarchy. (Normally the governor-general held the rank of 2A, while the governor's rank was 2B, though either might hold more senior ranks by virtue of posts held concurrently in the central government.[5]) Unlike governors, who frequently had the final step to the governor-generalship yet to make, the governor-general was more likely to retire or be promoted to one of the highest offices in the capital after reaching the pinnacle of provincial service. Thus, his career pattern was more likely to be near completion than that of a governor.

The first book-length study to attempt a reasonably complete statistical breakdown of both sets of officials throughout the dynasty, emphasizing changes in ethnic composition by period, was published in Taipei in 1963 by Fu Tsung-mao.[6] Unfortunately, Fu's study is based on a sample of 571 governors and governors-general rather than all who held either post and therefore tends to distort the data on many of the issues of concern to us. His sample was drawn from the group of office-holders who warranted biographical entries in the *Ch'ing-shih kao* and *Ch'ing-shih lieh-chuan*, and these men, by definition, were more successful than their excluded colleagues.

An important early article by Lawrence D. Kessler, "Ethnic Composition of Provincial Leadership During the Ch'ing Dynasty," appeared in the *Journal of Asian Studies* in 1969.[7] While our statistics do not always agree, our conclusions on aspects of common concern generally do. Kessler's study is unlike ours in that it includes governors, although for purposes of many of his analyses he isolates the governors-general. It also differs from our analysis in that it is limited to the question of ethnic composition.

Our master list of governors-general with initial ethnic identification was compiled from the *Ch'ing-shih* and checked against other sources such as Yen Mao-kung's 1931 compilation, *Ch'ing-tai cheng-hsien lei-pien*; the official banner history, *Pa-ch'i t'ung-chih*; Ch'ien Shih-fu's *Ch'ing-chi chung-yao chih-kuan nien-pao*; and Wei Hsiu-mei's *Ch'ing-chi chih-kuan piao*. Biographical data was obtained from one or more of the Ch'ing biographical collections such as *Ch'ing-shih lieh-chuan*, *Kuo-ch'ao ch'i-hsien lei-cheng ch'u-pien*, *Pei-chuan chi*, *Hsü pei-chuan chi*, *Pei-chuan chi pu*, and *Kuo-shih lieh-chuan*. In addition, data was also culled from the biographical sections of the *Ch'ing-shih*, *Ch'ing-shih kao*, *Pa-ch'i t'ung-chih*, *Liao-hai ts'ung-shu* (which contains some biographies of Manchus who are not included in the *Pa-ch'i t'ung-chih*), and local gazetteers. Obviously many of the most important governors-general appear in Hummel's *Eminent Chinese of the Ch'ing Period*, and some of those who held the office very late in the dynasty appear in Boorman's *Biographical Dictionary of Republican China*.

The collected writings *(wen-chi)* of leading governors-general were also used for checking biographical information, particularly the chronological biography *(nien-p'u)* and posthumous biographical writings included in the collected writings of some governors-general. The *nien-p'u* provided dates of birth and death, and recorded when examinations were passed, appointments received, and official duties taken up, as well as the reasons for administrative punishments, important events in the official's career, and key information on family background.[8]

Most collected writings have a section which consists of memorials written by the subject. These often will include two particularly valuable kinds of memorials. One type, the *hsieh-en che*, was written by an official on the occasion of his appointment to express his gratitude to the emperor. These provide the date on which the appointment was to take effect. The second, the *tao-jen che*, reported the official's arrival at the new office. As officials were frequently appointed to posts that were never actually assumed, these memorials are particularly valuable in verifying that a post was indeed taken up and in providing the date upon which the new appointee arrived at his office.

The memorials of governors-general were extremely important for other reasons. Official works such as statutes, the regulation of boards, and imperial edicts provide a picture of what was supposed to happen, but do not always provide a reliable description of what actually took place. The memorials offer a more complete picture of the way an official functioned, how he got along with colleagues and subordinates, the limits of his power, and his relationship with the emperor.[9] In some collected writings, information in the memorials is supplemented by copies of official correspondence, dispatches, and comments on the reports of subordinates; these add yet another dimension to the portrait of an official in action.

A large number of rather arbitrary and discretionary decisions had to be made in the process of compiling and analyzing the data on which this study is based. For most categories of analysis, the complete sample was broken into three political-ethnic groups: Han Chinese, Manchus, and Chinese and Mongol Bannermen. We have followed standard practice by considering the bannermen as a single group for purposes of comparison with the Han Chinese, particularly where questions of ethnic control, loyalty, and dynastic confidence or lack of it were involved. In areas for which sufficient information was available, a separate analysis of the Mongol data was performed. However, as only thirteen Mongols served as governors-general throughout the dynasty and complete biographical information is available for only some of them, the sample was in most instances too small to analyze separately. In some areas information on the Mongols was excluded from consideration because it seemed to distort the analysis rather than clarify it. We also separated the complete sample into groups according to the native provinces of the governors-general, which provided a basis of comparison within the Han Chinese group.

In compiling our master list of 504 governors-general, we adhered to customary procedure by including the governor-generalships of water conservancy and grain transport. We excluded those who served only as acting officials and those who were given the full title but appear for one reason or another never to have actually assumed the post. While these exclusions may have distorted certain aspects of the analysis, it seems to us that their inclusion would have presented more significant aberrations. As a result, our complete sample does not coincide with that used in similar studies such as Kessler's.[10]

Data was gathered for the twenty categories listed in appendix 1, but availability varied markedly according to the ethnic group, period of tenure in office, and native province of a governor-general.[11] For the entire sample, information was more complete in some areas than in others. For example, in over 90% of the cases, information was available on degrees held or other initial qualifications, the post held immediately prior to a man's first appointment as governor-general, and reasons for eventually leaving the office. This contrasts sharply with the category in which information was least complete, namely, ages of appointment and retirement, for which the availability of complete data on our entire sample was only 37.5%. Nevertheless, it was encouraging that for the full sample, 37.5% was the lowest figure for completeness of information. This percentage would be recognized by most analysts engaged in this type of research as more than adequate for such a large sample. Indeed, age of appointment and retirement was the only one of twenty categories of bigraphical information in which, for the entire sample of governors-general, the amount of relatively complete data fell below 60%. In the majority of categories the figure was well above 80%.[12]

On the other hand, complete biographical data in all categories of analysis over the entire sample was available for only 22.6% of the governors-general. The fact that this figure varied from 37.8% for the Han Chinese group to 15.4% for Mongols, 14.6% for Chinese Bannermen, and 10.8% for Manchus, increases the possibility of distortion in our comparative statistical analysis. However, these differences lose some significance in light of the relatively complete information obtained for each group in our twenty categories of data (see appendix 1). There, the lowest percentage of available information occurs in the age of appointment and retirement category for all ethnic groups, where availability varies from 58.5% for the Han Chinese to roughly 32% for Chinese Bannermen, 31% for Mongols, and 14% for Manchus. However, in the vast majority of categories, information return for all groups is well over 50%. Thus, both in absolute and comparative terms, our analysis should prove generally reliable. In the case of the Han Chinese group, all twenty information categories have over 50% complete data. For Manchus, only two categories (age of appointment and retirement, and years between first official appointment and first appointment as governor-general) report less than 50% complete data. Chinese Bannermen have three categories with complete information below 50%, the above two, plus number of years between the last degree and the first appointment as governor-general (32%, 42.7%, and 43.7% respectively). The small Mongol group has a total of five data categories with less than 50% complete information, but in four of these the percentage is over 45%.

In terms of differences among Han Chinese representatives, the least amount of data was available for those who came from the Northeast, Kansu,

Chihli, Kwangtung, Anhwei, Kiangsi, and Hupei. It is difficult to read any significance into this, and low availability probably occurs because a relatively high number of men from these provinces had less than distingushed careers, and most of them served in the early years of the dynasty, for which biographical information is more scarce. A much more serious problem was the relative weakness of biographical data for the earliest periods of the dynasty. This implies problems of possible distortion against which no foolproof check was available, since the early years saw a predominance of the Chinese Bannermen and the later years a predominence of the Han Chinese. Generally speaking, our analysis increases in reliability as the dynasty wears on.

Despite the problems inherent in this kind of study, we have chosen not to adopt any hard and fast rule for evaluating the reliability of our information on the basis of sample size and the ratio of complete information. Rather, we have sacrificed the attraction of rigorous and consistently applied absolute standards, and our criteria for maximum discretionary judgments are based essentially on common sense. Normally we do not assign a high degree of reliability to figures based on less than 30% information availability, and percentages higher than 30% are considered suspect if the sample involved is very small. Usually, when we have noted trends or even presented hard statistics for which we feel the sample is too small or the information only marginally adequate, we have stated our reservations in the text. In some cases we have attempted to check statistical patterns against the patterns which emerge from larger samples based on estimated information. For instance, in the case of age of first appointment as governor-general, the figures for the sample with actual ages given was checked against another sample based on estimated age. In these cases, age was estimated by using the average age of attainment of the *chin-shih* degree for each ethnic group, providing, of course, that the year the degree was awarded is known. In most cases, the pattern that emerged from such estimates tended to confirm the analysis done on hard data. In any event, interpretations based on or influenced by this kind of estimate are always clearly noted in the text.

The data in this study were gathered and evaluated entirely without the assistance of a computer. Errors that may be discovered, mathematical or interpretive, are thus entirely man-made, and we make no attempt to "pass the buck" to technology or technician. Despite these many problems and pitfalls, we are confident that the general patterns and trends we trace are accurate, even if not all the markings along the way are as clear to view or free of error as we would wish.

Abbreviation of Sources

CWHTK	*Ch'ing-ch'ao hsü wen-hsien t'ung-k'ao*
CSWP	*Huang-ch'ao ching-shih wen pien*
CWHTK	*Ch'ing-ch'ao wen-hsien t'ung-k'ao*
HCCSWHP	*Huang-ch'ao ching-shih wen hsü-pien*
HT	*Ta-Ch'ing hui-tien* (1733 and 1899 editions)
HTSL	*Ta-Ch'ing hui-tien shih-li* (1899 edition)
LPCFTL	*Ch'in-ting ch'ung-hsiu liu-pu ch'u-fen tse-li*
LPTL	*Ch'in-ting Li-pu tse-li*
SL	*Ta-Ch'ing li-ch'ao shih-lu*
THL	*(Shih-i ch'ao) Tung-hua lu*

Chapter I
Historical Survey and Powers of the Office

In the Chinese provincial bureaucracy, the offices of governor-general *(tsung-tu)* and governor *(hsün-fu)* were collectively known as *tu-fu*. As we shall see the scope and purpose of the *tu-fu* system changed over time. Generally speaking, however, each province (except Chihli and Szechwan) had at the top of its adminstration a governor, and, with some exceptions, a governor-general was put in charge of two provinces. These two officials had direct control over all aspects of provincial or local administration (terms often used interchangeably). The provincial hierarchy included district magistrates, sub-prefects, prefects, intendants of circuit (taotai), and judicial and financial commissioners, as well as other posts related to the examination system and salt monopoly. The governors-general and governors had military, judicial, and financial powers and were generally responsible to Peking for the peace, order, and good government of the provinces over which they had jurisdiction. The relationship between the two officials as well as changes in their duties over the course of time will be described below.

By the time of the Ch'ing dynasty, the governor-generalship, sometimes referred to by Europeans as the "vice-regal," was the highest office outside the capital. It originated, however, centuries earlier during the Ming dynasty. In 1441 a rebellion broke out at Lu-ch'uan in Yunnan Province and the minister of the Board of War, Wang Chi, was dispatched to direct the campaigns against the rebels with the additional title of *tsung-tu chün-wu* (in complete charge of the direction of military affairs).[1] Thereafter, a number of high-ranking, central-government officials were given this title when on military missions in the provinces. From the reign of the Ching emperor (1450-57) on, all high-ranking, central-government officials sent to the provinces on military assignments were given the title *tsung-tu.*

During a southern military campaign led by the emperor Wu-tsung (1506-22) the emperor called himself *tsung-tu chün-wu.* It then became inappropriate for officials to take this title and, in place of it, those sent to the provinces on military missions were called *tsung-chih* (to control all). In the middle of the Chia-ching reign (1522-67) it was decided that the term *"chih"* (to control) would not be used by officials and the title *tsung-chih* was changed back to *tsung-tu.*

The office of governor appears to have originated in 1391 when the Hung-wu emperor dispatched the heir apparent to *"hsün-fu"* (tour and soothe) the

1

province of Shensi. In 1421 the Ch'eng-tsu emperor dispatched twenty-six high officials to *hsun-fu* different parts of the empire. When an official returned to the capital and submitted his report, his *hsün-fu* commission was complete. The governors sometimes held additional titles such as *fu-chih liu-min* (to soothe and settle the refugees), *tsung-li ho-tao* (to superintend the river works), *cheng-ch'ih pien-kuan* (to manage the border defense), or *t'i-tu chün-wu* (to superintend the military affairs).[2] Later, officials were sent as imperial delegates to designated areas and by 1430 this custom "fell into a stable pattern."[3] In the following years, governors in various provincial, special frontier, or strategic locations began to serve as resident coordinators for longer and more indefinite periods of time.

As military crises dictated regional coordination on a broad scale, the governor-generalship system became more institutionalized. The need for this kind of coordination was described by a Ming author noted for his writings on governmental institutions.

> When a disturbance erupted in one province, the governor-general could mobilize the military supplies and soldiers of the neighboring provinces to make a concerted effort to attack the rebels from the front, block them from the rear, and press them from the left and right. . . . After this was over, troops were sent back to their [original] provinces. . . . There is a saying that it is more effective to hit with the fists than to fillip the ten fingers.[4]

While the position was essentially a military one, governors-general were also appointed to supervise river conservancy and grain transport.[5] The first resident governor-general was appointed in 1452 when a rebellion of the Miao tribe broke out in Kwangsi, and the government wanted to maximize coordination between that province and neighboring Kwangtung. In 1465 the governor-general of Liangkuang (Kwangsi and Kwangtung provinces) was concurrently governor of Kwangtung.[6] Most other governor-general appointees during the Ming were responsible for more than two provinces, for example, one official had jurisdiction over Szechwan, Shensi, Honan, and Hunan, and another was responsible for Chekiang, Fukien, Kiangsu, and Kiangsi.[7]

The practice of appointing governors-general became increasingly common in the second half of the fifteenth century. Many remained in the hinterland for long periods of time and served concurrently as governor of one of the provinces under their jurisdiction. After 1453, any minister or vice-minister sent to the provinces, either as governor-general or governor, was given the concurrent title vice-censor-in-chief to enhance his status vis-à-vis the provincial censors. This was the court's reaction to its belief that in earlier years the governors-general had feared the censors and gone too far out of their way to please them.[8] These Ming practices began to change the offices of governor and governor-general from temporary commissions in the provinces held by officials who retained their substantive appointments at the capital, to fully institutionalized posts at the top of the provincial hierarchy.

The final step toward institutionalization was taken by the Manchu rulers. In the early decades of the Ch'ing dynasty, a number of important changes in the tu-fu system occurred. Between 1661 and 1665 each province was provided with its own governor-general. Governors at subprovincial levels were eliminated, and by 1667 each province had its own governor as well. The regime continued to experiment with the regional jurisdictions of these offices well into the eighteenth century.

Strategic considerations frequently dictated changes in the jurisdictional boundaries of governor-generalships. For example, the area administered by the governor-general of Ch'uan-shen (Shensi, Szechwan, and Kansu provinces) was changed in 1748 to cover only Shensi and Kansu. A new post was created to handle Szechwan because the area was considered too large and strategically sensitive to be governed effectively from Sian in Shensi province.[9] Other posts were split temporarily for similar reasons, as when the Min-che region (Fukien and Chekiang), was divided in 1648.[10]

On at least two occasions the competence of individual appointees determined the redefinition of jurisdictional boundaries. In 1727, for instance, Kao Ch'i-chuo, governor-general of Min-che, was perceived by the emperor to be "short of ability to look after the affairs of two provinces." A new governor-general, Li Wei was appointed to administer Chekiang province, although the emperor made it clear that this was not to be considered a precedent.[11]

Just as governor-general posts could be divided for less capable incumbents, new ones could be created for exceptionally competent officials or court favorites. During the Yung-cheng reign, T'ien Wen-ching, governor of Honan, was appointed governor-general of that province and later of Hotung (Honan and Shantung provinces), new jurisdictions created because no other governor-generalship was available. The emperor made it clear that "this appointment reflects special imperial grace and should not be taken as a precedent."[12] In other cases, changes were implemented in an attempt to effect greater coordination of areas sharing common characteristics or problems. In 1734, the province of Kwangsi was removed from the jurisdiction of Kwangtung and temporarily placed with Yunnan and Kweichow because "Kwangsi and Kweichow are areas inhabited by the Miao people. If they are not placed under the control of one governor-general, coordination will often present a serious problem."[13]

The thirty-one different governor-generalships were, for the most part, amalgamated into eight jurisdictions by 1760. The sole exception was the governor-generalship of the three northeastern provinces, which was established in 1907.[14] The provinces of Shantung, Shansi, and Honan were ruled directly by a governor who did not fall within the jurisdictional purview of a governor-general. On the other hand, two provinces, Chihli and Szechwan, were without governors and were ruled directly by governors-general who resided at Pao-ting-fu and Chengtu, respectively. Kiangsu, Anhwei, and Kiangsi, commonly referred to as Liangkiang, were grouped together and administered by a single governor-general with headquarters at Nanking. The other provinces were grouped in pairs: Shensi and Kansu (known as Shen-kan) with headquarters at Lanchow; Fukien and Chekiang (Min-che) at Foochow; Hupei and Hunan (Hukuang) at Wuch'ang; Kwangtung and Kwangsi (Liangkuang) at Canton; and Yunnan and Kweichow (Yun-kwei) at Yunnan-fu or Kunming.

In addition to the provincial posts, other governors-general were appointed to administer river conservancy and grain transport. The number of river conservancy posts varied from one to three, but in their most settled form they carried such titles as director-general of the conservation of the Yellow river and Grand Canal, southern section (chiang-nan ho-tao tsung-tu) and director-general of the conservation of the Yellow river and Grand Canal, eastern section (ho-tung ho-tao tsung-tu) The grain official was called the director-general of grain transport (ts'ao-yun tsung-tu) . All three officials held the same rank as the provincial governors-general (2A) and often served in provincial posts as well. In addition to these, the court from time to time appointed special governors-general.

Concurrent Titles

The early Manchu rulers appear to have experimented liberally with concurrent titles for governors and governors-general. Both offices began with concurrent titles on the Board of War, but, as we shall see later, the military authority and titles of governors changed in different locations over time. The policy on granting concurrent titles to governors-general in the early years is not entirely clear. It appears that prior to 1692 the Ming tradition of providing governors-general with appointments on the Board of War and the Censorate was generally followed. It is not certain that all governors-general in these early years held concurrent posts, but it is clear that those who did always held them with the Board of War and the Censorate.

In 1692 the practice of giving governors-general concurrent titles became more regularized. At that time governors-general promoted from governorships were appointed concurrently junior vice-president of the Board of War and the Censorate. An official promoted to governor-general from a board vice-presidency received a concurrent post as either senior or junior vice-president of the Board of War and the Censorate, depending upon his seniority on a board prior to his new appointments.[15] In 1723 the regulations were changed to include the stipulation that those who had held a previous appointment as president of a board would henceforth be given the concurrent titles president of the Board of War and president of the Censorate. The only variation on this general rule was that the governors-general of Ch'uan-shen and Liangkiang, because of the great strategic importance of their regions, would be appointed concurrently president of the Board of War and junior president of the Censorate, regardless of their previous appointments.[16] The last major change appears to have taken place in 1749. Thereafter, whatever the region of their appointment, governors–general received the concurrent titles junior president of the Censorate and, at the discretion of the emperor, either president or vice–president of the Board of War.[17]

Other concurrent titles were given to governors–general of certain regions. The concurrent position of controller of the salt gabelle was given to the governors–general of Chihli, Liangkiang, Min–che, Shen–kan, Szechwan, and Liangkuang.[18] The title governor–general of water conservancy in charge of the northern section of the Yellow River was given to the governor–general of Chihli, and a similar appointment for the southern section went to the governor–general of Liangkiang.[19] The concurrent titles, superintendent of trade for the northern ports (pei-yang t'ung-shang ta-ch'en) and superintendent of trade for the southern ports (nan-yang t'ung-shang ta-ch'en) were given to the governors–general of Chihli and Liangkiang in 1870 and 1866 respec- tively.[20] Governors could not hold the posts of controller of the salt gabelle, imperial commissioner, or either of the two superintendent of trade positions to which governors–general were appointed concurrently with the governorship. In 1907 the administrative organization of Manchuria was changed. The positions of military governor of Mukden and prefect of Feng-t'ien were abolished and their responsibilities assumed by a newly created governor–generalship for the three eastern provinces. The incumbent in this post also was given the title "concurrently in charge of the affairs of the military governor" (chien-kuan chiang-chün shi-wu).[21]

Governors–general with responsibility for only one province were appointed concurrently governor of that province. This occurred in Chihli (1763) and Szechwan (1748) and for short periods of time in Kwangsi (1723), Kansu (1759– 61), and Fukien (1670). The governorship of Fukien was permanently abolished in 1884. In 1904 and 1905 all other governors–general, with the exception of the governor–general of Liangkiang, were given the concurrent title of governor of the province in which their headquarters were situated. Thus, separate governorships were abolished in Yunnan (1904), Hupei (1905), and Kwangtung (1905). This change was the result of considerable criticism that it was unwise to have these two powerful officials headquartered in the same city.[22]

In 1899 all governors–general and governors were appointed ministers in the Tsungli Yamen, posts they held only until 1901 when this office was re- placed by a Ministry of Foreign Affairs. The imperial edict ordering the appointments indicated that trade matters on the coast and missionary affairs in the interior made it impractical for anyone other than the highest official on the spot to deal directly with foreigners. It also was hoped that the appoint- ments would facilitate better coordination of regional government and the capital, and would force the provinces' highest officials to assume responsibility for this coordination, a task they apparently had been avoiding with the excuse that they were not members of the Tsungli Yamen.[23]

As we shall see below, a number of the more distinguished governors- general held various other concurrent posts in different ministries, in the Grand

Council, and in the Grand Secretariat. But even the regular concurrent ministerial and censorial titles, allowing as they did more direct access to the throne, gave the Ch'ing governors-general immense power and prestige.

Powers and Responsibilities of Governors-general

It is difficult to define the precise functions of the office of governor-general. Generally, he was "to rule over all subjects, control all civil servants, and command all military officers—in short, to be a general manager in the realm to which he was appointed."[24] As the highest provincial official, the governor-general exercised considerable power in the administrative, judicial, financial, and military jurisdictions of provincial government. He was the overseer of the entire provincial administration, ultimately responsible for the maintenance of peace, order, and good government within his jurisdiction. The geographical area of his responsibility could be vast and its population might number in the tens of millions. The duties of the office, the rank of its incumbent, and the distance a governor-general might reside from the imperial capital placed him in a position in which the exercise of great discretionary power was inevitable, and the growth of extraordinary personal power was always a potential threat to the court. That the court recognized the inherent danger in this situation is obvious from the elaborate system of checks and balances created to curb the governor-general's power. In administrative, judicial, financial, and military matters, the autonomy of the governor-general was seriously limited by a labyrinth of rules, regulations, and bureaucratic tensions, particularly in the relationship between his office and that of the governor, the vested interests of local groups, the moral inhibitions of Confucian ideology, and direct imperial control.

The governor-general was officially senior to the governor, but their overlapping duties and the various government policies which required that they consult with each other, submit many joint reports, and impeach each other in cases of wrongdoing ensured that each office would act as a check on the other. This was particularly important at the top of the provincial administration, where in the same geographical jurisdiction the two offices normally were held by representatives of different political–ethnic groups.

While the relationship between the two offices afforded the court an important check on the rise of individual power in either, it also encouraged confusion and provoked various attempts to define a distinction between them. In a 1657 edict, the Shun–chih emperor attempted to define their respective duties.

> The responsibilities of a governor-general are different from those
> of a governor. The governor is in charge of a province. Everything
> that has to do with criminal punishment, revenue, granaries, the

people's livelihood, and official administration falls into his realm of responsibility. As to the office of the governor-general, it is a post established specifically to respond to the needs of a location. The governor-general has overall charge of military matters and has the authority to check or restrain [*chieh-chih*] the powers of the governor, provincial military chief, and other civil or military official. He should devote all his attention to important matters such as making strategic battle plans and dispatching troops. If he is also asked to take charge of the details of criminal punishment, revenue, and the granaries, not only will he be exhausted, but he will be unable to function properly. This will create a situation in which everyone attempts to shift responsibility to others and things will be held up for a long time. If such a situation persists, how can we achieve the goal of accomplishing our tasks by assigning specific responsibilities to a single office?[25]

The emperor then asked his court officials to call meetings to discuss ways of clearly distinguishing the duties of the governor-general and governor on the basis of a given situation in a region or the nature of the matter to be dealt with. The historical record provides no clue as to whether these meetings were held, and, if so, their outcome.

The closest the Ch'ing rulers came to a separate definition of each office was in an imperial edict issued in 1723, during the Yung-cheng reign. In this edict to provincial officials, the emperor referred to the governor-generalship as the post upon which the throne depended most heavily.

A governor-general controls the area of two provinces and has power over both the civil and military administration. He must make certain that the military officers and civil officials work in concert and harmony, and that both the soldiers and people are pacified. Only then can he be considered worthy of his appointment.[26]

The emperor went on to identify the specific functions of the governor-general, pointing out the importance of each, and the consequences of mismanagement or dereliction of duty. The functions were defined as the selection and recommendation of meritorious subordinate officials for appointment, the commissioning of subordinates for special tasks, the maintenance of a pure and honest officialdom, the impeachment of officials, the assurance that all criminals and oppressive officials would be punished, and the responsibility to train troops and check and approve military provisions.[27]

The same edict stated that the office of governor carried with it a heavy responsibility for the selection of officials, the maintenance of peace and order, the transport of grain tribute, the assurance of an abundance of military provisions, and for all matters in a province related to the scrutiny of officials. More specifically, the governor was charged with: maintaining a pure and honest officialdom; selecting and recommending competent and upright officials for appointment; evaluating subordinates fairly for promotion, demotion, or dismissal; impeaching officials; ensuring honesty in the provincial treasury; maintaining adequate food supplies for times of famine; and properly training the troops he maintained for defense against bandits. The governor was also responsible for ensuring that minority populations had an adequate means of livelihood and remained peaceful. Finally, the governor was charged with preventing evil and powerful elements in the community from oppressing innocent people.[28]

Of all known Ch'ing documents, this edict provides the clearest official description of the duties of each office. However, it is important not because it appears to have exclusively assigned a few duties to one or the other office, but because certain specified responsibilities and the general authority of each were similar or even identical. The most significant feature of the edict, in fact, is its lack of a clear distinction between the responsibilities of the two offices. In several places the document both implicitly and explicitly identifies the overlap of duties and the checks and balances intended by it.

A survey of the collected works of seven leading Ch'ing governors-general and governors confirms the broad sweep of shared jurisdictions and shows how the overlap distinguished them from other Ch'ing officials.[29] Both governors-general and governors had the power to impeach any official, a right shared with no other provincial officer other than censors. Both had statutory authority to recommend the appointment or promotion of subordinates to positions up to a rank of 3B, and each had the authority to evaluate subordinates in the triennial "great reckoning" (ta-chi), when all provincial officials with the exception of governors-general and governors were evaluated by their immediate superiors. The governors-general and governors could communicate directly and independently with the central government and with their counterparts in other regions. They also shared the right to communicate directly with the emperor by means of imperial audiences, regular memorials (t'ung-pen), or palace memorials (tsou-che). Regular memorials reported on routine matters and might be referred to the appropriate department or board for comment before a decision was made by the emperor. Palace memorials were usually secret and, unless referred to the Grand Council for comment, were handled only by the emperor. In these ways they could influence court decisions on a broad range of issues including extensions of terms of office, tax remission and famine relief, and changes in the administration of the empire that could reach far beyond their own territorial jurisdictions. Governors-general and governors also shared the right to directly and independently supervise subordinates. They were empowered to command troops under their jurisdiction, to jointly or independently issue public proclamations, and to establish regulations and rules. They could jointly or independently launch an investigation, on their own initiative or as ordered by the emperor, and each could serve as examiner in the provincial, civil, or military examinations.

At one point the 1723 edict states that a governor-general's power extends over all military and civil officials within his jurisidiction, with the specific authority to restrain the powers of the governor. Yet, in the same edict the emperor warns the governors-general that their relationship with the governors was to be one of fellow officials or colleagues of equal status, with the implication that they, as well as provincial military leaders, must consult each other on all official matters.

In general, the imperial demand that the top provincial civil and military officials consult with each other as "colleagues" appears to have been adhered to, particularly by officials who resided at the same location. Sharing some similar or even identical duties, and holding joint responsibility for all the affairs of their region, the pressure to consult was considerable. Certainly it is apparent in a number of documents that they recognized the court's expectations. References to consultations occur in many of the memorials expressing thanks to the emperor for appointing a man to office (hsieh-en che). For example, in 1832 when Lin Tse-hsü was appointed governor of Kiangsu, his memorial declared, "I will discuss all official matters with the governor-general and cooperate wholeheartedly with him."[30] The governor-general he intended to consult, T'ao Chu, had made an almost identical declaration in his memorial upon an earlier appointment to the governorship of the same province.[31] In another example, Governor-general T'ao Mo's memorial upon arrival at his new office at Liangkuang in 1900 clearly stated what was expected of him in his relationship with the governor: "When important matters arise, I shall deliberate and examine the matter carefully with the governor. In no instance would I dare act rashly or arbitrarily."[32] Chao Shen-ch'iao, appointed governor of Hunan in 1704, was much more blunt about the need for consultation: "Since my office is restrained [chieh-chih] by the governor-general, it is inappropriate for me to take things into my own hands and act alone. As soon as I arrived in my office, I immediately corresponded with the governor-general and the provincial commander-in-chief to discuss matters."[33]

The language of consultation became routine in the memorials of governors-general and governors throughout the dynasty. The terms "hui-shang" (to meet and discuss), and "han-shang" (to discuss through correspondence), "mien-shang" (to discuss in person), and "i-chien hsiang-t'ung" (our views are the same) are almost routine phrases. Consultation was not only expected, but reference to it helped persuade the court that the region's affairs were being responsibly coordinated and managed and that the system of checks and balances was in fact working. For the top provincial officials it afforded some protection against charges of rash or arbitrary actions if things went wrong, in which case, as will be discussed below, they would by administrative regulation share the same responsibility and suffer the same penalty.

The topics on which consultation took place covered the landscape of provincial affairs, from the need to raise funds for famine relief to personnel, tax, irrigation, military, and judicial matters.[34] If issues crossed provincial boundaries, the consultations or meetings would take place between governors and governors-general throughout the region. For example, in 1833 when T'ao Chu, governor-general of Liangkiang, attempted to find ways to prevent the smuggling of Huai salt into Chekiang Province, he met with the governor-general of Min-che and the governors of Chekiang and Kiangsu. The meeting resulted in a joint memorial bearing the names of all who participated.[35]

When consultation led to agreement, the officials memorialized the throne in one of two ways: a memorial jointly drafted and signed, or a memorial jointly agreed to but primarily drafted by one, which could be either the governor or the governor-general. (For examples of topics addressed in memorials and the names signed to them, see appendix 2.) Consultation did not always lead to agreement and both governor-general and governor could act alone against the wishes of the other. For example, in 1710 the governor of Kiangsu, Chang Po-hsing, consulted the Manchu governor-general Ke-li about the need to memorialize the throne seeking relief from a famine in the northern part of the province. Ke-li was disinclined to inform the emperor of the famine, probably because the previous year he had failed to report the flood that had caused it, and he attempted unsuccessfully to dissuade Chang from sending the memorial. The court finally responded positively to Chang's request.[36] In the same year Ke-li objected to Chang's attempts to use the triennial evaluation then underway to purge some of their corrupt subordinates. Negotiations between Chang and the governor-general took place over a period of several months and in the end the governor again prevailed.[37]

Of course, the official records of the dynasty and most collected writings of its leading officials deal more fully with instances of consultation and agreement than with the lack of it. Location of the residences of a governor and his superior was one of the factors which determined the degree to which the norm was met. As might be expected, consultation was far more prevalent in jurisdictions where the governor-general and governor resided in the same city (for example, the governor-general of Yun-kwei and the governor of Yunnan living at Yunnan-fu), or in the same province (such as the governor-general of Liangkiang residing at Nanking and the governor of Kiangsu at Soochow). For instance, while Sun Lo was governor of Kiangsi (1688-92) and residing in Nan-ch'ang, not one of the twenty-four memorials included in his collected works indicate that any discussion took place with his superior, the governor-general of Liangkiang whose residence in Nanking was separated from Nan-ch'ang by the province of Anhwei. Yet the memorials he sent as governor of Kiangsu (1692-1705), when he was living close to Nanking in Soochow, frequently referred to consultation and discussion with the governor-general of Liangkiang.[38]

The degree of consultation and cooperation between a governor-general and a governor could also be influenced by personality, administrative style, or the status of the incumbents and their personal relationships to the throne. Perhaps one of the best illustrations of this is the career of Yeh Ming-ch'en, who became provincial treasurer of Kwangtung in 1846, governor of the province the following year, and both imperial commissioner for foreign affairs and governor-general of Liangkuang in 1852, posts he held until 1858. The relationship between Yeh, when he was governor, and Hsü Kuang-chin, then governor-general, was excellent. Working together in Canton during a critical period in Sino-British relations, they seemed to share similar views and administrative methods.[39] When one or the other was out of the city, they corresponded on an almost daily basis, soliciting each other's views, each changing his own opinion on the advice of the other, and, as the correspondence indicates, acting "as one man."[40]

On the other hand, the later relationship between Governor-general Yeh and Governor Po-kuei of Kwangtung was not that of equals. Yeh was Han and Po-kuei a Mongol. Yeh was younger, more industrious, and, while only one rank higher than the governor, had the added prestige of being an imperial commissioner, junior tutor of the crown prince, and a first-class baron.

> These differences in status alone were sufficient to make Po-kuei acutely conscious of his inferiority, apart from the fact that he had been accustomed to receiving orders from Yeh in the Hsü-Yeh era, first as grain intendant of Kwangtung in 1848, than [sic] as provincial judge in 1849, and finally as provincial treasurer from September of the same year.[41]

The gap in status widened when Yeh was appointed deputy, and later, grand secretary. Unlike the constant consultation with his governor-general that Yeh had enjoyed as governor, he frequently ignored Po-kuei, often, for example, neglecting to forward imperial edicts that did not directly affect him. A note written by Yeh's chief office clerk attached to a draft report that he was to send to Peking most graphically illustrates the nature of the governor-general's relationship with the governor: "Last time Your Lordship made the report alone; shall we ignore the governor again?"[42]

Part of Yeh's great personal power derived from his direct and close links with the throne. The same may be said of Chang Chih-tung, governor-general of Liangkuang (1884-89). Both men ignored the affairs of Kwangsi as much as possible, and Yeh, in fact, never went there. Chang "functioned more like a 'super-governor' of Kwangtung than a supervisor of both provinces under his nominal control. He dealt with the Governor of Kwangsi more or less on a basis of equality, probably due to the great distance between them."[43] Chang's domination of Kwangtung affairs, including two long periods without a governor, was "also indicative of a generally neglected institutional trend of the late Ch'ing period. Governors-general increasingly usurped the position of the Governors of the provinces in which they were stationed; these governorships would later be abolished briefly in 1898, and permanently in 1905."[44]

The style of individual officials varied enormously. It filled the spectrum from the aggressively involved, active style of Yeh Ming-ch'en to the more typical reactive, supervisory, and monitorial style of less famous men serving in periods and locations less dynamic than nineteenth-century Canton. Whatever their style, most recognized the importance of establishing, or appearing to have, a common position arrived at through the expected consultation and cooperation. In 1861, while governor-general of Liangkiang, Tseng Kuo-fan wrote the governor of Kiangsi, Yü K'o, about its importance.

> In regard to the financial matters about which we ought to memorialize, we should be especially careful and use as few memorials as possible. Perhaps the best thing would be for you to draw up a draft letter and send it to me for discussion. Once we have satisfactorily settled things between ourselves, then we can respectfully present just one memorial to the Throne.[45]

Virtually all Ch'ing documents that refer to the responsibilities of both offices are characterized by lack of clarity in distinguishing the duties of each. This was a deliberate element of a system of checks and balances, although it continued to frustrate the court as a cause of administrative inefficiency and "buck passing." Imperial exasperation is best reflected in an edict issued in the first year of the Ch'ien-lung emperor's reign stating that, as a result of this lack of a clear line of authority between the two offices, "orders are often changed, things are held up without being done, and people do not know what and whom to follow. Subordinate officials do not know whose orders to obey, decisions often cannot be made, and the whole province suffers."[46] It was a cost the Ch'ing rulers were willing to pay, for, as the Ch'ien-lung emperor also noted, "The original purpose of establishing the offices of both governor-general and governor was to have them check and investigate [ch'i-ch'a] each other."[47] Illustrations of the way this system worked may be seen in the following general description of key areas of provincial power and the constraints on the officials in control.

1. *The Selection and Evaluation of Officials*

Although the power and influence of the governors-general and governors in the selection of subordinate officials was seriously circumscribed, they had statutory authority to recommend to the throne the transfer or promotion of officials to positions of rank 3B or below,[48] and in practice they sometimes recommended promotions to such senior positions as financial or judicial commissioner.[49] Moreover, in the "great reckoning" every third year, the governors-general and governors could recommend various promotions. They also could memorialize the throne asking for a change in an existing appointment. This appears to have been a relatively common practice during the early nineteenth century, for an edict of 1806 deplored the fact that governors and governors-general were far too confident that "such deviant recommendations" would be approved as "imperial favor."[50] The governor and governor-general both had discretionary power in making acting appointments to any office up to first-class subprefect.[51] Frequently the emperor asked governors-general and governors to recommend men of extraordinary talent, whether they held office or not, for appointment to government service. Their advice was also solicited in the rapid promotion of existing officials with superior ability.[52]

Shared authority in this area was sometimes questioned by the governor. On at least one occasion the throne was memorialized by a governor who suggested a specific division of authority. In 1862, Ts'en Yu-ying, governor of Yunnan, in 1862 informed the throne of the tradition in his province.

> In the past, when a civil post became vacant in Yunnan the governor was primarily responsible for finding a person to fill it. The governor-general would be consulted and would signify his support of the recommendation by adding his title and name to the governor's in a memorial to the throne. The process was reversed if a military post was to be filled. This practice was established at the time of the K'ang-hsi emperor [1667-1723] with the intention of encouraging more mutual support between the governor-general and governor. Over the years, however, when unusual situations arose, the practice was always amended to suit the circumstances. This has now become the standard practice. Certain civil posts in the province are filled by persons chiefly selected by the governor, and others are filled by persons chiefly selected by the governor-general. [In other words,] the same task is carried out by different officials. There is no assignment of responsibility to a single office or official in this situation. As to the current practice of filling military posts without consulting the governor, this also seems to be something that was not done in the old days.[53]

The governors and governors-general exercised enormous power in the evaluation of local officials, particularly during the triennial "great reckoning." It is interesting that, while they had the power to impeach each other, one normally could not evaluate the other unless specifically asked to do so by the emperor during an imperial audience. Moreover, financial and judicial commissioners were given separate evaluations by the governor and governor-general. In this explicit attempt to provide a system of checks and balances at the top of China's regional administration, evaluations were to be submitted directly to the capital, and the governors-general and governors were not to exchange views on them. This was an overt attempt to prevent the two top regional officials from "scheming together."[54]

Beneath these high offices, minor provincial officials were initially evaluated by their immediate superiors. These evaluations passed through the hands of the governor and governor-general on their way to the Board of Civil Appointments. Uncertainty as to who was responsible for initiating the triennial evaluation often led to a reliance on tradition. An interesting example of this occurs in an exchange of correspondence in 1679 between the governor of Fukien and the governor-general of Min-che concerning responsibility for undertaking the triennial evaluation of civil officials in the province. New to his post, the governor sought advice from his financial commissioner, who admitted that he too had no idea! Eventually the financial commissioner asked his secretary and was told that traditionally the governor assumed primary responsibility for the triennial evaluation of civil officials and the governor-general for the evaluation of military officials. Consulting his files, the financial commissioner confirmed this and reported his finding to both his superiors.[55]

Since both governors and governors-general could be held responsible for the conduct of these officials and might suffer demotion or dismissal as a result of the misconduct of any of them, performance evaluations were prepared with as much care as available information permitted.[56] Since the normal tenure of a governor or governor-general was relatively short, and they had few means of establishing direct contact with officials below the level of prefect, their contribution to the evaluation process for the lower bureaucratic levels was very limited, a point that occasionally attracted imperial criticism.[57]

Despite the severity of punishment that could be, and was, handed out to officials who abused their prerogatives in the areas of appointment and evaluation, it was not unusual for governors-general and governors to accept bribes. Cash and gifts were frequently offered for the highly favorable evaluation ("outstanding and distinctive") which usually led to an imperial audience and promotion, or for a cover-up of misconduct or mistakes that might have led to demotion or dismissal. In a K'ang-hsi edict of 1666, the emperor acknowledged that some governors-general and governors openly accepted bribes during the year of the "great reckoning" and that the value of these gifts was related directly to the level of office involved.[58] Another imperial edict of 1681 noted that top provincial officials frequently provided unjustifiably high performance ratings at the request of colleagues of the same rank, in expectation that the favor would one day be returned.[59]

As mentioned above, the powers of the governor-general and governor in appointing officials was seriously limited. While the governor-general and governor were answerable to the throne and not to the various boards, the Board of Civil Appointments had great power over the civil bureaucracy below the level of governor-general. With the exception of a few posts reserved for nominations by the governors-general and governors (pen-sheng t'i-tiao), appointments were made by the throne on the recommendation of the board. In the process of evaluation, too, the Board of Civil Appointments and the throne made the final judgments. In these areas, however, the governors-general and governors undoubtedly exercised greater discretionary power in practice than in theory, for their recommendations carried enormous weight. The system itself underlined the importance of the principle of "checks and balances" within Ch'ing governmental practice.[60]

The administrative power enjoyed by governors-general and governors, particularly in the area of appointment, grew during the mid-nineteenth century. The creation of new armies, taxes, and bureaus to collect them, as well as self-strengthening establishments such as arsenals, led to the establishment of a number of important bureaucratic and military positions over which the governors-general and governors had considerable authority.[61] Military exigencies also led to increased use of "military merit" as a basis for appointment to various posts, and to far greater exercise of the power to make "acting" appointments.

It was soon apparent that the throne, as well as the boards, viewed these trends with some concern. In 1868 and 1869, edicts cut in half the number of posts open to candidates with "military merits" and then excluded such candidates from appointments to either financial or judicial commissioner unless they also held regular high degrees.[62] In further edicts of 1876 and 1877, the number of acting appointments that could be made by governors-general or governors at the *chou* and *hsien* levels was reduced to 10% of total posts, and certain kinds of vacancies ("dismissals, retirements, demotions, mourning leaves") were specifically reserved for nomination by the Board of Civil Appointments.[63] Even in times of national crisis, which saw the emergence of such eminent governors-general as Li Hung-chang and Chang Chih-tung, Peking easily asserted its traditional control over the administrative powers of China's top regional leaders.

2. *Judicial and Impeachment Powers*

It appears that the governors-general and governors did play a major role in the normal conduct of judicial affairs. At the provincial capital the judicial commissioner or provincial judge (*an-ch'a-shih*) handled most of the region's legal affairs, except cases of a purely civil nature which commonly went to the financial commissioner (*pu-cheng-shih*). The judicial process usually began at the lowest level of provincial government, that is, at the official office (*yamen*) of the district magistrate, but, except for the most minor cases, decisions were reviewed and confirmed at higher levels. The most important ultimately went to the emperor. At the provincial capital the judgments of the judicial commissioner required the ratification of either the governor or governor-general, but "the fact that the judicial commissioner owed his first responsibility to the Board of Punishments in Peking gave him considerable autonomy."[64] The role of the governors-general and governors appears normally to have been one of ratification and transmittal rather than detailed review or initiation. However, if the case was one for which the penalty might be more severe than permanent exile, they could ask the judicial commissioner to retry it. If they were dissatisfied with the retrial, they could then try the case with the judicial commissioner and report it back to the Board of Punishments.[65] Less serious cases were transmitted periodically and collectively to the Board of

Punishments, while those of a more serious nature were sent on to Peking individually.[66] In civil suits, the financial commissioner's primary responsibility was to the Board of Revenue. However, most civil suits were handled by him and did not go on to Peking.[67]

Within the judicial system, the governors-general and governors did have special discretionary powers and responsibilities. In the Ch'ing dynasty all sentences had to accord with law or statute and could be based on decisions in prior cases only if these had been declared precedents. "Only the governor-general and governor were authorized to cite a prior case and request the approval of the Board of Punishments."[68] The governors-general and governors also were responsible for retrying all cases involving the death sentence.[69] Moreover, it was common for the Board of Punishments to reverse decisions made at the provincial level. When this happened the case would be "remanded to the provincial governor-general or governor with stated reasons for the reversal and instructions to reconsider the case accordingly."[70] The new judgment would again be submitted to Peking for final approval. Frequently a reversal by the Board of Punishments was accompanied by a rebuke of the governor-general or governor. As in all other areas of provincial government, the ultimate responsibility of the top officials for the good conduct and competence of officials beneath them meant that the failure of the judicial process, or more particularly the misconduct or incompetence of its officers, could lead to the disgrace by demotion or dismissal of governors-general and governors.

As the highest provincial officials, with concurrent positions in the Censorate, the governors-general and governors had important powers of impeachment. During the years of "great reckoning" they could investigate and impeach provincial officials who had committed one or more of the "eight proscriptions."[71] At any other time they had the power of special impeachment (t'e-ts'an) over any official in the government, inside or outside their own jurisdictions, who had committed such serious offenses as bribery, acts of obvious incompetence, mishandling of a trial, or cowardice that resulted in military defeat.[72] No other provincial official enjoyed this prerogative.

The exercise of this power was usually based on the report (chieh-pao) of the immediate superior of the man to be impeached, who in turn was liable to severe punishment if such cases were not reported to the top officials.[73] The governors-general and governors did not always rely upon the reports of their subordinates, but often initiated investigations that led to impeachment. As soon as the removal of an official from his post was reported to the throne, the governor-general or governor could "remove his seal of office and his grade-signifying button, and 'keep him under custody' awaiting judicial inquiry."[74] An interesting aspect of the checks and balances system that evolved in Ch'ing government was the stipulation that inquiries initiated by the governor be conducted by the governor-general and vice-versa.[75] While these men had extraordinary power in initiating the process of impeachment, they had no authority whatsoever in determining the nature of the punishment.

A more remarkable aspect of the checks and balances system was the power of the governors-general and governors to impeach each other, as well as subordinates and other officials, including their counterparts in other provinces. Derived from their concurrent positions in the Censorate, this power was defined by the Ch'ien-lung emperor as one designed to "make them check and investigate each other," thereby avoiding situations where they might be tempted to conspire to conceal each other's faults and crimes at the expense of the nation.[76]

In fact, governors-general and governors rarely exercised the power to impeach each other, much to the chagrin of the censors. As early as the Shun-chih reign one censor commented that "the governors-general and governors have been repeatedly ordered by imperial edict to impeach each other, but this [directive] has never been carried out."[77] Later in the dynasty, during the K'ang-hsi reign, another censor remarked that "in the last few years, there has not been a single case of impeachment against the governor by the governor-general of the same province, or vice-versa."[78] That the court considered this a serious problem is reflected in a 1670 proclamation by the K'ang-hsi emperor establishing a new regulation that called for the demotion by three ranks and transfer of any governor-general or governor who failed to impeach a colleague whose misconduct was later discovered.[79] It appears that the threat of demotion did little to correct the situation, for toward the end of the dynasty an official, Hsüeh Fu-ch'eng, complained that "when the governor-general and governor are both improper they will tolerate and conceal each other's faults so that their own [illegal] adventures will not be jeopardized in the future. There is no benefit to speak of from mutual restraint and control."[80]

The difficulty encountered by the court in enforcing this aspect of impeachment was due as much to the complexity and thoroughness of Ch'ing administrative law as it was to the more obvious reasons stated by Hsüeh Fu-ch'eng. The comprehensive administrative regulations under which Ch'ing officials worked made it easy for a high official to transgress a rule which could lead to serious administrative penalties. Ultimately responsible for virtually everything that happened within their vast jurisdictions, the governors-general and governors could be found wanting in any number of ways by a colleague determined to accuse them. They were sensitive to their own vulnerability and were not eager to invite counterattack by accusing others. Ironically, the very rules and regulations originally designed to ensure greater efficiency, morality, and loyalty to the throne sometimes had the opposite effect.

3. *Financial Powers*

There were clear constraints on the financial powers of governors and governors-general, even during the latter half of the nineteenth century when new taxes and other sources of regional revenue improved their positions somewhat. The key official in charge of a province's finances was the financial commissioner, whose rank (2B) was the same as that of the governor.[81] Although governors and governors-general were responsible for evaluating the performance of the financial commissioner, they did not have powers of appointment, promotion, or demotion. The financial commissioner, by statute, was directly responsible to the Board of Revenue as well as his provincial superiors. This unusual arrangement gave the board direct access to the chief financial official and his affairs without going through the offices of his superiors.[82] The board could and sometimes did recommend imperial reprimands of the governors and governors-general. The financial commissioner also had the right to memorialize the throne without prior consultation with them.[83] This direct access to the throne, even if exercised infrequently, enhanced the degree of autonomy the financial commissioner enjoyed within his region. It also tended to restrict the scope of the governor-general or governor's fiscal authority and discouraged abuse of that authority for personal gain. In all of these ways a system of dual responsibility, or checks and balances, effectively limited the growth of regional power and underlined the fact that there were distinct limits to the power of governors-general and governors.

The governor-general's authority in collecting and spending provincial revenues was severely limited. The single most important source of revenue, the land tax, was fixed in accordance with the *Complete Book of Taxes and Labor Service*, (Fu-i ch'üan-shu) which was prepared by the office of the financial commissioner. The collection of taxes from local government offices and their deposit in the provincial treasury were also the responsibility of the financial commissioner.[84] However, semiannual reports on the state of the provincial treasury were prepared by the governors and governors-general and sent to the capital. The Board of Revenue decided what amount could be withheld by the province for approved expenditures and how the balance was to be dispersed.[85] Annual budgetary estimates and reports of expenditures made to Peking by the governors-general and governors were based on the reports of the financial commissioner.[86] These were audited, approved or rejected, and returned to the provinces by the Board of Revenue. Final budgetary approval was an imperial prerogative.[87] In addition to allocations for estimated expenditures specified in the annual winter estimates *(tung-ku)* the provinces, with the exception of Chihli, were given a reserve fund *(liu-ch'u)* for exigencies. The amount of this fund was fixed for each province and the governors-general and governors were clearly instructed not to use it without prior approval from the central government. Failure to comply with this regulation often led to the dismissal, and even imprisonment, of a governor-general or governor.[88] Control over funds for large projects such as famine or flood relief and military operations was retained by the central government. Even during crises, when relief was urgently required, it appears that the governor-general did not have the right to transfer funds from one of his provinces to another without prior imperial consent.

The allocation of land and miscellaneous taxes to provincial and local governments was never sufficient to cover required expenditures, and only the existence of a surcharge system prevented major deficits.[89] Of all the surcharges, the largest was the so-called meltage fee *(hao-hsien)* which originally was collected to supplement officials' salaries, meet deficits, and pay certain types of public expenses such as the cost of repairing government offices.[90] In practice, the rate for this tax was decided by the district *(chou and hsien)* government in consultation with leaders of the local gentry. Only after the mid-nineteenth century was the responsibility for setting this rate gradually shifted to the governor-general and governor.[91] Even then, they could not use these funds without imperial approval for any amount in excess of five hundred taels of silver. For amounts between three and five hundred taels, the governor-general or governor could authorize payments but had to report the nature of the expenditures to the Board of Revenue.[92]

The powers of these officials were limited severely in other areas of tax collection and expenditure. For instance, while the salt tax was administered by a salt intendant who was under the supervision of the governor-general, the tax was for the exclusive use of the central government. In exercising control over this area of revenue collection, the governor-general acted more as an imperial agent than a chief executive in charge of the provincial salt administration.[93] Similarly, provincial customs duties were administered by superintendents, some commissioned by the emperor, some recommended by the Board of Revenue, and some delegated by the governors-general and governors. In all cases, however, they came under the direct jurisdiction of the Board of Revenue rather than that of the governors-general and governors.[94]

The governors-general and governors did increase their financial powers in the second half of the nineteenth century. This derived in particular from administration of the likin—new internal transit and exise duties. The governor-general and governor appointed the administrators of bureaus set up to handle likin receipts and expenditures, while the financial commissioner had authority over more junior personnel. While the court ordered the provinces to submit semiannual reports on likin funds in 1857, this did not become standard practice until the 1870s, and even then the figures reported were not precise. Moreover, likin funds were deposited, not in the accounts of the financial commissioner, but in the headquarters of the provincial likin bureaus. These were controlled by officials appointed by the governor-general and governor, who also authorized expenditures of the funds.[95]

In much the same way, the governors-general and governors of coastal provinces won greater financial power because they supervised imperial maritime customs receipts. Although the assessment was administered by a foreign officer, the funds were paid into native banks commissioned by the superintendent of customs. This official "was usually concurrently the taotai [intendant of circuit] of the treaty-port area who came to be among the few regular provincial officials nominated by the governor-general or governor."[96] While 40% of these monies were allocated to a special fund in the Board of Revenue, the provinces retained a good deal of the remaining 60%, and the governors, governors-general, and taotai exercised some control over the timing of remittances. Along with this greater financial power went a corresponding increase in control of the provincial bureaucracy. In general, most new offices, bureaus, and agencies were created and staffed through appointments made by governors-general and governors rather than the Board of Civil Appointments.[97] These new financial and administrative powers were offset somewhat by increasing provincial and national demands for larger assessments from new sources of revenue, as well as by the creation in 1863 of fixed annual quotas for provincial contributions to the capital.[98] In post-Taiping China, the governors-general and governors enjoyed increased financial autonomy largely through the creation of new sources of revenue more directly under their administrative control. At the same time, however, a multitude of new demands for expenditure of these resources—provincially, nationally, and within the capital—placed additional pressures and frequent professional perils in the lap of the governors and governors-general.

4. *Military Powers*

The alien Manchu rulers were particularly sensitive to the potential threat of Han regional leaders with any kind of military power. Within a century of the founding of the Ch'ing dynasty, the banner forces deployed throughout the land as a check on regional power and internal rebellion ceased to be an effective military force. Perhaps as early as the end of the seventeenth century, the Green Standard Army became the main fighting force of the Ch'ing dynasty.[99] Almost three times the size of the banner forces, its six hundred thousand predominantly Han officers and soldiers were spread out across the vast empire. The Manchu rulers implemented a number of measures to ensure that a large military force of Han Chinese, combined with the highest regional officials of Han origin, did not pose an awesome threat to the dynasty's internal security.

While governors-general were nominally the supreme commanders of provincial forces, there were a number of checks on their real authority. The direct authority of the Board of War over the empire's armies was emphasized by each governor-general's concurrent title of president or vice-president of the board. The Board of Revenue placed another serious constraint on the potential military power of the governor-general, as its approval was required for all military expenditures, including salaries and provisions.[100] While weapons were usually made locally, any expenditure on them in excess of one thousand taels of silver required prior approval from Peking.[101]

With the exception of lieutenant (*ch'ien-tsung*) and sublieutenant (*pa-tsung*) the governors-general in most provinces had no power to appoint middle-grade officers to positions ranging from second captain (*shou-pei*) to colonel (*fu-chiang*). For appointments below the top regional military post of provincial commander-in-chief *(t'i-tu)* and brigadier general *(tsung-ping)*, the governor-general could recommend candidates to the Board of War, which made a final recommendation to the throne.[102] Normally the governor-general made his recommendation before the position became vacant.[103] While this system, known as *yü-pao* (recommending candidates before a vacancy occurs) was not an inflexible regulation, few positions were filled on a governor-general's recommendation after vacancies occurred.[104] The military "great reckoning" *(chün-cheng)* took place every five years, and the governor-general played an important, though not completely independent, role in it. While initial evaluations were submitted by an officer's superior, reports on officers from colonel to lieutenant required the governor-general's approval and comments before it was forwarded to the Board of War.[105] Senior officers (colonel and lieutenant colonel) were evaluated jointly by the governor-general, governor, provincial commander-in-chief, and brigadier general. Recommendations for promotion from colonel to brigadier general, based on outstanding achievement, were made jointly by the governor-general and the commander-in-chief.[106]

The system of checks and balances included the relationship between the most senior military and civil officials. Early imperial edicts reflect a deliberate effort to make the two highest civil and military offices work both as a team of equals and as a constraint upon the powers of the others. The 1723 edict from the Yung-cheng emperor instructed all governors-general to consider governors and provincial commanders-in-chief as their "colleagues of equal status" and ordered that with regard to "all local affairs, military or civil, you should consult and discuss with each other . . . and avoid being obstinate in your views."[107]

The governor-general in theory and practice held the supreme military position throughout the dynasty, but the military authority of the governors varied according to period and location. They had considerable military responsibility during the first reign of the dynasty, as reflected in the wording of their titles. All were concurrently vice-presidents of the Board of War, and a significant number of them had as part of their official terms of appointment the words *"t'i-tu chün-wu"* (to command and supervise military affairs) or *"tsan-li chün-wu"* (to assist in the management of military affairs).[108] Moreover, they had regiments under their direct command varying in size from fifteen hundred to two thousand troops. These responsibilities were altered in 1662 when the court apparently decided that governors should devote all their attention to civil administration and be relieved of their military duties. The words *"t'i-tu chün-wu"* were removed from their titles, and their concurrent vice-presidential appointment was transferred from the Board of War to the Board of Works. Their troops were placed under the command of the governors-general.[109]

With the outbreak of the Wu San-kuei Rebellion in 1673, Peking again changed its policy on provincial military authority. In order to improve the coordination of civil and military administration at the regional level, particularly in areas affected by the rebellion and specifically in those provinces without a resident governor-general (for example, in Kiangsi or Kweichow), the governors were again assigned military responsibilities. Their concurrent vice-presidential title reverted to the Board of War, and they were given troops to command.[110]

When the rebellion was stamped out, the number of troops under the governors' control was generally reduced, but their concurrent titles with the Board of War remained. Apparently, until the middle of the nineteenth century the governors of provinces that fell within the jurisdiction of a governor-general no longer were expected to play a significant military role and for the most part did not do so. However, in Shantung, Shansi, and Honan—provinces which did not come under the jurisdiction of a governor-general—the situation was very different. The governors of those provinces were given the concurrent titles of provincial commander-in-chief in 1743, 1734, and 1740 respectively, and each controlled the entire Green Battalion of his province.[111] Of all the governors, these three exercised the greatest military authority, but at different times others were given considerable control. The governors of Anhwei and Kiangsi were appointed provincial commander-in-chief in 1803 and 1749 respectively. The governors of Kweichow, Kwangsi, and Hunan, in 1753, 1731, and 1724, were given official appointments that included the words "chieh-chih t'ung-sheng ping-ma" (to control all the troops in the province).[112]

With the onset of rebellion and war in the mid-nineteenth century, the military authority of provincial leaders became far less clear. The military role of the governors often depended on the exigencies of the moment and the individual's relations with other regional leaders and the central government. Expediency, pragmatism, and personal opportunity could lead to a greatly expanded military role. The ability of a provincial leader to organize an army, to raise revenues to support it, to deal effectively with emergencies, and to win on the battlefield became more important than tradition, titles, or terms of appointment.

With their ex-officio positions in the Censorate, the governors-general and governors had the power to impeach all provincial military officers. However, both commanders-in-chief and brigadier generals had the right to submit memorials directly to the throne, by-passing the governors and governors-general and reporting not only on general local conditions but on specific affairs, particularly on matters their provincial superiors failed to report (presumably in the hope of avoiding responsibility for them).[113] These military officers also had the right to request an audience with the emperor. This direct access to the throne enjoyed by their military colleagues obviously placed severe limits on the real and potential military power of the governors and governors-general.

The command structure of the provincial military forces provides another excellent example of the Manchu rulers' determination to institute a complex system of checks and balances. While the governor–general was nominally in charge of the entire Green Standard Army, in fact he had only a small detachment *(tu-piao)* under his direct personal command, and had only general control over the other forces in the province(s) under his jurisdiction. He could exercise his power of command only by issuing orders to the provincial commander-in-chief, who in turn had direct control only over his own detachment *(t'i-piao)*, and was forced to exercise his broader responsibilities through the brigadier generals. While the size of the detachments varied significantly, those of the provincial commander-in-chief and the brigadier generals were invariably larger than those of the governor–general.[114]

In times of peace, the governors–general and governors had to obtain imperial approval for the deployment of troops within their areas of jurisdiction. While these requests were normally granted, it is significant that approval had to come from Peking. During large–scale campaigns, military command was usually assumed by an imperial commissioner who was frequently either a prince or a high central–government official. While there were a number of reasons for this practice, one of the most obvious was the added control it gave Peking over the region's highest resident officials.[115] On other occasions, especially in the nineteenth century, a governor–general often was given a concurrent appointment as imperial commissioner, which greatly enhanced his military authority.[116]

In the final half–century of the dynasty, rebellion, war, and a weakening central government augmented the military power, as well as financial resources, of the governors–general and governors. Their increased military authority in post-Taiping China has been discussed in a number of studies and need not be documented here.[117] The exigencies of war and rebellion led to the development of a new type of army, the "brave battalions" *(yung-ying)*, mainly directed by the governors–general and governors, the largest of which was Tseng Kuo-fan's Hunan Army, which numbered 120,000 men. These were the armies that suppressed the rebellions and served as the main provincial security force. Unlike the regular army, key officers in the "brave battalions" were appointed by the governors and governors–general, in a procedure known as "commissioning by letter" *(cha-wei)*. Apparently the appointment of these commanders did not require the prior approval of the emperor or of the Board of War, unless a commander also was given a rank in the Green Standard forces.[118] However, many officers sought concurrent titles or posts in the regular army, for it gave them added perquisites and prestige. The court was more than willing to oblige because those who held concurrent positions were under Peking's direct control. This weakened their ties to the governors–general and governors and imposed yet another limit on regional autonomy. Moreover, "once such lofty appointments were made, the fortunate commanders were required to come to Peking for an audience with the throne, thus to be reminded where real authority lay."[119]

Conclusion

It is readily apparent that even during the final decades of the Ch'ing dynasty, the power of the governors-general was severely limited, in no small part by the wide range of responsibilities they shared with the governors and the system of checks and balances between them. Constraints were imposed from above by the throne and the various boards and from below by a complex network of vested interests. These limits were reinforced by a host of inhibitions placed on bureaucratic autonomy in general by Confucian ideology and morality. The throne retained absolute power over the appointment, demotion, and dismissal of a governor-general almost to the end of the dynasty, while the boards retained a remarkable degree of control over this regional bureaucracy. By an elaborate system of checks and balances in which "Peking controlled the appointment of key personnel, the military and financial power of the governors-general and governors was severely circumscribed."[120] Local vested interests in both the military and financial spheres imposed other limitations on their autonomy. Moreover, the extraordinary emphasis placed on loyalty to the monarch within Confucian ideology, reinforced when the governors-general personally received imperial instructions, resulted in an atmosphere in which even the most powerful regional leaders "would hardly have regarded separatism or insubordination as real possibilities."[121] The combination of direct control from above, indirect control from below, and the pervasive range of moral and ideological inhibitions against the growth of great personal power meant that throughout the Ch'ing dynasty the authority of the governors-general was very seriously circumscribed.

Nevertheless, as the highest regional official, the governor-general could and did exercise very real power. That power was in itself an important check on the growth of despotism.

> Any notion of increasing despotism in Ming and Ch'ing times should be balanced against the fact that "appellate" decision-making, with many decisions being proposed by the governors and governors-general, was a major part of the executive process in those periods. In other words, power is not only the power of ultimate decision but also the power of making proposals, and we seem to see a long-term tendency in Chinese history for the latter kind of power to be diffused from the prime office in the capital to high regional offices.[122]

That the alien Manchu rulers recognized both the real and potential power of their highest regional officials is apparent from the elaborate system of checks and balances discussed above. It will be equally apparent in the chapters that provide an analysis of the career patterns of governors-general. The analysis demonstrates the court's determination to impose other checks as well, for example, short tenures, frequent transfers, and strict emphasis on civil rather than military appointments.

Within the framework of general national policy, as outlined by imperial edict, administrative codes, precedent, and custom, the governor-general unquestionably possessed a considerable degree of administrative autonomy and "appellant" or "policy-influencing" power. And yet, almost by definition, this power was normally exercised with great caution, for order, control, and the protection of the status quo, not innovation, were the hallmarks of government in imperial China. Along with the privileges of high government office went its perils. The miscarriage of justice at any level in the provincial administration; the revelation that administrative incompetence, miscalculation, or corruption had not been handled with a firm hand; the failure to provide sufficient corvée or taxes; the outbreak of banditry or rebellion—these and many other misfortunes could befall governors-general who at any time might face demotion, dismissal, banishment, or even execution. As we shall see, over a quarter of the tenures in office of all governors-general ended in either demotion or dismissal.[123] Clearly, it was an office of the utmost importance throughout the Ch'ing dynasty, and one in which extraordinary demands were made on the more than five hundred men who held it.

Chapter II

Ethnic Composition and Dynastic Control

In his role as the highest government official residing outside the capital, the governor-general was the critical link in a chain of command which extended from a small group of alien rulers in Peking to the hundreds of millions of Chinese across a vast empire. If the Ch'ing court gave a high priority to the governor-general's function as a key official in the Manchus' control of an indigenous Han population, loyalty must have been as important a criterion as ability or any other consideration in the selection of men for this office. The court's concern with loyalty, as well as with competence, was reflected in the men it chose and the ways they were appointed.

Eligibility

According to the *Ch'in-ting li-pu tse-li* (Imperially endorsed [compilation of] regulations of the Board of Civil Appointments) those eligible for appointment to the position of governor-general were the president of the Censorate, the governors, and the vice-presidents of boards. Although the post held immediately prior to appointment varied according to both ethnic group and period, the most common route to the governor-generalship was an immediately preceding governorship. Other offices from which appointments to a governor-generalship were common were board presidencies and vice-presidencies (including positions in the Censorate), provincial commander-in-chief and other high military posts, and, to a lesser extent, grand councillor and grand secretary. Assistant grand secretaries were also occasionally appointed governors-general.

On the question of the ethnic identity of governors-general, there appear to have been implicit constraints according to period and location, but the Manchu rulers evidently made only one formal ethnic restriction. This occurred in 1669 when the court ruled, for reasons to be discussed in the next chapter, that only Manchus could serve as governor or governor-general in the Shensi-Shansi area. This restriction was rigidly enforced until it was officially abandoned in 1723.[1] Indeed, it was the only governor-generalship in which, during the course of the entire dynasty, Manchus held over 50% of the tenures. They also held it for a higher percentage of total time (47%) than any other governor-generalship. Only 25% of the tenures in Shen-kan were held by Han Chinese (for 26% of the time), while the Chinese Bannerman-Mongol group also held 25% of the posts (for 27% of the time). In fact, Han Chinese were appointed less often in Shen-kan than in any other region in the empire.[2]

Methods of Appointment

Throughout the Ch'ing dynasty, the selection of high officials (rank 3 and above) remained an imperial prerogative. The degree to which it was directly exercised varied from period to period, as did the criteria for selection and the procedures of recommendation. These changes are of considerable importance because they reflect the overall evolution of Ch'ing government, its loci of effective control, and the dynamic nature of power relationships between the throne and the empire's highest officials. While no single method of selection was used to the exclusion of others in any given reign, there were three basic procedures, each employed with different rates of frequency in different periods.

1. The Method of Hui-t'ui

During the first half-century of Manchu rule, the emperor normally asked one of the two most powerful consultative bodies, either the Assembly of Nine Ministers and Censors, or, much less frequently, the Assembly of Deliberate Princes and Ministers, to meet and make nominations for appointment to vacant governor-generalships. Names of the nominees were recorded in a list of joint nominations (hui-t'ui-pen) which supposedly included detailed information on the nominee's qualifications and past administrative performance.[3] This list was submitted to the emperor by the president of the Board of Civil Appointments for a final decision.

Like many Ch'ing institutional practices, this method of selecting governors-general, known as hui-t'ui was inherited from the Ming dynasty. It was probably instituted during the reign of Hsien-tsung (1465-87), when hui-t'ui and t'e-chien (special imperial appointment) were the two predominant methods of selecting high officials.[4] It is not clear when the hui-t'ui method of selection was first practiced in the Ch'ing dynasty. It is certain that it was institutionalized in 1649 when the Shun-chih emperor decreed that governors-general and governors would thereafter be selected by this method. It is interesting that the emperor also decreed that any member of the assembly could include his own name in the list of nominees. While the assembly as a whole did not assume responsibility for the future conduct of its nominees, an individual nominator did if he chose to place his name beside that of a specific candidate he had nominated.[5]

The list of nominations sent to the emperor indicated the assembly's first choice and alternative. The emperor did not always accept these recommendations. On occasion he referred the matter back to the assembly for further consideration, and at other times he rejected the list and made his own appointment.[6] However, the imperial veto was rarely exercised for it represented a clear "vote of no-confidence" in the powerful assembly.

A number of problems developed in this method of selection. For example, the assembly was directed to meet and decide on the second day following imperial notice of a vacancy, which did not allow adequate time for thorough deliberation.[7] Another problem involved the criteria for selection; in particular, the factor of seniority. Despite imperial instructions of 1654 stating that the assembly should disregard rank and give priority to ability, the nominees were usually chosen on the basis of seniority.[8]

During the K'ang-hsi reign a number of other problems arose which eventually led to the abandonment of this form of selection. Nepotism and factionalism became major determinants in the nomination process. Not only did assembly members increasingly recommend their former students, fellow graduates, relatives, acquaintances, and fellow provincials, but deals were frequently made among assembly members, who would win votes for one nomination with the promise of support for other candidates at subsequent meetings.[9] Moreover, the assembly came to be dominated by a few powerful members, usually Manchus, who were able to "pack" the lists with their favorites.[10] Assembly members seldom provided anything more than a general description of their candidates' abilities, and even the emperor noted that members appeared more interested in rapid decisions and quick adjournment than serious or protracted consideration.[11]

Although the *hui-t'ui* system was officially abolished in 1671, it lingered on in practice until 1712, probably because the emperor, insecure in his own position, was reluctant to withdraw too abruptly a privilege enjoyed by the powerful assembly for more than two decades.[12]

2. The Method of K'ai-lieh

Instituted in 1671, the *k'ai-lieh* (listing) system was the predominant method of selecting governors-general after the Ch'ien-lung reign. Under this system, when vacancies occurred, the Board of Civil Appointments memorialized the throne asking the emperor if he wished to fill it by special imperial appointment (see section 3, below). If the emperor did not plan to make the appointment himself, he would instruct the board, or in subsequent reigns either the board or the Grand Council, to forward a list of candidates to him. The number of candidates varied from time to time, but there were always at least ten names on the list.[13]

Each list had a prescribed order. The first group, known as *ying-kai* (due for change), included the names of officials holding posts of equivalent rank to the governor-generalship, such as the president of a board or the Censorate. The next group, *ying-tiao* (due for transfer), consisted of officials who held similar posts, usually governors-general in regions. The third group, *ying-sheng* (due for promotion), included officials of lower rank than the governor-general such as governors and vice-presidents of boards.[14]

Names within each group were ordered according to seniority.[15] While the emperor reserved the right to ignore seniority and appoint whomever he wished, the information on each candidate was normally so minimal that he would usually make his decision on the basis of this ranking. The dilemma faced by the emperor, that tended to dictate a decision based on seniority, was explicitly identified by the Chia-ch'ing emperor in an 1801 edict: "Ability and seniority are equally stressed in the appointment policy of the country. There is no reason why seniority should be ignored. When a list of candidates is submitted, how can I know all the candidates well? Naturally, I cannot and therefore make an appointment based on seniority."[16]

The *k'ai-lieh* system had certain clear advantages over the *hui-t'ui* method of selection. It allowed consideration of a greater number of candidates and permitted the throne more discretion in making a final choice. While the earlier system did not bind the emperor to a choice of either of the two candidates recommended, frequent rejection of the assembly's recommendations would have created an unfortunate tension between the court and its highest officials. Moreover, the *k'ai-lieh* method was inherently more objective and less susceptible to factionalism or favoritism. The lists were compiled according to the records of candidates' performance which were kept by the Board of Civil Appointments. No documentary evidence suggests that it was in any sense as subject to abuse as the earlier method.

3. *The Method of T'e-chien*

Throughout the Ch'ing dynasty the emperor reserved the right to select high officials without consulting any government body.[17] This system was known as *t'e-chien* (appointment by special imperial decree) and officials chosen in this way were called *t'e-chien-kuan*. In the first two reigns of the dynasty, high officials were usually selected by the *hui-t'ui* or *k'ai-lieh* methods, and *t'e-chien* was used only in extraordinary circumstances. However, appointment by special imperial decree became commonplace in the Yung-cheng reign. The explanation for the Yung-cheng emperor's personal appointment of most high officials probably lies in his own background. Having witnessed the severe factional struggles for power that characterized the latter part of his father's rule and the resulting promotion of a large number of incompetent men to high office, the emperor initiated a number of moves designed to increase his own power and direct control over the Chinese bureaucracy. His creation of the Grand Council, consisting of a small group of hand-picked confidants vested with various areas of authority formerly held by different power groups, and his increased use of secret palace memorials to ensure the loyalty and competence of his high officials, were designed to tighten his own autocratic rule.[18]

The Yung-cheng emperor was fully conscious of the dependence of effective autocratic power on the success of policy execution, which could only be guaranteed by loyal and competent officials. He thus attached immense importance to the selection of the empire's highest officials. The Yung-cheng emperor paid little attention to seniority, but adhered to a policy of "*sui-ts'ai shih-yung, liang-neng shou-chih*" (to use a person according to his talents and to appoint an official according to his strength).[19] In an edict of 1729, the Yung-cheng emperor made it clear that even a district magistrate or prefect could be appointed governor or governor-general provided he had the required ability.[20]

Succeeding emperors reverted to a policy of selecting their high officials after consultation and usually through the *k'ai-lieh* system. Appointment by special imperial decree again became the exception. The *t'e-chien* method became common during the second half of the nineteenth century, as various crises facing the dynasty seemed to dictate greater imperial intervention in the selection of officials and less emphasis on the traditional criteria of seniority and career background.

Ethnic Composition

The restrictions on eligibility for the governor-generalship and the care with which its incumbents were chosen are indicative of the recognized need for competent and loyal governors-general. The degree to which the court was concerned with the control feature of this office and the loyalty to the throne of the men who held it are reflected in the high number of governors-general, particularly in the early decades of Ch'ing rule, who were selected from among Manchu, Chinese Bannerman, and Mongol candidates, regardless of their relative lack of experience in local government. Conversely, the same concern is suggested by the fact that increasing numbers of Han Chinese were appointed to this office as time passed, suggesting the alien rulers' growing confidence in this group. Another indication suggesting the court's concern with control of this office is the region to which appointments from the different groups were made. Han Chinese, especially in the earlier years, received appointments to those areas closest to the capital.

The court's concern for the loyalty of all governors-general, particularly among the Han Chinese, also is reflected in a rapid rate of change in these offices. The frequent transfer of governors-general to other provinces suggests dynastic concern about the potential growth of regional power focused in the hands of a single official. While this concern is reflected in the number of transfers within all groups, it is more obvious in the length of tenure of Han Chinese, particularly in the early years of the dynasty. The same concern is seen in the frequency of transfers, not only within the provincial services, but between the provinces and the capital.

It is clear that the early Manchu rulers faced a serious dilemma in filling the highest provincial posts. On the one hand, as aliens who had just assumed imperial rule, they were reluctant to trust Han Chinese in posts that involved the exercise of great power over vast expanses of land often distant from the capital. On the other hand, they could not supply enough candidates for the posts from among themselves, for in the early years of the dynasty few Manchus had either proficiency in the Chinese language or much experience in local government. The solution was to appoint an inordinate number of Chinese Bannermen, candidates who were ethnically and linguistically Chinese, but politically more reliable.

The role played by the Chinese Bannermen in the early years of the dynasty and the reasons for the rapid waning of their influence in the early eighteenth century provide an interesting perspective on the nature of alien rule in imperial China. The first Chinese Bannermen were Chinese who joined the Manchus during the first three decades of the seventeenth century and were later given the status of bannermen. They were originally local residents or soldiers of the Ming garrison in the northeast, particularly in the area around Liaoyang and Shenyang. Around 1620, after their capture by or surrender to the Manchus, they were subjected to great humiliation and hardship. Some were offered to the Manchus as the booty of war; many served as laborers or slaves. But, in the early 1630s their situation began to improve. Some of the more successful, such as Ning Wan-wo and Fan Wen-ch'eng, earned the trust of their rulers and gained some influence in the inner circles of power. Others fled Manchu control or worked secretly with the Ming government.

Confronted by these developments, the Manchu ruler, Abahai, began to change the policy toward this group, seeking their support and confidence. The majority were given their own land and freedom, and in 1631-32 Abahai formally established a Chinese Bannerman military detachment.[21] This move was an explicit admission by the Manchus that as they moved south in their conquest of China they would require the support of a politically reliable group of Chinese-speaking soldiers and administrative personnel. By 1642 the number of Chinese Bannerman detachments had increased to eight, with a total of 158 companies—comparable in size to about half the entire army of Manchu Bannermen.[22] In 1683, two years after the suppression of the Rebellion of the Three Feudatories, the last major expansion of the Chinese banner troops took place as they absorbed the troops formerly under the three feudal princes.

During the first two decades of Manchu rule, few Chinese Bannermen were given important positions in the central government. Not until 1651 were two Chinese Bannermen appointed to the powerful Court of Deliberative Officials, an elite, predominantly Manchu cabinet created to discuss major military measures and civil policies. Even then, the bannermen were not allowed to take part in discussions of military affairs, a prohibition that was not lifted until 1661.[23]

In the provinces, however, Chinese Bannermen played a critical role. In these early years, the Manchu rulers were forced to leave the reins of local government in the hands of Han Chinese elites. During the Shun-chih reign,

Han Chinese constituted 90.4% of all prefects, 89.3% of the empire's magistrates of independent departments, and 96.6% of the county magistrates.[24] The resulting polarization of power between the Manchu–dominated central government and the newly conquered Han Chinese at the local level presented the court with a dangerous situation. By appointing a large number of Chinese Bannermen to the highest provincial posts, the Manchus created a link between the two levels of government that was perceived to be reliable and functionally effective.[25]

There were other reasons for the extensive use of Chinese Bannermen in high provincial posts during the first sixty years of Manchu rule. From the outset of the dynasty, the court was plagued by a power struggle among different factions of the Manchu nobility. The appointment of Manchu nobles to high provincial posts carried with it the risk of enveloping provincial government in this factional strife.[26] "Manchus were not as trustworthy as Chinese Bannermen in the emperor's struggle for political supremacy over influential Manchu princes."[27] Having supported the Manchus in their conquest of China, the Chinese Bannermen had no real alternative to supporting the Manchu court during these early years. From the Manchu point of view, the Chinese Bannermen had the obvious advantages of inconspicuousness within the Chinese population, fluency in the Chinese language, and greater familiarity with the Chinese social and political structure and traditions.[28]

Our statistics emphasize the importance of the role played by Chinese Bannermen in these early years. During the reign of the first Ch'ing emperor, Shun–chih (1644-61), Han Chinese were given only five of a total of thirty–seven possible provincial governor–generalships, an additional three grain posts, and one river appointment. Even more revealing is the fact that in the same period Manchus held only one of these posts, the directorship of grain transport. All other governor–generalships were held by the Chinese Bannerman. Their predominance continued throughout the rest of the seventeenth century, although representatives of the Han and Manchu groups grew in number and began to be appointed to an increasing variety of locations. No Mongol served as governor-general until the early Ch'ien–lung period (1736-55).

During the reign of the second Ch'ing emperor, K'ang–hsi, the court's attitude toward the role of each political–ethnic group in senior civil–service positions began to change. K'ang–hsi, recognizing that the court could not rely forever upon the small group of Chinese Bannermen to fill these top provincial posts, made a direct appeal for the explicit support of Han elites. The first major sign of his intention was an official invitation to the many known scholars who had earlier refused to work with the Manchus to take part in the first *po-hsüeh-hung-tz'u* examination, given in 1679. His initiative proved extremely beneficial, as forty of the fifty successful candidates were from the Kiangsu and Chekiang areas, the stronghold of Ming loyalist elites. This examination "signaled the beginnings of a Manchu sharing of power and cooperation with the non–collaboratory Chinese,"[29] and the acceptance of the "legitimacy" of Manchu rule by this group. Two years later, the Rebellion of the Three Feudatories was suppressed. Soon after the Ming loyalists in Taiwan surrendered, concluding almost forty years of major opposition to the dynasty by a Ming restoration movement.

By 1685, Manchu power under the K'ang-hsi emperor was secure and the court began to appoint fewer Chinese Bannermen and more Han Chinese and Manchus to the highest posts in both the provincial and central governments.[30] This shift in policy was the result, not only of the passage of time, but of the recognition that more Han Chinese would have to be given important appointments. Two other factors undoubtedly influenced the court. First, after forty years in power a new generation of Manchu officials, more experienced in the structure of Chinese society and government, were available to play a role in the affairs of state outside the court and imperial household. Second, the Manchu rulers were increasingly disenchanted with the performance of Chinese Bannermen in official positions.

The changing perception of the Chinese Bannermen was an important historical phenomenon and an interesting one to document. In a 1683 edict, the K'ang-hsi emperor bluntly addressed this group and the problems he saw in it.

> Since the founding of the empire by our ancestors, Chinese Bannermen and Manchu officials have always been treated equally. In the past, many [Chinese Bannermen] even made some outstanding contributions. However, in recent times, the performance of the Chinese Bannermen has steadily deteriorated. Whenever they are appointed to a provincial post, they bring along large numbers of attendants and servants. They live lavishly and wastefully, and have shown no interest in anything other than increasing their personal fortunes. They have caused great suffering to the people, behaved recklessly, and frequently do not even abide by the law. . . . From this time on, you should completely reform your minds and change old habits. . . . If you persist, and demonstrate no repentance, the laws of the country will make no exception for you.[31]

The emperor reprimanded them again a few years later, claiming that they were "extravagant and vainglorious," and remonstrating that "all they ever do is compare the lavishness of their dress and engage in heavy drinking and the pursuit of pleasure. . . . These are traits that cannot be found among Manchus and [non-Bannermen] Chinese."[32]

One can speculate that these imperial views were influenced by the criticism Han officials levelled at the Chinese Bannermen, as the following memorial to the K'ang-hsi emperor would suggest.

> Other than the Manchus and the Han, there is this odd category of people called "Chinese Bannermen." It is a fact that many of them have occupied prominent positions in the government. Nevertheless,

they behave as if they are the private possessions of a family. . . . As soon as they see their master, they bow their heads in total obedience, only worrying that they have not done enough to please [him]. They have no hesitation in doing the kind of things that are despised and condemned by the rest of the people. They dare not utter a single word of disagreement. . . . They show obedience merely in the hope of keeping their positions and winning the hearts of their masters. How can one expect people such as these to render useful service to the country? Why does your Majesty not think of a way of disposing of this problem?[33]

The frequency and influence of this kind of attack by Han officials on Chinese Bannermen is not known, but it may well have played some part in shaping the Manchu rulers' perceptions, which soon influenced policy.

An interesting passage, found in an edict of 1701, indicates that the court's unfavorable impressions of the Chinese Bannermen did have a direct effect on the emperor's choice of governors-general. "In normal circumstances, the [non-Bannermen] Chinese are more suitable for the positions of governor-general or governor. The Chinese Bannermen are too extravagant in their expenditures and subsequently cause harm to the people."[34]

The statistics on appointments to the top provincial post document how these perceptions influenced policy. From 1704 to 1722, the pattern of appointments to governor-generalships changed decisively and Manchus became the predominant group holding this office. During these years, Manchus held sixteen of twenty-five provincial governor-generalships, and received just over 48% of new appointments.[35]

Perhaps the most interesting feature of this pattern in the early years of the dynasty is what appears to be a sudden reversal of appointment policy and practice during the short reign of the Yung-cheng emperor (1723-36). Of thirty-nine new governors-general appointed during this period, 43.6% were Han Chinese, 30.8% were Chinese Bannermen, and only 25.6% were Manchus. This remained the highest percentage of new appointments for Han Chinese until the beginning of the nineteenth century. Equally striking, it represented the lowest percentage of new appointments for the Manchu group for the periods 1704-22 and 1862-74.[36]

This apparent aberration in the general pattern for the dynasty as a whole may be explained in part by the unusual circumstances surrounding the Yung-cheng emperor's ascendancy to the throne, which he won by military power and intrigue. He attempted to consolidate his rule by a number of devices designed to weaken the power of rival Manchu factions. Ironically, the quest for greater personal power and the evident paranoia behind it, which made the reign of the Yung-cheng emperor the most autocratic of the dynasty, appear to have been manifested in the greater trust shown toward the Han Chinese at the expense of the emperor's Manchu rivals at the top of the regional government hierarchy.

The Yung-cheng emperor was determined to destroy existing cliques and prevent the rise of new ones. In 1725 he issued his famous "Discourse on Parties and Cliques" *(P'eng-tang lun)* a direct warning to the empire's great officials, particularly its powerful Manchu princes and their followers.[37] A year later he demanded that the great Manchu officials, "quickly wake up and show remorse . . . the formation of cliques constitutes the greatest concern to the court. . . . If you ever harbor the idea of scheming behind my back, you will be condemned as traitors, and tolerated neither by the laws of our ancestors nor of our country."[38] That he feared the potential threat of powerful Manchu leaders developing regional loci of power appears evident in the dramatic drop in the number of Manchus appointed to governor-generalships during his reign.

While suspicious of many fellow Manchus, the Yung-cheng emperor also accused the Chinese Bannermen of collusion, intrigue, and incompetence.[39] He also seems to have been unusually sensitive to the quality of senior Han officials and the importance of making appointments on the basis of competence and character, rather than ethnic grounds and the early assumptions of loyalty related to them. In an edict of 1727, the Yung-cheng emperor stressed the importance of competence and morality in the selection of officials.

> If one differentiates between Manchus and Chinese, one will only create mutual distrust and suspicion. This is certainly not the way to govern. It is a law of nature that the talents of people, Manchu and Chinese alike, are unequal. Some are better than others. What should concern us at the time of making an appointment is the qualifications of the person. The ethnic difference between Manchu and Chinese should not be taken into consideration.[40]

While one of the emperor's most trusted advisors was a Chinese Bannerman, the Yung-cheng emperor stressed that fewer and fewer were qualified for senior posts and that he had "great pity for them."[41]

The pattern in appointment policy changed dramatically in the early years of the Ch'ien-lung emperor's reign (1736-96). More than half the new governors-general appointed by this ruler were Manchus. While appointments of Han Chinese did increase in the second half of the reign, the most important secondary effect of more Manchu appointments was the extraordinary decrease in the number of Chinese Bannermen. This group plunged from a high of 77.6% of new appointments in the first years of the dynasty, through a still significant 30.8% in the Yung-cheng period, to approximately 10% of new appointments to Ch'ing governor-generalships.[42]

While this pattern is most marked in the category of new appointments, it is also apparent in a calculation of total governor-general tenures throughout the reign. In this case, Manchus held 72% of all tenures during the Ch'ien-lung period, while the other two groups split the remainder evenly, as many Chinese Bannermen appointed in the preceding period continued to serve in the early years of the new reign. Realizing that as a group their status was on the decline, many Chinese Bannermen sought to relinquish their bannerman status. Some tried to register as ordinary citizens, while many military officers requested transfers to the regular Green Battalion.[43]

Another interesting feature of the Ch'ien-lung years is the beginning of a preference for Han Chinese in the grain and river governor-generalships. By the middle of the reign, Han Chinese held the majority of these posts and essentially retained their domination for the duration of the dynasty. More precisely, from the middle of the eighteenth century to the end of the dynasty, Han Chinese held 68% of all grain and river governor-generalships, while the figures for Manchus and the Chinese Bannermen-Mongols were 24% and 8%, respectively.

If the grain and river posts are excluded, the Ch'ien-lung emperor's preference for Manchu incumbents in the highest provincial posts becomes even more obvious and significant. An explanation for this change offered by some Chinese historians is that, of all the emperors of the dynasty, the Ch'ien-lung emperor, despite his own personal and deep appreciation of Chinese culture, had the worst record in mistreating Han Chinese. The historian Hsiao I-shan, for example, argues that the Ch'ien-lung emperor blatantly and consistently oppressed the Han Chinese.[44] While this would be difficult to prove, the statistics certainly confirm that a disproportionately high number of Manchus were appointed to the posts of governor-general and governor during his reign.[45]

One explanation of this is undoubtedly the large number of military campaigns launched to quell rebellions during this period. The so-called ten meritorious campaigns covered an immense expanse of territory and involved the mobilization of an unprecedented number of troops. With the exception of the Taiwan campaign, most top military posts were held by Manchu generals and a large number of battles were fought by Manchu banner troops. These campaigns provided an excellent opportunity for the rapid promotion of Manchu leaders, many of whom moved on to senior posts in the provincial government. This is demonstrated by the large number of governors-general during the Ch'ien-lung reign who earlier had served as tartar-general or lieutenant general.[46]

Another explanation for the high number of Manchus in governor-generalships during these years is the simple one that with the passage of time increasing numbers of Manchus with the required knowledge and experience in government were available. In the early years of the dynasty most Manchus were appointed to posts either in the central government in Peking and Mukden or in the banner garrisons stationed in various strategic cities. Few were involved in local government on any level. An edict of 1742 explained the reasons for this, and pointed out that times were changing.

> Previously, Manchus were not appointed to the posts of prefect or
> district magistrate. This was due to a lack of qualified people.
> There were only enough people to fill the positions at the capital.

> Now, after a hundred years of instruction, there are many times
> more talented [Manchu] people than in previous years.[47]

The emperor went on to order that in the future Manchus should be appointed
to positions in local government from district magistrate up.

As a result of this change there was a sharp increase in the number of
Manchus appointed to posts such as prefect, district magistrate, and magistrate
of independent departments. In his study, *"Ch'ing-tai chi-ts'eng ti-fang-kuan
jen-shih shan-ti hsien-hsiang chih liang-hua fen-hsi"* (Quantitative analysis of
the careers of prefects and magistrates in the Ch'ing dynasty), Li Kuo-ch'i
shows that more Manchus were appointed to these posts during the Ch'ien-lung
period than in any other reign in the Ch'ing dynasty.[48] The extent of the shift
is emphasized by just one statistic. The number of Manchus appointed to
prefect positions during the Ch'ien-lung period surpassed the combined total for
the Shun-chih, K'ang-hsi, Yung-cheng, Hsien-feng, T'ung-chih, Kuang-hsu, and
Hsuan-t'ung reigns.[49] It is evident, therefore, that the unusually high number
of Manchus appointed governor-general during the reign of the Ch'ien-lung
emperor was not an isolated phenomenon, but may in large part be explained by
the general increase in appointments of Manchus to various local government
posts.

As Kessler has shown in his article "Ethnic Composition of Provincial
Leadership During the Ch'ing Dynasty," the increase in appointments of Han
Chinese to top provincial posts did not occur after the Taiping Rebellion, as
was customarily assumed, but in the opening years of the nineteenth century.
In terms of new appointments, the period 1796-1820 saw 54% of the new
governor-generalships going to Han Chinese. By the time of the Tao-kuang
reign, Han Chinese held 57% of all governor-generalships, and the Manchus
29%. This trend strengthened throughout the nineteenth century. Indeed, over
the last sixty years of the dynasty, 72% of all governor-general tenures were
Han Chinese and only 20% were Manchu.[50]

Do patterns of frequency of turnover, number of appointments held by an
individual, and length of service in the same location offer further evidence of
a dynamic policy in which the issues of ethnic control, the initial inadequacy of
Manchu candidates, and a heavy reliance on Chinese Bannermen were major
factors? One would expect such a hypothesis to be borne out by evidence that
Han Chinese governors-general held their posts for shorter periods of time than
either of the other groups, particularly in the early years of the dynasty.

Duration of Tenure and Multiple Postings by Ethnic Group

Out of a total of 504 governors-general, 222 (44%) were Han Chinese, 166
(33%) were Manchus, 103 (20%) were Chinese Bannermen, and 13 (3%) were
Mongols. Thus, Han Chinese were outnumbered, 56% to 44%, by the other
three groups combined. The discrepancy between political-ethnic groups is
even greater when we look at total man-years of service in this office.

Excluding for the moment the grain and river governor–generalships, the statistics are particularly revealing. Calculating the total man-years of all provincial governors–general for the entire dynasty, Han Chinese held these offices only 34% of the time, compared with a figure of 38% for the Manchus. Thus, it is apparent that Han Chinese, who held 44% of all Ch'ing governor–generalships, but for only 34% of the time, were transferred much more frequently than the other groups, in part, no doubt, because they were not as thoroughly trusted.

In the case of the grain and river posts, Han Chinese again held a higher percentage of the tenures, but for less of the total time. Roughly 52% of the grain posts were held by Han Chinese for 44% of the time, while Manchus held 36% of these posts for 39% of the time, and the Chinese Bannerman-Mongol group held 12% of them for 17% of the time. The river posts saw an even stronger predominance of Han Chinese, who held 56% of these tenures for 50% of the time. The Manchus, who held river posts for an identical percentage of time, occupied only 18% of them. The most surprising figure is for the Chinese Bannermen-Mongols, who held 25% of the river governor–generalships for 32% of the time.

If grain and river posts are included, we find that Han Chinese held 40% of all Ch'ing governor–generalships for 37% of the time, Manchus held 36% of the tenures for 35% of the time, and the Chinese Bannermen-Mongols held 24% of the tenures for 27% of the time. While other studies indicate that the imbalance reflected here was somewhat compensated for by a much higher percentage of Han Chinese in Ch'ing governorships, the fact remains that over the course of the dynasty the highest provincial posts were held by Han Chinese for just over one-third of the time.[51] While these figures may be subject to other explanations, they do seem to show the importance of both the question of loyalty and the court's view of this office as a critical link in the control of the empire by an alien group.

Throughout the dynasty, governors–general held each of their posts for an average of two years and nine months. Since they tended to keep their positions longer in the first half-century of Ch'ing rule, when Chinese Bannermen held the majority of posts, it is not surprising that the average length of tenure in this group (3 years, 11 months) was the longest of the three political-ethnic groups. Rather more interesting is the fact that the average length of tenure for Han Chinese and Manchus was nearly identical—2 years and 8.6 months for Han Chinese, and 2 years and 7.3 months for Manchus.

Many Ch'ing governors–general held more than one post, sometimes in widely distant parts of the empire, but often in the same province at different times. To be precise, 201 of the 504 officials served as governor–general more than once. The extent to which Chinese Bannermen were used in the early years of the dynasty is again reflected in the fact that a higher percentage of them (44.8%) held multiple postings. Of those holding more than one appointment as governor–general, the difference in percentage between the Manchus

(34.9%) and Han Chinese (33.8%) is not statistically significant. The average length of time governors-general of all groups served in such posts was five years and two months. While almost equal numbers of Manchus and Han Chinese experienced a second or subsequent appointment to this office, individually the rate of reappointment was lowest for Han Chinese (1.5 compared to 1.8 for each of the other groups). While these variations are open to other interpretations,[52] it is probable that they also reflect the court's relative reluctance to keep successful Han Chinese at the top of the bureaucracy in the provinces for long periods of time.

An analysis of both the higher number of multiple appointments (to the same province or to different ones) as time went on, and increasingly longer aggregate tenures in all governor-generalships by the same official, points again to the growing confidence and security of the middle years of the dynasty, particularly from the middle of the Ch'ien-lung reign to the late Tao-kuang period. With the exception of the final quarter of the nineteenth century, Ch'ing officials were more likely to receive two or more postings as governor-general during the Ch'ien-lung reign than in any other period.

With the high incidence of multiple postings during this period, it is not surprising that the total length of time these officials spent in all of their postings as governor-general was also unusually high throughout the Ch'ien-lung reign and into the 1830s. The national average for total service in all posts as governor-general (five years, two months), in the Ch'ien-lung reign rose to an average for all political-ethnic groups of seven years, two months. The average decreased only slightly for the years 1796-1838. Equally unsurprising is the fact that the period of shortest aggregate service occurred roughly between the 1840s and the 1870s, years of frequent war and rebellion. However, while multiple postings and total years of career service as governor-general were highest in the century between the 1730s and 1830s, the average length of each tenure was shorter than in most other periods. Thus it could be argued that, while the court's greater sense of security was reflected in high total years of career service, the shorter length of tenure in one location revealed its continued concern with the question of loyalty. Indeed, this conclusion is supported particularly by the average length of individual tenures of Han Chinese, which fell from four years and eleven months at the outset of the Ch'ien-lung reign to a low point of three years at the end of the reign. The Ch'ien-lung emperor seemed to be saying to all groups, but in particular to the Han Chinese, that "We trust you enough to keep you at the top of the provincial administration longer than before, but only if it is not in the same province!"

A more significant factor in any attempt to consider the degree of security or insecurity felt by the court at different times, as reflected in the amount of trust placed in the highest provincial officials, may be the frequency with which the same man was reappointed to the same governor-generalship. Throughout the dynasty just 8.9% of incumbents served as governor-general in the same post more than once. Manchus were more likely to receive postings more than once in the same area than Han Chinese. A total of sixteen Manchus (almost 10% of total Manchu appointees) were so honored, some of them for third and fourth tenures. For the Chinese Bannerman-Mongol group the figure was 11.2%, while only 7.2% of Han Chinese were trusted with multiple postings in the same location, and of these over one-third held grain or river posts.[53] These figures seem to reflect a general concern at the court to avoid repeat postings, presumably in part because of the potential for the development of rival power bases.

Equally significant is the reemergence of earlier patterns that reflect increased confidence on the part of the court during the Ch'ien-lung reign. During that period, reappointment of men to the same governor-generalship was most common, peaking in the years 1776-95. This trend is most clearly marked among the Manchu group, for whom all but two of the appointments to the same location were made in the Ch'ien-lung period. Only one Han Chinese received multiple postings to the same region before the Ch'ien-lung reign, while 81% so honored received their second postings to the same governor-generalship after 1800.[54]

Subsequent and Concurrent Service as Governor and Governor-general

As we shall see in the next chapter, most governors-general served as governor at some point in their careers. This was particularly true of the Han Chinese. Experience as governor and governor-general in the same area was not common (26%), and direct promotion from governor to governor-general in the same province even more unusual (15%). The analysis in chapter 3 indicates that this phenomenon generally occurred in the frontier provinces, which suggests that factors such as logistics or special requirements for long local experience made this a sensible practice.[55] The difference in frequency of such occurrences between the political-ethnic groups for the dynasty as a whole is marginal. Thus, a major concern at court for preventing the rise of regional power bases encouraged by long service, particularly by consecutive service in the same area, is far from proved by these statistics. Nevertheless, had the court felt no concern at all, it is likely that more than 15% of the empire's governors-general would have been appointed directly from a governorship in the same location.

The same concern may help explain why so few governors-general held a concurrent governorship. Of the fifteen men who held both posts concurrently, nine were Manchus and only three were Han Chinese. The problem of logistics again seems to have been the main cause of this rare occurrence, for it happened most frequently in the geographically distant areas of Liangkuang (five times) and Yun-kwei (four times).

Appointment of Han Chinese governors to positions as governor-general in the same area, either directly or at some later date, became increasingly common from the early eighteenth century on, with the only major dip in the upward trend occurring in the 1860s and early 1870s. No doubt this reflected the special circumstances of the Taiping Rebellion and its immediate aftermath. The general trend seems to confirm the increasing confidence and sense of security enjoyed by the alien Manchu rulers as time passed. It does, however, differ in one respect from earlier evidence leading to the same conclusion. In this case, the trend begins, not in the reign of the Ch'ien-lung emperor, but during the preceding Yung-cheng reign. This apparent anomaly adds further weight to our earlier suggestion that the unusual way in which the Yung-cheng emperor came to power led him to rely more heavily on Han Chinese in high provincial posts.[56]

Appointments by Region and Ethnic Group

Perhaps the most convincing evidence of the court's concern about the control feature of this post and its reluctance, lessening as time went on, to place its full trust in Han Chinese, is demonstrated in an analysis of the most common regions to which Han Chinese were sent as governors-general.

Table 2.1 provides an indication of changes over the course of the dynasty in the number of tenures held by the different political-ethnic groups in each of the governor-generalships. Table 2.2 demonstrates graphically, in terms of both percentage of tenures and the total length of time they were held, that, with the sole exception of Liangkuang, Han Chinese were kept in governor-generalships close to the capital.

This is particularly interesting because 73% of the Han appointments in Liangkuang, the major point of contact with the Western powers, were held during the last century of the dynasty. The only provincial governor-generalship held for more than half the time by Han Chinese was Chihli, probably due to the section on "Avoidance" in the Statutes and Precedence of the Board of Civil Appointments, which excluded Manchus and Chinese Bannermen from this post except by special permission.[57] The law of avoidance also excluded Chinese Bannermen from positions in metropolitan prefectures. The reasons for this exclusion were enunciated in an edict of 1726.

> Chihli is in close proximity to the capital, where relatives and acquaintances of Chinese Bannermen can be found everywhere. Moreover, a large proportion of their bannerland is also located there. How could one be sure that there were no cases in which the officials [Chinese Bannermen] would use their influence to advance their own interests and show special favor toward their acquaintances?[58]

Table 2.1

Number of Governor-generalships According to
Period and Political-ethnic Group, 1640–1911

Period	Group*	Chihli	Liangkiang	Shen-kan	Szechwan	Min-che	Hukuang	Liangkuang	Yun-kwei	Grain	River
1644–61	H	2	0	2	0	0	2	0	0	4	3
	M	0	0	0	0	0	0	0	0	1	0
	B/M	5	3	5	5	5	4	5	2	2	12
1662–83	H	1	1	2	1	1	0	1	1	1	3
	M	0	2	1	3	0	0	0	1	1	0
	B/M	1	3	2	4	9	3	6	6	1	5
1684–1703	H	0	3	0	0	2	3	0	0	3	1
	M	0	2	1	2	0	0	0	1	1	1
	B/M	1	2	0	1	6	4	3	3	4	4
1704–22	H	0	0	0	0	1	0	1	0	0	1
	M	0	4	2	1	1	2	0	3	1	0
	B/M	0	0	0	1	2	4	2	1	2	1
1723–35	H	4	0	0	0	1	1	1	0	3	5
	M	0	1	0	0	0	1	1	2	2	3
	B/M	1	4	0	1	3	2	2	1	0	1
1736–55	H	3	0	0	0	0	2	1	0	2	2
	M	1	9	2	2	5	9	9	2	7	6
	B/M	0	2	2	1	2	2	1	2	0	3
1756–75	H	2	0	0	1	1	1	1	1	4	8
	M	0	2	6	6	4	9	2	9	3	2
	B/M	1	0	2	0	2	1	4	1	0	2
1776–95	H	6	2	0	3	2	3	2	0	2	5
	M	0	6	4	6	8	8	4	7	3	1
	B/M	0	0	0	2	0	0	1	1	0	3
1796–1820	H	6	3	0	0	3	7	3	0	8	19
	M	1	4	5	4	6	5	5	6	6	0
	B/M	0	3	6	1	0	3	3	0	1	4

Table 2.1 (Continued)

Period	*Group	Chihli	Liangkiang	Shen-kan	Szechwan	Min-che	Hukuang	Liangkuang	Yun-kwei	Grain	River
1821–38	H	2	3	1	2	4	6	4	3	9	9
	M	3	1	2	3	1	2	0	2	5	2
	B/M	1	2	2	1	1	0	0	1	1	5
1839–50	H	0	6	0	0	4	2	4	6	4	5
	M	2	2	4	1	2	2	1	1	0	2
	B/M	0	1	1	1	1	0	0	0	0	1
1851–61	H	1	3	1	4	3	2	5	5	3	4
	M	2	1	3	1	3	1	0	1	1	3
	B/M	2	0	0	1	0	2	0	0	0	1
1862–74	H	3	3	2	2	5	2	3	4	4	5
	M	1	0	1	0	3	0	2	0	1	0
	B/M	0	0	0	0	0	0	0	0	0	0
1875–84	H	1	4	3	3	2	3	5	3	4	4
	M	0	1	0	0	0	0	1	0	2	2
	B/M	0	0	0	0	1	1	0	0	0	0
1895–1900	H	2	2	5	5	3	1	3	3	2	3
	M	2	1	0	1	0	1	0	1	2	1
	B/M	0	0	0	0	1	0	0	0	0	0
1901–11	H	3	4	0	3	2	4	5	3	3	1
	M	1	1	2	1	3	1	0	0	2	0
	B/M	0	0	1	3	1	1	0	1	0	1

* H=Han Chinese; M=Manchus; B/M=Chinese Bannermen/Mongols

Notes: These figures include any tenure that existed during the period, i.e., regardless of whether it began in the preceding period or extended into the succeeding one. Thus, this table should not be used to determine average length of tenure.

Table 2.2

Number and Duration of Governor-generalships Held
by Political-ethnic Group, 1644-1911 (percentages)

Post	*Group	Percentage of Posts	Percentage of Time
Chihli	H	51	60
	M	19	23
	B/M	30	17
Liangkiang	H	36	34
	M	42	43
	B/M	22	23
Shen-kan	H	25	26
	M	51	47
	B/M	25	27
Szechwan	H	29	26
	M	43	46
	B/M	28	27
Min-che	H	38	36
	M	33	30
	B/M	29	34
Hukuang	H	32	36
	M	43	36
	B/M	25	28
Liangkuang	H	44	38
	M	29	23
	B/M	27	40
Yun-kwei	H	36	29
	M	43	44
	B/M	21	27
Grain	H	52	44
	M	36	39
	B/M	12	17
River	H	56	50
	M	18	18
	B/M	25	32

* H=Han Chinese; M=Manchus; B/M=Chinese Bannermen/Mongols

Presumably the same reasons help explain the absence of Manchu appointments to Chihli in any significant number before the nineteenth century.

Aside from Chihli, only the grain and river posts were held for considerably longer periods by Han Chinese than by either the Manchu or the Chinese Bannerman-Mongol groups. Min-che was held slightly longer by Han Chinese than by either of the other groups, while Hukuang was held for exactly the same length of time by Han Chinese as by Manchus. In the case of Shen-kan, Yun-kwei, and Szechwan, our statistics reveal that during the reigns of the K'ang-hsi, Ch'ien-lung, and Chia-ch'ing emperors a very high percentage of the governors-general were Manchus. This was not coincidence. The empire's statutes, the Ta-Ch'ing hui-tien, reveal that in 1688 the K'ang-hsi emperor issued an order to the effect that only Manchus could be appointed to the posts of financial commissioner, judicial commissioner, governor, and governor-general of Shensi, Shansi, and Kansu.[58]

As there are many similarities between the problems faced by the court in Yun-kwei and Shen-kan, one can assume that the same concern for security in border regions led to few Han appointments in the southwest as well as in Shen-kan. Strategically, these provinces formed a single line of defense protecting the western front of the heartland of China and her southern border from potential military threats by Sinkiang, Mongolia, and Tibet (over which Ch'ing control was loose), or by the southern tributary states of Annam and Burma. Traditionally these provinces were labelled "strategically important border regions" (yen-chiang). They also contained a large number of minority groups that frequently engaged in riots and uprisings. The top provincial posts in these volatile and vulnerable provinces required men of military experience and political reliability. A K'ang-hsi edict of 1712, transmitted to the Council of Princes and High Officials, to grand secretaries, and to presidents and vice-presidents of the boards, is explicit in revealing why so few Han Chinese were appointed governor-general in the border areas.

> The country has been in a state of peace for a long time. Han
> Chinese officials are now only able to compose essays of no sub-
> stance and utter words of no consequence. As for important mili-
> tary work, they have generally demonstrated incompetence. . . . I
> have repeatedly told them that, since they cannot ride horses or
> stand hardship, I must appoint bannermen to do the work whenever
> an emergency arises in the border areas. . . . Moreover, Han
> Chinese officials often decline to take up an appointment in the
> northern and western border areas with the excuse that they cannot
> ride horses and that they find it too difficult to move around on foot
> in large areas where there is little water. . . . Therefore, only
> Manchus are appointed governor-general and governor of
> Ch'uan-shen [Szechwan, Shensi, and Kansu]. When Chang Po-hsing
> [a favorite Han Chinese official of the emperor K'ang-hsi] was the
> governor of Kiangsu, he was frightened once, panicking at the mere
> sight of a few fishing boats which he mistakenly thought were pirate

ships. If he were assigned to handle matters in the border areas, he would unquestionably fail in his duty. When Li Chih-fang [another Han Chinese official] was the governor-general of Min-che, he personally led the troops to attack bandits. How could one say that there is no Han Chinese without military ability? The problem is that there are just too few of them.[60]

For the most part, significant numbers of Han Chinese were appointed to the governor-generalship of these sensitive border provinces only in the final century of Ch'ing rule.

Conclusions

While not providing incontrovertible evidence, the statistical analysis in this chapter points toward the control feature of this office and therefore to the loyalty of the men appointed to it as a major concern. It indicates that, because of this concern and particularly in the early years of the dynasty, alien Manchu rulers were reluctant to appoint Han Chinese to these posts or keep them in the same area for long periods of time. Despite the relatively small number of Han Chinese in these high positions, several early emperors insisted that Manchus were not being favored with high posts to the disadvantage of competent Han Chinese officials. The Ch'ien-lung emperor made the claim for himself and his predecessors in stating that "all the emperors of this reigning dynasty, from my grandfather, and my father, to me, have held fast to the principle of impartiality, without a trace of favoritism."[61] Ironically, the Yung-cheng emperor, who, as we have seen, appointed more Han Chinese governors-general than his predecessors, responded to Manchu accusations that he favored the Han by stating bluntly that there were not enough competent Manchus, and he would not favor them simply because they were Manchus.[62]

Particularly in the early years, the imperial claim to impartiality, best exemplified in such slogans as "Manchus and Chinese are all of one family" *(Man-Han i-chia)* and "Manchus and Chinese are given the same consideration" *(Man-Han i-t'i hsiang-shih),* appears to have been more symbolic than substantive, at least in terms of appointments to the empire's highest provincial posts. However, the partiality that did exist seems to have been based on political considerations rather than racial ones. This interpretation appears to be supported by the heavy reliance the court placed in the early decades of the dynasty on the ethnically Chinese, but politically more reliable, Chinese Bannerman group. Equally significant, and much more interesting, is the manner in which almost all the statistics of this chapter graphically chart the increasing sense of security and confidence of the Manchu court, most convincingly from the Ch'ien-lung reign on. Throughout the Ch'ing dynasty such changes in practice, if not always in policy, show dramatically the dynamic nature of Manchu rule in China.

Chapter III

Career Patterns

A Ch'ing governor-generalship was not a sinecure reserved for court favorites or easily survived by officialdom's fools. It was a difficult, demanding job, which carried with it as many perils as it did privileges and perquisites (for a discussion of salaries and salary supplements see appendix 3). The office served not only as a critical link in the chain of command by alien rulers over a vast, sprawling empire, but also as a pivotal post in all important administrative, military, fiscal, and judicial matters that tied capital to county, and emperor to distict magistrate and the common people. What kind of men were selected to serve in the empire's highest provincial office? How well qualified were they in terms of education and experience in government service in the provinces or capital? What career patterns did they take to the office and follow after they left it?

Initial Qualifications

1. Educational Background and Degrees Held

The majority (64.9%) of Han Chinese who reached the top of the provincial bureaucracy began their careers with the *chin-shih*, the empire's highest degree. Of the Manchu governors-general, 19.3% had the *chin-shih*, as did 12.6% of the Chinese Bannermen and 7.7% of the Mongols. Han Chinese could attain the *chin-shih* only by taking the regular provincial, metropolitan, and palace examinations. Manchus and Mongols could receive a *chin-shih* after successfully completing a much less competitive examination (the *fan-i hui-shih*) in the Manchu or Mongolian languages. This examination was introduced in 1739 and lasted, with several short interruptions, until the end of the dynasty.[1] The success rate for those who took it was very high: one out of every five or six candidates.

Of the eighty-two Han Chinese governors-general for whom we have both birth dates and dates of attainment of the *chin-shih*, we find that the average age of receipt of the degree was 29.6 years. Of the 14 Manchus for whom the same information is available, the average age of receipt of the *chin-shih* was 26.0. If we calculate the average age of *chin-shih* degree-holders from the biographies of Hummel's *Eminent Chinese of the Ch'ing Period*, the age of Han Chinese jumps to 31.2 and that of Manchus falls to 25.2. Combining the two averages, we still find an age differential between the two groups of about five years. It is interesting to note that these average ages are considerably lower than those given by other studies which estimate an average age of 33 to 36.[2] This would tend to confirm a basic assumption of this study, that the men who reached the governor-generalship were by definition among the most successful Ch'ing bureaucrats.

In the case of Han Chinese governors-general, 7.2% who did not have the *chin-shih* did have the next lowest degree, the *chü-jen*, leaving less than one-third (27.9%) who attained the governor-generalship with neither degree. Another 14.6% of the Manchu governors-general and 6.9% of the Chinese Bannerman-Mongol group had the *chü-jen*. Thus, while close to three-quarters of Han Chinese governors-general had at least a *chü-jen*, and most of these held the *chin-shih* as well, only about half of all the empire's governors-general had one of the top two degrees.

For success in entering and climbing the bureaucratic ladder, possession of the empire's leading degree was not as important for Manchus as it was for Han Chinese. The statistical evidence for this, provided below, is very similar to that offered in a study by Ch'en Wen-shih, who found that of the 305 most successful Manchu civil officials, only 27.5% possessed a *chin-shih* degree of either type.[3]

The statistics underline the dilemma faced by the Manchus as a minority alien group confronted with dual and sometimes contradictory needs: they had to become sufficiently sinicized to rule the country effectively, but short of the point where their own cultural identity was endangered. This was particularly true in the dynasty's early and middle years. By the beginning of the nineteenth century the very process of sinicization diluted the issue as a pragmatic concern, and issues of ethnic and cultural identity within China began to be less important than concern for the preservation of Chinese culture in the face of Western imperialism.

The tension between these contradictory needs in the early decades of the Ch'ing dynasty is well demonstrated by the court's ambivalence toward the issue of Manchus seeking the empire's most coveted degree. The early Ch'ing emperors realized that a significant number of Manchus must develop fully their expertise in the broadest possible spectrum of Chinese civil service practices and bring their knowledge of Chinese language and literary studies to the level of competence required to pass the examinations. On the other hand, they recognized that Manchus must also be exhorted to preserve their own language and concentrate on their mastery of the martial arts. The tension between the two was recognized, but a balance that would satisfy the court proved elusive. Even when Manchus were allowed to take the examinations, they were subject to constant imperial exhortation not to devote too much time and energy to Chinese learning. This attitude, as well as periodic prohibitions against Manchus taking the exams and the recognition that Han Chinese were better qualified to pass them, limited the number of senior Manchu officials who attained the *chin-shih* degree.

In 1657 the Shun-chih emperor ordered the suspension of the privilege
allowing Manchus to take the regular provincial examinations.

> The founding of our nation was entirely the result of our military
> achievements. Now people in the Eight Banners tend to favor the
> pursuit of literary studies and consequently have neglected the study
> of the martial arts and their military duties. This has happened
> because, once they have passed the provincial and metropolitan
> examinations, they can be appointed immediately to an official
> position or receive a promotion.[4]

In 1676 the K'ang-hsi emperor explained that his prohibition on Manchus taking
the provincial and metropolitan examinations was meant to encourage young
Manchus to concentrate on military training.

> I am afraid that if they concentrate in literary studies, they will be
> lax in their military training. We are presently in a time when a
> great deal of military action has been taking place. If the children
> of the Eight Banners are allowed to take the civil examinations
> together with Han Chinese, they will inevitably be inclined to con-
> centrate on studying and therefore neglect their military training.[5]

During the next fifteen years not one Manchu wrote the *chin-shih* examination.

The same concern with the conflict between literary and military training
was expressed in 1724 by the Yung-cheng emperor, who also addressed another
aspect of the problem.

> The truth is that no matter how hard they [the Manchus] work at
> their studies, they cannot expect to compete with the Han Chinese
> from Kiangsu, Chekiang, and Anhwei. Why should we abandon the
> skills in which we have always excelled in order to pursue something
> in which we cannot possibly be superior?[6]

Ironically, it was the great patron of Chinese literature, the Ch'ien-lung
emperor, who was most reluctant to allow Manchus to attempt the examinations. At one point he expressed the view that Chinese learning and the exams
relied on "florid writings and inconsequential words," while the main attribute
of the Manchus was their pragmatism.[7] Perhaps his own deep appreciation for
Chinese learning led him to discourage Manchus from engaging in Chinese
studies, for in his view Manchus could not attain the same profound depth of
knowledge the Han Chinese possessed. The Manchu attempt at doing so had
made them "the laughing stock of the Han Chinese,"[8] and his own sensitivity to
this issue appears to have been acute.

> The writings of the Manchus who study in order to pass the civil
> service examination have always been shallow and inferior. After
> they have passed the examinations and obtained their *chü-jen* or
> *chin-shih* degrees, they are at times asked questions about literature
> by Han Chinese scholars. They use being a Manchu as an excuse for

their inability to answer the questions. When they are asked about the Manchu language and the arts, or archery and equitation, they claim that, being scholars, they cannot possibly know things that are familiar only to soldiers. They evade questions from both sides and always find themselves in a great dilemma. They have become useless people and have incurred my great disgust.[9]

In 1760 the Ch'ien-lung emperor ordered that thereafter Manchu bannermen should devote themselves to the study of the Manchu language and the arts of archery and equitation. "If you can learn these well, I shall surely appoint you to an official position. Whether you have studied literature is a matter of no concern to me."[10] This kind of attitude helps explain why relatively few Manchu governors-general held the *chin-shih* degree in the early reigns of the dynasty. During the reign of Ch'ien-lung, for example, nearly half of the twenty-seven *chin-shih* examinations produced three or fewer Manchus with the degree.[11]

While success in the examinations was the normal route by which Han Chinese entered the civil service and climbed to the top, Manchus had available a number of other acceptable avenues. For all groups, entry into the civil service could result from hereditary privilege, the purchase of a title, or the method of *i-hsü*, an evaluation system by which unranked government workers could be promoted to a position with rank. From the outset of the dynasty, it was possible for Manchus to obtain a ranked position in the government by passing a Manchu-language examination which essentially involved the translation of Manchu into Chinese.[12] It was relatively easy to pass, for those who did not read and write Chinese could demonstrate their competence in the Manchu language only and be employed as copy clerks.[13] The examination could be taken even by bannermen who had neither position nor salary in the banner forces.[14] It was held frequently and there appears to have been no restriction on the number of attempts a candidate could make.

After passing this examination, a Manchu was eligible for appointment to the ranked position "bithesi," or *pi-t'ieh-shih*, (Manchu clerk). Originally the term in the Manchu language meant "man of letters."[15] These men constituted the largest group of lower-level Manchu officials (ranks 6 to 9), engaged primarily in translating and transmitting Manchu-language documents.[16] Some performed these functions in the provincial capitals, the garrisons of the Banner forces and Mukden, the Manchu's subsidiary capital. In the central government alone there were 1,750 "bithesi" positions, of which 85% could be filled only by Manchus.[17] While it was not difficult to attain this status, it was considered a respectable starting point for Manchus in the civil service. As the Yung-cheng emperor noted "these are the people who eventually may be selected for positions such as presidents, vice-presidents and directors of the Boards."[18] The study of Ch'en Wen-shih discovered that over 20% of the Manchus who attained a rank of 1A or B and whose biographies are included in the *Ch'ing-shih-kao*, *Ch'ing-shih*, and *Ch'ing-shih lieh-chuan*, began their careers as bithesi.[19] This figure could in fact be higher, as not all biographies provide information on the subject's first appointment.

The majority of governor-generalships held by Han Chinese went to men with the *chin-shih* in every period of the dynasty except three (1662-83, 1756-75, and 1776-95).[20] As table 3.1 indicates, an analysis of the number of *chin-shih* among new appointments in each reign provides the same general pattern.

Table 3.1

Governors-general with the *Chin-shih* Degree

Reign	Percentage of Han governors-general with the chin-shih*	Percentage of all governors-general with the chin-shih
Shun-chih	70.0	20.0
K'ang-hsi	60.0	31.8
Yung-cheng	66.7	45.5
Ch'ien-lung	54.8	36.4
Chia-ch'ing	80.4	68.4
Tao-kuang	90.9	81.3
Hsien-feng	90.5	82.8
T'ung-chih	68.8	61.9
Kuang-hsü	64.6	55.0

*Since one man may have held more than one governor-generalship, these percentages do not represent the number of men with *chin-shih* degrees, but rather, the number of governor-general tenures. They provide a reflection of the extent to which the post at any given time was in the hands of men with the degree.

Perhaps the most interesting feature of this pattern is the steady decline in the tenures of Han Chinese with the *chin-shih* throughout the Ch'ien-lung reign. The number of *chin-shih* holders among Han Chinese governors-general increased during the thirty years preceding the reign of Ch'ien-lung, but fell to their lowest point for the dynasty in the final years of his rule. It is interesting to note also that during this reign the second lowest number of *chin-shih* degrees were awarded at the regular triennial exams.[21] Thereafter they rose sharply and steadily, peaking in the 1850s and then falling off again in the last half of the nineteenth century. The main outline of the pattern for Manchu governors-general with the *chin-shih* is essentially the same, although the variations are not as great. Chinese Bannermen governors-general who held the top degree were scattered throughout most of the dynasty, although again it may be significant that none held office in the Ch'ien-lung reign.

We know from comments by the Yung-cheng emperor that a relatively low number of *chin-shih* appointments to the top provincial post was not always a historical accident. It sometimes reflected an explicit bias against those with advanced degrees, as an edict of 1729 makes dramatically clear.

> You people with the *chin-shih* and *chü-jen* degrees . . . like to form cliques to advance your own personal interests. In order to climb to high office you have given each other undue assistance and protection. For these purposes you sometimes distort the truth and twist facts. If necessary you even trump up charges for the sake of revenge. There is nothing you will not do. Nothing in this world can demoralize people more than this kind of evil practice. Since I ascended the throne, many people have warned me not to trust officials with the two highest degrees. However, I have always tried to treat you people with great trust and expectations, believing in my own mind, "Who other than scholars like you should be given the responsibilities of an official?" Now, if you choose to continue evil practices such as engaging in favoritism by helping the careers of those who obtained a degree in an examination in which you were the examination officer, or to those who received a degree in the same examination as you, as your emperor I will not be able to give you an official position even if that were my wish . . . . Was there ever an ancient sage who held a degree? Degree holders always show contempt toward people without a degree. In fact, the feeling is very much a reciprocal one. This is just like the people of Kiangsu and Chekiang who always scoff at people from Shansi and Shensi, saying that they are vulgar and rustic. On the other hand, people from Shansi and Shensi are contemptuous of those from Kiangsu and Chekiang for being weak and cowardly. What has this got to do with one's moral fibre? . . . As long as people with the *chin-shih* and *chü-jen* degrees continue to do this there will be no justice on earth. You must quickly repent and forego these evil practices which have been handed down from generation to generation.[22]

During the Yung-cheng reign, just over 50% of Han Chinese governors-general held the *chin-shih*, although 66.7% of his new appointments held the top degree.

Han Chinese governors-general who held only a *hsiu-ts'ai* degree were relatively few (17 men or 7.7%), but they were represented in most periods of the dynasty. The term "*hsiu-ts'ai*" was a popular designation for the *sheng-yüan*, the lowest degree-holders. People with this qualification had a higher social status than commoners and are sometimes classified by modern scholars as members of the lower gentry. This degree did not normally provide an opportunity for government position and those holding it should be differentiated from *kung-sheng* (tribute students) and *chien-sheng* (students of the Imperial Academy) who were eligible to take other tests that would qualify them for a minor official appointment. Such a differentiation has not been made in this study, where the term *"hsiu-ts'ai"* includes these other groups.[23]

In biographical works, extremely few Manchu, Chinese Bannerman, or Mongol governors-general are listed as being graduates of bannermen schools *(kuan-hsüeh)*. This term described various types of schools for children of bannermen, including the one for members of the imperial clan. Founded in 1644, these schools provided basic education to selected children between the ages of ten and eighteen. Curricula varied slightly, but normally consisted of the Manchu language, Chinese classics, and the arts of archery and equitation. Students might spend from three to ten years in one of these schools. Enrollment was limited, and in some periods only one or two children attended from each unit of 300 bannermen. At other times the numbers were even smaller. In 1743, for example, only 100 children (60 Manchus, 20 Chinese, and 20 Mongols) were selected from each banner.

That restricted enrollment and curriculum did not imply an elite status for graduates is reflected in the infrequency with which the compilers of Ch'ing biographical collections bothered to note graduation from a banner school. When this information is missing, there is no mention of "qualification" and only the first official appointment is provided. Bannermen obviously did not need this background for entry into the civil service as it was relatively easy to become a bithesi by examination or purchase. In time the institution began to disappear, especially after the Chia-ch'ing reign, when among Manchus the practice of purchasing official titles became commonplace.

Graduates of the banner schools could follow a number of career paths, depending in part on their family background and academic ability. Those who excelled in Chinese might be transferred to the Imperial Academy for further study of the Chinese classics and history, and eventual appointment to the civil service by examination or recommendation. Students who completed their studies in a banner school might take an examination and obtain an appointment as a bithesi of rank 7 or 8, a position such as secretary of the Manchu-Chinese translation office. Graduates of the school for the imperial clan could take an examination arranged by the imperial clan court, which might result in appointment as a second-class secretary in that court.[24]

2. Hereditary, Military and Other Backgrounds

The initial qualifications of Han Chinese governors-general who did not begin their careers with a degree varied. Five of the earliest appointees began their careers with hereditary titles. Only one Han Chinese governor-general prior to the middle of the nineteenth century appears to have begun his career with primarily military credentials. However, in the final quarter of the nineteenth century, 22% of all Han Chinese officials, seven men, began their careers in a military capacity. This is no doubt explained by the opportunity for rapid promotion provided to military men by the wars and rebellions of this era and by the late Ch'ing attempts to modernize the country's armed forces.[25]

About one-third of Han Chinese governors-general in the dynasty's first reign can be classified as "Ming turncoats." The highest percentage of Chinese Bannerman governors-general in the Shun-chih reign can also be classified as "Ming turncoats." This term has been deliberately chosen to describe a specific group of high-ranking Ming military and civil officials who surrendered in the early stages of the Manchu conquest of China and, by virtue of that action and their active collaboration with the Manchus, were appointed to positions of equivalent rank in the new government. In the perception of the Manchus, they were more loyal and reliable than other former Ming officials who assumed office in the new government only after the Ch'ing dynasty was fully established. It is therefore a more precise term than alternatives such as "former Ming official," and represents a form of "qualification" for high official rank in the Ch'ing government, not only by virtue of former governmental experience, but by that added perceived attribute of loyalty and reliability. As early as 1667, a Chinese scholar-official with the *chin-shih*, Ch'u Fang-ch'ing, defined "changing allegiance to the new government" *(t'ou-ch'eng)* as one of the seven acceptable ways of entering government service.[26]

The percentage of governors-general from the other two political-ethnic groups who began their careers with exclusively or predominantly military credentials was surprisingly low. Only 10% of the Manchu tenures can be classified as such, or at most 15% of those for whom the relevant information is recorded. Only eight representatives of the Chinese Bannerman/Mongol group for whom this information is recorded fall into the same group. The percentage of their tenures never exceeded 30% at any time, and was normally less than 10%. Nevertheless, as will be demonstrated later, a larger number of governors-general from both these groups began their careers with other qualifications and did in fact follow career patterns that included extensive military service.

Only seven Manchu governors-general began their careers with hereditary positions, and with one exception they held their posts in the 1732–1820 period. Fifteen men from the Chinese Bannerman/Mongol group began their careers with a hereditary position and most of their appointments were concentrated in the early decades of the dynasty. That relatively few Ch'ing governors-general entered government service with hereditary positions should not be surprising. This privilege was conferred only on the eldest child of officials of rank 4 (rank 3 for provincial officials). In the event that the eldest son could not take advantage of this privilege, it was extremely difficult to have it transferred to another son. This usually occurred only when the emperor wished to bestow a very special imperial favor upon the family. Also, it was standard practice of the Ch'ing dynasty not to extend the inheritance of positions beyond two generations. The eldest son of a high official dismissed from office became ineligible if he had not yet received his own first government appointment.[27] The statistics of this study are confirmed by those of Li Kuo-ch'i; his figures for

Ch'ing local officials who began their careers with inherited positions are as follows.[28]

Table 3.2

Ch'ing Local Officials Who Began Their Careers

with Inherited Positions (by ethnic group)

Position	Percentage of Han Chinese	Percentage of All Bannermen*
District magistrate	0.9	0.2
Department magistrate	4.8	1.6
Independent department magistrate	2.9	0.9
Prefect	5.7	1.8

*These figures include Manchus, Chinese Bannermen, and Mongols.

Career Pattern Prior to Appointment as Governor-general

Of greater interest and significance than this analysis of the initial qualifications of these men is a study of the patterns of positions they held prior to becoming governors-general, their first government appointments, and the relationship between the two, as well as variations in these patterns according to political-ethnic group and periods of appointment.

Minor variations in career patterns charted from first posting to appointment as governor-general are, of course, almost limitless. However, the vast majority of governors-general followed just four basic patterns, which have been differentiated by the amount of experience gained in provincial (including local posts outside the provincial capital), central (including the grand secretariat, grand council, and Hanlin Academy as well as the six boards), military, and imperial (such as posts in the imperial clan court and imperial household) appointments.

As might be expected considering the nature of the job, the pattern most commonly followed (by 34.9% of all governors-general) involved significant periods of service in both provincial and central government prior to the first appointment as governor-general; at least one major appointment and normally several years in more than one position. Evidently it was believed that the responsibilities of the post demanded considerable first hand experience at both levels of government. The result of this analysis clearly indicates that experience in local government was considered more important for governor-general candidates than experience in Peking.

The second most common career pattern among Ch'ing governors-general was for an official to have held predominantly provincial posts prior to his appointment as governor-general, as was the case for 15.4%. Those who held exclusively provincial posts are the third largest group (12.4%). Almost one in ten (9.9%) of the governors-general experienced significant lengths of service in at least three of the four areas (provincial, central, military, and imperial), but only 7.3% took the route of predominantly central appointments before becoming governor-general, and an even lower 4.1% appear to have held exclusively central offices prior to their first appointment to the top provincial post. Less than one percent had their experience exclusively or predominantly in imperial posts.

Perhaps the most surprising result of this analysis is the relatively small percentage who followed a predominantly military career pattern. As the governor-general had very important military responsibilities, this finding was rather unexpected. In almost all documents that describe the duties of governors-general, there is an emphasis on the equal importance of his military and civil duties. Ch'ing documents describe the governor-general as having "power over both civil and military officials"; as a man who "should try to make the generals and civil officials work together in harmony," and one who "should ensure that soldiers as well as civilians are properly governed."[29] Yet the statistics indicate that, based on a calculation of all career patterns in which significant military service appeared, only 14% of governors-general followed this route. Even more remarkable is the fact that only 4.1% followed an exclusively military pattern, and another 4.4% a predominantly military career, prior to appointment as governor-general.

Analysis of career patterns in each of the three political-ethnic groups revealed that the majority of governors-general in all groups had substantial prior experience in provincial government.[30] Predictably, the Han Chinese had by far the greatest amount of local government experience, with approximately 80% of them serving significant lengths of time in the provinces. Of these, the majority followed career patterns that were predominantly, and sometimes exclusively, in local service.

Virtually no Manchus (1.4%) held exclusively provincial posts prior to the governor-generalship, whereas 18% of Han Chinese and 17.2% of the Chinese Bannerman/Mongol group climbed to the top via that route. The largest group of Manchus (39.2%) followed the pattern of significant provincial and central service.[31] On the other hand, about 60% of the Manchus had significant central government experience, compared to a figure of about 45% for both the Han Chinese and the Chinese Bannerman/Mongol group.[32]

Not surprisingly, relatively few Han Chinese had significant military experience before their appointment as governor-general (11%). Of course, the figure for the Chinese Bannerman/Mongol group is the highest (19%). Rather unexpectedly, a relatively small percentage of Manchus (14%) had significant experience in military posts prior to becoming governor-general.[33]

The predominance of provincial experience in the careers of men so successful that they achieved the dynasty's top provincial post was in part simply a reflection of the relatively few positions in Peking compared to the number in the provinces. This was not only reflected in the number of officials who began their careers in local posts, as we shall see later, but also in the fact that others who began their careers in Peking received a provincial appointment at some point early in their careers. For both groups, opportunities for transfer to Peking were limited.

Li Kuo-ch'i's study of Ch'ing dynasty provincial officials provides some interesting statistics on the few men who succeeded in obtaining appointments in Peking. Only 7% of district magistrates left their local posts for appointments in Peking. For department magistrates the figure was 8.9%; for magistrates of independent departments, 1.7%; and for prefects, 0.6%. In each case, between 40% and 54% of the remaining officials continued in provincial government positions. The balance were either demoted or dismissed, died in office, or retired. Among prefects, for example, 14.7% retired, 15.5% died, and 5% were either demoted or dismissed.[34]

The contrast in the availability of positions at the two levels of government was particularly marked for positions under the rank of 3B. According to the Kuang-hsü edition of the Ch'ing statutes, 250 positions in the central government with ranks from 4A to 7A were available to Han Chinese. If we add to this approximately eighty positions in the Hanlin Academy,[35] the total is even smaller than that of all positions within the same ranks in the three provinces of Chihli, Shantung, and Kiangsu alone.[36]

There was also a problem in the distribution of ranks at the 5 and 4 levels. The total number of rank 5A and 5B positions in the central government available to Han Chinese was 146, but at the ranks of 4A and 4B the number was only fifteen.[37] At this level the real bottleneck in upward career mobility occurred, and because of it the system attracted some criticism at various points in the dynasty. In 1726, Wang Ching-ch'i, the famous victim of the Yung-cheng literary inquisition, noted that "one does not get a transfer in ten years; one does not become a department director until old age."[38] Tseng Kuo-fan commented in 1850 that

> the six boards have been overcrowded with officials [waiting to be transferred]. It often happens that one does not get a transfer for as long as twenty years. Some can never hope to reach the position of department director. Often members of the Grand Secretariat and the Hanlin Academy do not get an assignment in ten years. All one has is a rank and a salary. Many talented people are really wasted.[39]

In theory, transfer between the capital and the provinces could take place at various levels, all of which were clearly defined in the regulations of the Board of Civil Appointments.[40] The restrictions in practice were rather severe. The same documents indicate that when a position of rank 3 or lower became vacant in the central government, officials at the capital were usually given priority.[41] Given the bottlenecks in the system and the numbers waiting for promotion and transfer in Peking, the result is hardly surprising.

Perhaps the most interesting feature of our analysis of career patterns is their similarity throughout the history of the dynasty. The variations that do exist are relatively few in number, limited in time, and essentially predictable. For example, the pattern of significant prior experience at both the provincial and national levels is predominant for Han Chinese until the 1820s. Thereafter there is somewhat greater variety, with Han governors-general during the closing decades of the dynasty experiencing greater lengths of service at the provincial level and in military posts.

The same pattern of significant experience in the provincial government and in Peking prevails for Manchus in every period for which adequate information is available except 1662-83. This pattern also prevails for the Chinese Bannerman/Mongol group up to 1723, and again after 1796. The major occurrence of career patterns which involved considerable military experience was during the 1723-96 period for the Chinese Bannerman/Mongol group, in the 1704-22 period and again in the 1850s for Manchus, and between 1704 and 1735 and again from 1875 to the end of the dynasty for Han Chinese. The majority of those who followed an exclusively provincial career pattern served as governors-general in the period 1750-1850.

Initial Post and Career Patterns

The overwhelming majority of governors-general began their official careers in only a handful of different posts. These included various military assignments which have been grouped as one, the Hanlin Academy, magistrate or subprefect, secretary or assistant department head, or clerk. Taking all Han governors-general as a group, we find that of the two hundred men for whom information on initial appointment is available, only four (2%) began their careers as clerks, fifteen (7.5%) started in a military post, forty-eight (24%) as magistrates or subprefects, forty-nine (24.5%) as secretaries or assistant department heads, and, by far the single largest group, eighty-two (41%) in the Hanlin Academy. Two men began in "other" posts.

The majority of Han Chinese with the *chin-shih*, (eighty-one men, or 56%) received an initial appointment in the Hanlin Academy, either as a student member *(shu-chi-shih)* or as an official. Every period of this study is represented by Han Chinese who began their careers in this way, although this pattern varied from a low of 10% of the tenures in the seventeenth century to a high of 65% by the middle of the nineteenth century.

The relatively high number who entered the Hanlin Academy shows that as a group the governors-general represented the elite of successful Ch'ing officials, for only a minority of those who received the empire's highest degree in any given year received Hanlin appointments. The three with the highest rating in each palace examination were admitted immediately to the Hanlin Academy as full members. One study estimates that approximately 23% of the remaining new degree recipients were selected to study in the Hanlin as student members.[42] After three years of study in the academy, these students were given an examination which normally resulted in about 70% receiving an appointment as a Hanlin compiler or corrector. In other words, in any given year only about 16% of all chin-shih recipients were made full members of the Hanlin Academy.

Of those Han Chinese with a chin-shih degree who became governors-general, none began as clerks and only two started in military posts. Twenty-two (15%), started their careers as magistrates or subprefects. Thirty-three (23%), began as secretaries or assistant department heads, and a few received appointments as secretaries in the Grand Secretariat or directors of studies at the Imperial Academy of Learning.[43] In fact, there were relatively few central government posts available. Ch'ing statutes indicate that there was a total of only ninety positions in these three offices, of which only a small percentage would be vacant at any given time.[44] This was a very small number indeed, compared, for example, to openings in the provincial service where in the province of Chihli alone there was a total of 123 district magistrate positions.

Only a minute fraction of chü-jen degree holders received initial appointments at the capital, normally in either the Grand Secretariat or the Hanlin Academy.[45] The most common first posts for this group were district magistrate, director of a local academy, assistant department magistrate, assistant district magistrate, rank 8 prefect, record keeper, or unranked prefectural salt examiner. Similarly, most kung-sheng who obtained their first appointment by examination went to the same kinds of provincial posts.[46]

Of the Han Chinese who did not have the chin-shih degree, 33% began their careers as magistrates or subprefects, and 20% as secretaries or assistant department heads. Another 17% began in military posts, while only four men began as clerks. One man who had a chü-jen degree received an initial appointment in the Hanlin Academy.

While only fifteen Manchus began their careers in the Hanlin Academy, their appointments occurred throughout the dynasty, except for the last sixty years. Most Manchus who began their careers in military positions reached the governor-generalship in the eighteenth century. Only four Manchu governors-general began as magistrates or subprefects. The overwhelming majority began their careers either as clerks (34%) or as secretaries or assistant department heads (31%). Until about 1821, those who began as clerks were predominant.

The Chinese Bannerman/Mongol group also had a high number of initial appointments as clerk. This figure is not surprising, for in the central government alone there were 125 such positions reserved for Chinese Bannermen and 109 for Mongols. An equal number (24%) began their careers in military posts. But, unlike the Manchus, a surprisingly high number (20%) began as magistrates or subprefects. While most members of the Chinese Bannerman group became governors-general in the first thirty years of the dynasty, few reached the top in the period 1684-1723 or in the nineteenth century. Representatives of this group who began their careers as clerks held most of their governor-generalships in the decades prior to 1755, while those who started as magistrates or subprefects held their high office in similar numbers throughout dynasty. The few (10%) who began as secretaries or assistant department heads were also appointed governors-general in the opening decades of the dynasty.

The majority (46%) of governors-general who began their careers as clerks followed career patterns that provided them with significant terms of service in both provincial and central government. Less than half as many (17%) followed predominantly provincial careers, while 12% registered experience in military, provincial, and central posts, and 15% followed a route to the governor-generalship of exclusively or predominantly central offices.

An even higher percentage (65%) who began their careers as secretaries or assistant department heads followed career patterns of significant lengths of service in both the provinces and the capital. Only 11% followed predominantly provincial patterns, while a very low 12% spent their early careers either exclusively or predominantly at the capital. Only 3% to 8% of this group registered any significant experience in military posts.

These figures, as well as those for men who began their careers in the Hanlin Academy, further demonstrate the difficulty, especially for Han Chinese, of serving long periods of time in the capital where there were relatively few vacancies and a long waiting list. Only 5% of those who began in the Hanlin Academy remained exclusively in central offices before becoming governors-general. Close to a third of this group (29%) followed patterns of predominantly provincial service, while as many as 63% to 76% spent at least a significant period of time in provincial posts before reaching the governor-generalship. Most of the nearly one-third of graduating Hanlin students received appointments in the provinces where they spent most of their early and mid careers. Many Hanlin officials, after reaching rank 5, were sent to the provinces as prefect, intendant, or provincial educational commissioner.[47]

Ch'ing governors-general who began their careers in military posts were likely to follow careers either exclusively (25%) or predominantly (21%) military. Between 64% and 86% followed careers with significant military service, while only about one in ten jumped quickly out of military office to follow a predominantly civil career pattern. One of the most interesting features of this group is that before their first appointment as governors-general, Han Chinese who began their careers in military posts were much more likely to remain either exclusively or predominantly in the military than either Manchus or the Chinese Bannerman/Mongol group.[48]

For Han Chinese there was a clear distinction drawn between military and civil appointments.[49] Under the system known as *wen-wu fen-t'u,* a Han Chinese who started his career in a military post normally could not be transferred to a civil position.[50] The only exception that appears to have been made on a regular basis was the appointment of a brigadier general or a provincial commander-in-chief to the post of governor or governor-general. The important military responsibilities of these two posts, particularly in strategically sensitive areas, explains the exception to the rule.[51]

In the case of the Chinese Bannermen, a maximun degree of career mobility between civil and military positions at all ranks was permitted. The regulations concerning this, including comparability of civil and military positions by rank and salary scales, were clearly spelled out in the regulations of the Board of Civil Appointments. Under these regulations a private in the banner forces, for example, could be selected as the ceremonial usher in the Board of Rites, a secretary of the board could be transferred to the position of captain, a colonel could be made a subdirector of the Court of Sacrificial Worship, and a lieutenant general might be made the president of a board.[52] Our own analysis indicates that this flexibility occurred in practice as well as in theory. Unlike Han Chinese, many Chinese Bannermen began their careers in military posts followed patterns of both civil and military appointments.

The most interesting aspect of this analysis of initial appointment and career pattern is the predominance of provincial experience. The simple fact that there were far more positions to fill in the hinterland than in Peking meant that most Han Chinese spent long periods of time in the provinces. It also meant that there were limited opportunities for transfer to a central post, and that most of those who began their careers at the capital received provincial appointments soon after and were likely to remain in the provinces for long periods of time.

Of all those who began their careers as magistrates or subprefects, an extraordinary 66% never held a post in the capital prior to their first appointment as governor-general. If we add to this figure those who followed predominantly provincial careers, the total jumps to 77%. Since few Manchus began as magistrates, the only useful comparison is between the Han Chinese and Chinese Bannerman groups. Interestingly, the pattern for both is virtually identical. In fact, the career pattern of the successful Ch'ing bureaucrat who began as a magistrate is most predictable of all. It involved a steady climb through the established hierarchy of provincial administration.

Native Province, Region of Appointment, and Career Pattern

A study of possible relationships between the native province of Han Chinese governors-general and the career pattern they followed is not particularly instructive, although it does reveal one or two interesting features. Perhaps most interesting is the fact that the most likely pattern for Han Chinese from the three northwestern provinces of Shensi, Shansi, and Kansu was one of exclusively provincial posts (35%), a higher percentage than from any other region in the empire. Moreover, a high proportion (20%) of men from this area followed career patterns of exclusively military posts as well. Those from distant Kwangtung and Kwangsi were also likely to follow either predominantly or exclusively local patterns (40%). The only apparent explanation of this finding is that fewer governors-general who were natives of these provinces had the *chin-shih* (55%) than those from other provinces (63%). As *chin-shih* degree holders had by far the best chance of having considerable experience in the central government, the correlation between numbers of *chin-shih* from a region and numbers of people from that area holding central posts is logical and confirms earlier findings related to career patterns.

There appears to be little significant correlation between the early career patterns of governors-general and the regions to which they were appointed. Some variations do occur, but it is difficult to evaluate their significance. For instance, relatively few governors-general of Shen-kan (8%) followed patterns with long periods of provincial service. This was probably due to the fact that twice as many Manchus served in this post as either the Han Chinese or Chinese Bannerman groups, and, as we have seen, Manchus tended to spend more time in central posts than did the Han Chinese. An unusually high percentage of Yun-kwei governors-general (35%) spent most of their early careers in provincial posts. These were primarily Han Chinese who, if they had a degree, had not served in the Hanlin Academy. The post to which governors-general with the most experience at the capital were most often sent was Liangkiang (15%).[53] This may be explained by the importance of Liangkiang's rice production to the national economy and the resulting high level of its tax contribution to the central government. It was important that its governor-general have previous central-government experience, a good understanding of the financial needs of the central government, and first-hand knowledge of the bureaucratic mechanisms for control, monitoring and distribution of tribute grain.

The same explanation is suggested by the fact that more grain than river governors-general had significant experience at the capital. In fact, the clearest correlation between career patterns and the post was found in these two groups. In both cases, as with the national average, the single most common pattern was the combination of provincial and central service (grain, 39%; river, 31%). However, for those in river posts provincial experience predominated, as half of these men had either exclusively or predominantly local career patterns. Long periods of provincial experience were considered critical for river appointments. Over 24% of appointees had exclusively local experience, while a grand total of 75% had significant local experience. Comparable figures for the grain governors-general reveal that 58% had significant provincial experience and only 19% had exclusively provincial experience. Exactly twice as many grain as river directors (22% vs. 11%) had exclusively or predominantly central government backgrounds. Only a handful of men in either post had exclusively military backgrounds. It is also revealing that 67% of grain governors-general had significant provincial experience in the provinces known as "the grain route" (Chihli, Shantung, Kiangsu, Kiangsi, Chekiang, Hunan, and Hupeh). If those with little or no provincial experience are excluded, the figure jumps to almost 100%. Many grain governors-general who spent most of their early careers at the capital had considerable experience in related work such as positions in the Imperial Granary.

Importance of Provincial Experience

Despite interesting variations related to period of appointment, initial qualifications, posts held, and the region to which the appointment was made, the fundamental conclusion of this statistical analysis is that the governor-generalship was looked upon essentially as a civil post in which both central and provincial experience were considered very important. While the desired mix of experience was a combination of provincial and central posts, the critical factor appears to have been the provincial experience. Thus, while between 70% and 80% of all Ch'ing governors-general served significant lengths of time in provincial administration, a much lower percentage, 50% to 60%, spent significant periods at the national capital.

These conclusions concerning the importance of provincial experience are based on the percentage of governors-general whose early careers included significant provincial service. The same finding emerges even more definitively if we study the total man-years spent in provincial service by individuals. In this calculation, further refinement has been attempted by distinguishing between length of service in junior and senior provincial posts. The position of provincial judge (rank 3A) has been selected to mark the point at which senior appointments began. This breakpoint is acceptable for several reasons. The selection of provincial judges was made by the emperor, in theory, at least, whereas appointments to the next lowest position, taotai were normally made by the routine methods of *pu-hsüan* (selection by the Board of Civil Appointments according to regular priorities) or *yüeh-hsüan* (monthly selection).[54] Moreover, while each province may have had several taotai, it has only a single provincial judge. Provincial judges had the power to recommend their subordinate officials for special promotion *(pao-chü)*, and important privilege that was not extended to taotai. Along with the financial commissioner, the governor, and the governor-general, the provincial judge also had the right to grant his eldest son the privilege of inheriting office.

Calculations based on total man-years spent in junior and senior, or lower and higher provincial posts provide some interesting and perhaps significant contrasts. Among all Ch'ing governors-general for whom adequate data is available, the average length of provincial service prior to the first appointment as governor-general is almost thirteen full years. Slightly more time was spent in posts at the rank of provincial judge or above (six years, four months) than in lower offices (six years, one month).[55] As in our earlier comparisons of career patterns we found that Han Chinese spent much longer than the national average in provincial posts (seventeen years, one month). The total for Manchus was nine years, three months, and for the Chinese Bannerman/Mongol group ten years, six months.

Equally significant is the contrast between Han Chinese and the other two groups in terms of the distribution of provincial service at junior and senior levels. Han Chinese tended to serve longer in posts below the rank of provincial judge (eight years, five months) than in posts at or above it (seven years, five months). However, while this distribution is relatively equal, Manchu governors-general not only reversed the pattern, but did so with a much more significant descrepancy. On average, they served three years in junior provincial posts and five years, six months in senior ones. In the case of the Chinese Bannerman/Mongol group roughly equal lengths of time were spent in junior (five years, six months) and senior (five years, one month) posts.

A number of conclusions may be drawn from these figures. First, it is apparent that Manchus tended to be appointed to the provinces at more senior levels than were Han Chinese. Thus, Manchus came to the governor-generalship not only with less experience in provincial administration generally, but with very little if any in the lower echelons. In many cases they moved directly from the capital to a governorship, then up to the post of governors-general. These findings are corroborated by other analyses which have produced the following statistics for the period 1796-1908.[56]

Table 3.3

Local Officials by Ethnic Group, 1796-1908

Position	Percentage Han Chinese	Percentage Manchus	Percentage Chinese Bannerman
District magistrate	94.35	1.76	1.50
Department magistrate	93.90	2.80	2.18
Independent department magistrate	89.30	4.52	2.40
Prefect	80.70	10.50	3.45
Provincial judge	74.16	19.12	3.36
Financial commissioner	75.06	17.85	2.24

For Han Chinese, local service was not only more common, but they spent more years in it. Some served in Hanlin posts before being sent to the provinces, but significant numbers climbed the provincial hierarchy after initial provincial appointments. Considering that in the lower ranks promotion came slowly, the Han Chinese governors-general tended to be more experienced in the full range of provincial administration than their colleagues from either of the other two groups.

The only statistically significant feature that emerges from a correlation of length of provincial service to the area of appointment as governor-general is that relating to Chinese Bannermen appointed to the grain and river posts. While total length of service for this group prior to appointment as governor-general varied from four and a half to nine years, in the case of grain posts it was over eighteen years and for river positions just over sixteen years.

Statistics relating length of provincial service to date of appointment as governor-general can only be plotted usefully for the Han Chinese and Manchu groups. In both cases, the second half of the eighteenth century is the period in which those serving as governor–general had the longest prior experience in provincial administration. With one slight variation, the total length of prior provincial service then falls off abruptly, until the last half of the nineteenth century, when again the court appears to have chosen men with progressively longer experience in provincial government. Another interesting feature of this correlation is that in the final half–century of the dynasty the provincial experience of governors–general tends to be relatively greater at the senior level than in junior positions. It appears that the increasing turbulence caused by war and rebellion in the late Ch'ing dynasty led to opportunties for more rapid promotion of provincial civil officials and the appointment of a greater number of men with military backgrounds to the post of governor–general.[57]

The importance of early experience in provincial administration, particularly at senior levels, is particularly obvious in the statistics for those who first served as governor. An extremely high 78% of all governors–general served as governor in one or more locations prior to their first appointment to the top provincial post. The figures, by group, are: Manchus, 72%; Chinese Bannermen/Mongols, 78%; and Han Chinese, 81%. In every period of the dynasty, over 60% of governor–generalships were held by men who had once been governors. The lowest percentage recorded was for the period 1736-55, which again points to the exceptional features of the Yung–cheng reign. In most periods at least three–quarters of the governors–general had held at least one prior post as governor.

Experience as governor appears to have been least important for appointments to the governor–generalships of the north and northwest. In both Chihli and Shen–kan, a high 28% of all governors–general had never served as governor in any part of the empire prior to their appointments there. Szechwan was also high, as 24% of its governors–general had never served as governor. The only other region with a figure above 20% was Liangkiang, where it reached 22%. Yun–kwei had the highest percentage (88%) of governors–general who did have experience as governors, perhaps another reflection of the problems of logistics and the greater likelihood of governors in this distant frontier area being appointed directly to the governor–generalship of the same province.

Almost half (48%) of the Ch'ing governors–general were appointed directly from a governorship, while another quarter went from acting governor–general to governor–general, and a very high percentage of these served as governor either immediately before or concurrently with their appointment as acting governor–general. Only 15% of the dynasty's governors–general were promoted directly from governor to governor–general of the same area, and, with the exception of Szechwan, this was most common in the frontier provinces.[58] However, a reasonably high 26% of all governors–general served as governor at some point in their careers in at least one of the provinces in which they were later appointed as governor–general. There does not appear to be any significant variation in these patterns in relation to period.

Appointment directly from governor to governor–general was more common among Han Chinese (55%) than Manchus (43%) or the Chinese

Bannerman/Mongol group (44%). Other posts from which governors-general were directly appointed included board vice-presidencies (6%), the presidency of a board or the Censorate (6%), a high Manchu or Bannerman military post such as lieutenant general of a banner or first-rank imperial bodyguard (5%), and a Grand Council or Grand Secretariat position (3%). These routes were slightly more common for the Manchu and Chinese Bannerman/Mongol groups than for Han Chinese. For instance, while only 1% of Han Chinese were appointed directly from a vice-presidency to a governor-generalship, the figure was 9% for Manchus and 8% for the Chinese Bannerman/Mongol group. Equally interesting, but more puzzling, is the fact that 8% of the Chinese Bannerman/Mongol group, but only 3% or 4% of Han Chinese and Manchu governors-general came to the post directly from a board or Censorate presidency.

Age at First Appointment as Governor-general and Later Careers

One of the consequences of the career patterns followed by Ch'ing governors-general, many of whom had considerable experience in both central and provincial positions, is that all were relatively advanced in years when they were first appointed to the top provincial post. The national average age throughout the dynasty was 54.5 years. While the average range of Manchus, Chinese Bannermen, and Mongols on their first appointment as governors-general was 52.1, 51.3, and 49.5 years respectively, that of Han Chinese was just over 56.[59] As Han Chinese normally spent longer periods in provincial government, especially at junior levels, it might be assumed that a slower rate of promotion in these posts accounts for the difference. Other available evidence does not support this. One study, for example, indicates that 46.7% of prefects spent less than a year in that position while 49% of district magistrates also left their positions also within a year's time, and of these more than one-third left for higher positions.[60] A more likely explanation is that Han Chinese began their careers at a later age as a result of the many years needed to acquire a regular *chin-shih*.[61] In any event, the office of governor-general was seldom held by young and inexperienced men. The job demanded mature, experienced officers, and for the most part the statistics demonstrate that this was recognized by the court.

Since the average length of a governor-general's tenure was about three years, most were in their late fifties when they left their first position. Most were given more subsequent postings and averaged a total of 5.2 years in all their governor-general posts. Therefore, the typical governor-general was about sixty years of age when he completed his provincial service. After their first as well as their final appointments as governor-general, these men were well advanced in years; few could expect to go on to lengthy appointments in the capital. While there were no regulations during the Ch'ing dynasty stipulating a retirement age, there were various review mechanisms that could lead to forced retirement at virtually any age. This kind of decision usually was made at the time of the triennial "great reckoning" or during an imperial audience if the emperor felt the official was too advanced in years or too physically infirm to discharge his responsibilities competently.[62] In a study which samples the ages of other high Ch'ing officials, the average age for those in positions of rank 3 and above was found to be sixty-five years, and for grand secretaries, seventy-one years.[63]

If we look at the career patterns of those who went on to other posts above the governor-generalships we are in fact considering less than half the national sample for whom this information is provided, since 60% of all governors-general were transferred to another tenure in the same office, demoted, dismissed, or died in office. As we shall see in the next chapter, 27% of all tenures ended in demotion or dismissal and the majority of those affected never returned to a post of comparable rank. However, of all governors-general promoted to higher offices, a total of forty went directly to either the Grand Council or Grand Secretariat. An even higher number (forty-seven) went on to the presidency of a board or the censorate. Twenty-two were transferred to high military posts (fifteen Manchus, five Chinese Bannermen/Mongols, and two Han Chinese), and eighteen went on to serve either as an imperial commissioner or in some other special capacity. While more Han Chinese (twenty-one) than Manchus (seventeen) or Chinese Bannermen/Mongols (nine) went on to a presidency, the numbers were very nearly identical for those appointed to the Grand Council or Grand Secretariat (Han Chinese, fourteen; Manchus, fifteen; Chinese Bannermen/Mongols, eleven). Of these men, only seven served exclusively, and another twelve predominantly, in provincial posts. That is to say, almost all governors-general who went on to serve in some high central office had already at some point in their careers spent some time at the capital.

No very clear pattern emerges from the attempt to relate these figures to different periods, although generally promotions to a presidency tended to be more common in the first century of Manchu rule than thereafter, while promotion to the Grand Council or Grand Secretariat was most common in the mid-eighteenth century and again throughout most of the final one hundred years of Ch'ing rule. Predictably, transfers to high military positions and to the post of imperial commissioner occured more often during periods of foreign pressure, upheaval, and rebellion, particularly from 1839 to 1862 and from 1875 to 1900.

Conclusions

For most Ch'ing bureaucrats who attained the governor-generalship, it was the peak of their careers. The climb to the top was a long and arduous one for all but a handful of the most brilliantly successful. For the most part, the court chose men highly experienced in the problems of government at both the provincial and national levels, with provincial experience apparently considered most important. These men were advanced in years by the time they attained the governor-generalship, and, as we shall see in the next chapter, the demands it placed upon them led to frequent demotions and dismissals. Many either died in office or retired from it. None of the statistics analyzed here would suggest that a Ch'ing governor-generalship was considered a sinecure to reward the faithful or flatter favorites. It was a demanding position—perhaps the most critical in the Manchu rule of China.

CHAPTER IV

Professional Mobility: Determinants of Success and Failure

A statistical analysis of the biographical information available for most of the dynasty's 504 governors-general provides material for a number of interesting interpretations of factors that appear to have affected rates of professional mobility, success, and failure. We have selected three basic sets of criteria to judge the degree of success enjoyed by our sample of officials: the age at which these men were first appointed governor-general, the length and number of tenures they held as governor-general, and their vulnerability to demotion or dismissal. In each case we have attempted to interpret the results by a correlation with a number of factors already discussed in other contexts, such as degrees held, political-ethnic group, first appointments, career pattern, native province, and period and province of postings. The patterns which emerge are not definitive, but they are suggestive.

Rates of Advancement

Estimated on the basis of all first appointments, both civil (including appointment to the Hanlin Academy) and military, Han Chinese were on the average 31.2 years of age when they began their careers, whereas Manchus were 25.6 and Chinese Bannermen 27.1. The difference in age at the time of first career appointment between Han Chinese and all the other groups combined was just under five years, which probably reflects the relatively high number of Han Chinese who began their careers with the *chin-shih* degree.

While our study is not reliable for the civil service as a whole, it is interesting that among high Ch'ing officials, in this sample at least, Han Chinese with the *chin-shih* degree were not only older than those without it when they entered the bureaucracy, but they never made up the extra years by more rapid promotion. Once their careers were launched, the rate of progress through the ranks was almost identical for members of all groups. It took the average Han Chinese 25.4 years to advance from his first appointment to the governor-generalship, while the combined average for the other groups was 25.6 years. Indeed, despite the fact that one might expect discrimination by the Manchu rulers against Han Chinese bureaucrats, their climb through the ranks was faster than that of the Manchus (26.5 years). The fastest rate of promotion was that of Chinese Bannermen, who reached the top of the provincial administration in an average of 24.2 years. This undoubtedly reflects the rulers' heavy dependence on this group in the early years of the dynasty and the resulting advantage loyal and capable Chinese Bannermen held in rapid career advancement.

The average age at time of first appointment did vary from period to period during the dynasty. For instance, there was a rise in average age during the eighteenth century for Manchus and Chinese Bannermen/Mongols. The most interesting feature of the correlation between age and period of first appointment is the steady increase in age during most of the Ch'ien-lung period, followed by a rather abrupt drop in the 1850s. This may reflect the relative stability of the Ch'ien-lung reign, and the uncertainty of the later period with its change of reigns and the need for the exigencies of rebellion to be met with young military leaders rather than aging civil ones. It does not, however, indicate a reluctance on the part of an aging emperor to change incumbents or appoint younger men, for the Ch'ien-lung emperor probably issued more orders to force older officials to retire than any other Ch'ing emperor.[1] As late as 1783 he made it a rule that during the triennial metropolitan inspection, when the performance of governors-general, governors, and officials in the central government were evaluated, he would give an audience to officials of rank 3 to determine who was too old or physically infirm to continue in office. The intention was to ensure that "these people would therefore not be able to block the path of others waiting to be promoted."[2]

Ironically the rate of promotion for Han Chinese within the bureaucracy was fastest for those without a degree. It took Han Chinese with the *chin-shih* eighteen months longer to advance from their first appointments to the governor-generalship than it did those without the degree (25.7 years and 24 years, respectively). On the other hand, it took Han Chinese with only the *chü-jen* even longer (28.8 years) to become a governor-general.

For Manchus with and without degrees our data base is much smaller, and probably inadequate for any definite conclusion. However, it does suggest an interesting trend. While the rate of promotion is almost identical for Manchus and Han Chinese who held only the *chü-jen*, Manchus with the *chin-shih* apparently were promoted much more rapidly. Manchu *chin-shih* degree holders took an average of 22.5 years from the time of their first career appointment to that of governor-general, compared to the 25.7 years found among Han Chinese with that degree. Curiously enough, while Han Chinese with the top degree moved more slowly through the ranks than those without it, the trend was reversed in the case of Manchus, who without the degree took 30 years to attain a governor-generalship. The rate of promotion for Chinese Bannermen did not differ substantially between degree holders and others (*chin-shih*, 25.1 years; *chü-jen*, 24.5 years; and no degree, 25.9. years). The most interesting fact remains the relatively rapid rate of promotion for Han Chinese without a degree. On average, these men received their first posting as governor-general eighteen months faster than Han Chinese with the *chin-shih*, and three years faster than either Manchus or Chinese Bannermen who lacked the top degree.

These variations are not explained by correlating different career patterns with rates of promotion. Unfortunately, we have inadequate data on rates of promotion for those who followed an exclusively or predominantly military career pattern, so a complete correlation is impossible. However, the data available would suggest that, with one major exception, career patterns did not affect rates of promotion by more than three years, and in most instances by not more than a few months. The exception involves governors-general who held exclusively central posts. The rate of promotion for this group was more than seven years faster than that of any single group for which we have adequate data. Those who followed careers of predominantly central posts reached the governor-generalship about eighteen months faster than those with predominantly provincial career patterns. The lengthiest route to the top seems to have been a relatively equal combination of provincial and central posts. These men took close to two years longer than those who held exclusively provincial posts, and nearly three years longer than those whose postings were primarily at the capital.[3]

The rapid rate of promotion for Han Chinese without a degree cannot be accounted for by exclusively or predominantly central career patterns, since no Han Chinese followed such a pattern. Nor did they win rapid advancement through military careers, for only 12.2% of this group followed exclusively military, and 8.2% predominantly military, career patterns. In fact, the most extraordinary feature of this group is that the highest percentage (36.7%) followed exclusively provincial careers, while another 18.4% held predominantly provincial postings. Within most career patterns there was less than six months difference in the rate of promotion experienced by the different political-ethnic groups. The exception proved to be Han Chinese who held exclusively provincial posts; these men moved much faster than the others (24.8 years, as opposed to 26.9 years for all other groups combined).

It is clear, then, that in most periods a significant number of Han Chinese attained the highest provincial post without holding either a *chin-shih* or *chü-jen* degree. One might have expected the cause to be predominantly military backgrounds among the men in this group, in which the opportunity for professional success rewarded by unusually rapid promotion would be greater than in strictly civil careers. This was not the case. In fact, most of these men worked their way up through the normal succession of local and provincial posts. Moreover few held central posts for any significant length of time. Han Chinese with the *chin-shih* degree never made up in their official careers the extra time it took them to acquire the degree. It appears that satisfactory performance and a full background of experience in the hierarchy of civil posts were more valued in the actual determination of promotion than was the level of formal educational qualifications. In short, the empire's highest degree was obviously important, but once in the civil service it seems to have had little impact on the more pragmatic determinants of career advancement.

It should be added that Han Chinese without either of the highest degrees held governor–generalships in all the periods. The largest concentration occurred in the final fifty years of the dynasty, when about one-third of their tenures were held. The second highest concentration was in the period 1776-1838, and the third highest was in the early years, 1644-83. While these periods of concentration are of interest, the most important finding is that Han Chinese without the highest degrees could and did reach the exalted post of governor–general in significant numbers throughout the dynasty.

Advancement and Native Province

Han Chinese governors–general without either a *chü-jen* or *chin-shih* came from most parts of the empire, but the highest number in both absolute and relative terms were from the northeast. Ten of the seventeen governors-general from this area did not have either degree. Fifty percent of those from Shensi and a surprisingly high ten of twenty-three from Hunan had neither degree.[4] No clear pattern emerges as to where these men served as governor-general, although the highest number of tenures among this group was in river posts, followed by the governor–generalship of Chihili.

A few tentative conclusions can be drawn about relative levels of success according to native province, as assessed by the age at which the *chin-shih* was awarded and the age of first appointment to the post of governor–general. From both our own sample and an analysis of the biographical entries in Hummell, men from the northwest and from Szechwan were considerably younger when they attained their *chin-shih* than those from any other area. The average age of receipt of the *chin-shih* for our entire sample is 29.6 years, while that for Hummel's biographies is 31.2 years. The provincial breakdown is as follows.

Table 4.1

Average Age at Attainment of *Chin-shih*

Native Region	Average Age at Attainment of Chin-shih	
	Chu-Saywell	Hummel[*]
Kwangtung-Kwangsi	30.7	32.0
Kiangsu-Anhwei-Hupeh	29.8	30.9
North (Chihli, Shantung, Honan)	29.6	30.4
Yunnan-Kweichow	29.0	29.7
Chekiang-Kiangsi-Hunan-Fukien	29.0	34.8
Northwest (Shensi, Shansi, Kansu)	25.3	24.8
Szechwan	25.0	23.7

* First column shows the average for our sample, the second is our calculation of information available on date of birth and *chin-shih* provided in Hummell's *Eminent Chinese of the Ch'ing Period.*

In correlating native province to age at first appointment as governor-general, it appears that Han Chinese from northern China were considerably older when they reached this post than those from other areas. Generally, the more distant the native province from the seat of government, the younger were the men when first appointed governor-general.

Table 4.2

Average Age at First Appointment as Governor-general

Native Region	Average Age at First Appointment as Governor-General
Kwangtung-Kwangsi	53.0
Kiangsu-Anhwei-Hupeh	57.2
North (Chihli, Shantung, Honan)	57.1
Yunnan-Kweichow	52.0
Chekiang-Kiangsi-Hunan-Fukien	55.4
Northwest (Shensi, Shansi, Kansu)	56.8
Szechwan	53.2

Interesting features also emerge from an analysis of the age at first appointment in the bureaucracy. The most surprising is the fact that, while the age of natives of most areas for which we have adequate data is between 27 and 32 years, an exceptionally low 21.4 years is recorded for natives of Kiangsu-Anhwei-Hupeh. Since men from this region were also the second oldest group when appointed governor-general, their professional mobility would appear to be the slowest of all. However, these figures should be treated cautiously and must be considered suggestive at best. They may be idiosyncratic due to the relatively small sample from which they were derived.

Length of Tenure and Frequency of Subsequent Postings

Length of individual tenures and the frequency of second and subsequent postings to the office of governor-general should provide another indicator for assessing levels of success. We have already seen (in chapter 2) that the rate of turnover among Han Chinese was considerably higher than that of the Chinese Bannerman/Mongol group, but almost identical to that of the Manchus. While the average length of tenure for the Chinese Bannerman/Mongol group was three years, eleven months, for Han Chinese and Manchus it was two years, nine months and two years, seven months respectively. The average length of tenure in many other provincial posts during the Ch'ing dynasty was also shorter than three years, as the following examples illustrate.[5]

Table 4.3

Length of Tenure in Provincial Posts

Office	Period	Percentage of Tenures Under Three Years	Percentage of Tenures Under One Year
Financial commissioner	1796–1908	81.6	45.9
Provincial judge	1796–1908	89.6	40.1
Prefect	1644–1911	76.1	46.7
Magistrate of independent department	1644–1911	80.5	51.3
District magistrate	1644–1911	78.8	49.0

While on average Han Chinese and Manchus served almost the same length of time in a governor-generalship, Han Chinese were the least likely to be given more than one posting. Calculating success on the basis of the total number of years all governors-general held their posts, the average was five years, two months. The Chinese Bannerman/Mongol group averaged a total of five years, eight months, while Manchus averaged a total of just over five years, one month. Perhaps the most interesting feature of the Han Chinese group is that those without either of the top two degrees spent a total of five years, two months, the average of all groups, in all governor-general posts, while those with at least one of the top two degrees spent the shortest total time in office, four years, seven months. It would again appear that those without the degrees were the most successful, but it must be remembered that those with the *chin-shih* or *chü-jen* reached the governor-generalship at a more advanced age, and thus were more likely either to retire at the end of their first posting or die while in office.

Those appointed to river posts were by far the most likely to receive multiple postings. The governors-general of Hukuang and Liangkuang were the next most likely group to receive a second or subsequent posting. Men appointed to grain posts or to Shen-kan were the least likely to receive a second posting. It was relatively uncommon for governors-general to be reappointed to the same post. The only significant exception was in river posts, where close to half of those who received multiple postings were reappointed to the same position. Repeat postings of this sort were virtually unheard of in the grain directorship or in Shen-kan.

In evaluating success rates by length of average tenure and relating this to region of appointment, we find a striking similarity across the face of the empire. The range is widest between the governors-general of Chihli, who served an average of 3.4 years, and those of Hukuang, who served 2.4 years. Most tenures were extremely close to the national average of 2.9 years.[6] A comparison of lengths of tenure and the frequency of demotion of dismissal also yields interesting results. In the case of Chihli, for example, the incidence of longer tenures was accompanied by more frequent dismissals and demotions. This also occurred in river posts, where governors-general had longer tenures than those in grain directorships, but were much more susceptible to demotion and dismissal. Not surprisingly, perhaps, it appears that the longer one held a governor-generalship, the greater was the chance of making a mistake or being caught for having done so.[7]

Retirement, Demotion, and Dismissal

The issue of vulnerability to demotion or dismissal and the causes of disgrace reveals much about the nature of Confucian attitudes in the governance of imperial China. (For examples of penalties, see translations of the regulations on administrative penalties, appendix 4.) As we have seen, a very high 25.6% of all governor-general tenures ended in either demotion and dismissal (9.1% ended in demotion, and 16.5%, almost twice as many, ended in dismissal). If demotions and dismissals are combined, the Han Chinese appear to have been most vulnerable, while the Chinese Bannerman/Mongol group experienced the lowest casualty rate. If the grain and river directorships are excluded, the figures do not change significantly. The demotion/dismissal rate of Han Chinese with the *chin-shih* degree was almost identical to the rate for those without the degree.

Table 4.4

Percentage of Governor-general Tenures Ending in Demotion or Dismissal:

General Averages

Group	Percentage for All Posts	Percentage Excluding Grain and River Posts
Han Chinese	31.2	32.7
Manchus	24.2	27.0
Chinese Bannermen/Mongols	18.8	14.6

By Political-Ethnic Group

	Percentage of Han Chinese	Percentage of Manchus	Percentage of Chinese Bannermen/Mongols
Demotion	13.5	6.6	5.8
Dismissal	17.7	17.5	13.0

While Han Chinese suffered almost double the rate of demotion experienced by Manchus, their rate of dismissal was almost identical. The casualty
rate also varied tremendously between regions of appointment, from Chihli,
where over 60% of all tenures ended in demotion and/or dismissal, to Min-che,
where the casualty rate was just over 16%. Besides Min-che, the "safest" post
was the grain directorship, with a combined demotion/dismissal rate of only
16.5%. Also below the national average were Szechwan, Yun-kwei, and Liangkuang.

It appears that the proximity of a post to the capital increased the likelihood that an official's mistakes would be noticed, for an extraordinary 53.5% of
all governors-general of Chihli were demoted and/or dismissed. As Table 4.5
indicates, this was by far the highest casualty rate in the empire. On the other
hand, military defeat could also result in dismissal or demotion. The relatively
high rates in Hukuang (27.7%) and Shen-kan (28.6%) reflect a high incidence of
rebellion and banditry in those areas. Similarly, problems created in the nineteenth century by the onslaught of Western imperialism help account for the
24.4% of Liangkuang's governors-general who were demoted or dismissed.

A striking contrast emerged between the "dangerous" river posts and the
relatively safe grain positions. Almost one in three river governors-general
were demoted or dismissed (32.2%), while for the grain posts the figure was a
low 16.5%. Obviously river posts were among the toughest posts outside the
capital, and it is interesting to speculate on why such a high percentage of Han
Chinese without either top degree held them. Were they less prestigious or did
they demand the appointment of men of a more practical bent of mind and
experience than was required by the provincial governor-generalships?

Demotion/dismissal rates also varied remarkably according to time. As
Table 4.6 reveals, the highest casualty rates occurred, not during the troubles
of the mid-nineteenth century, but between 1756 and 1820. Even more remarkable is the fact that forty-one demotions and dismissals, or just over 19% of the
total for the entire dynasty, were registered in the twenty-four years between
1796 and 1820. This represents close to 75% of all tenures during those years.
This period was particularly difficult in more than one respect. The figures
undoubtedly reflect the impact of the White Lotus Rebellion, which covered
much of Hupeh, Szechwan, Shensi, Honan, and Kansu during the years 1795-
1803. Many governors-general, such as Pi Yüan, were severly punished for
military defeats related to this rebellion. In the early years of the Chia-ch'ing
reign, many officials, including such prominent governors-general as Ching-an,
Li Feng-han, and Ch'in Ch'eng-en, were removed from office because of their
personal corruption or connection with Ho-shen during the final twenty years or
so of the Ch'ien-lung reign. The Chia-ch'ing reign was also a period of repeated
failure in flood control and as a result, river directors were frequently demoted
or dismissed.[8]

Table 4.5

Percentage of Governor-general Tenures Ending in Demotion or Dismissal
(By Region)

Governor-generalship		Percentage Han Chinese	Percentage Manchu	Percentage Chinese Bannermen/Mongols	Percentage of Total
Chihli	Demotion	31.8	0.0	8.3	18.6
	Dismissal	36.4	66.6	8.3	34.9
	Total	68.2	66.6	16.6	53.5
Liangkiang	Demotion	18.5	8.3	11.1	12.3
	Dismissal	18.5	16.7	5.6	14.8
	Total	37.0	25.0	16.7	27.2
Shen-kan	Demotion	15.4	6.5	0.0	6.3
	Dismissal	30.8	22.6	15.8	22.2
	Total	46.2	29.0	15.8	28.6
Szechwan	Demotion	8.3	11.1	0.0	7.3
	Dismissal	20.8	19.4	0.0	14.6
	Total	29.2	30.5	0.0	22.0
Min-che	Demotion	5.7	6.1	0.0	4.1
	Dismissal	14.3	12.1	10.0	12.2
	Total	20.0	18.2	10.0	16.3
Hukuang	Demotion	12.5	10.3	8.7	10.6
	Dismissal	15.6	20.5	13.0	17.0
	Total	28.1	30.8	21.7	27.7
Liangkuang	Demotion	11.8	8.0	4.3	8.5
	Dismissal	14.7	16.0	17.4	15.9
	Total	26.5	24.0	21.7	24.4
Yun-kwei	Demotion	14.8	7.9	0.0	8.5
	Dismissal	11.1	13.2	17.6	13.4
	Total	25.9	21.1	17.6	22.0
Grain	Demotion	7.8	0.0	25.0	7.2
	Dismissal	11.8	5.9	8.3	9.3
	Total	19.6	5.9	33.3	16.5
River	Demotion	16.1	0.0	9.4	11.3
	Dismissal	19.4	19.0	25.0	20.9
	Total	35.5	19.0	34.4	32.2

Note: Often a governor-general would be first demoted and later dismissed, presumably as accumulating evidence indicated a more serious transgression than was first realized.

Table 4.6

Number of Governor-general Tenures Ending in Demotion, Dismissal, or Both (by period)

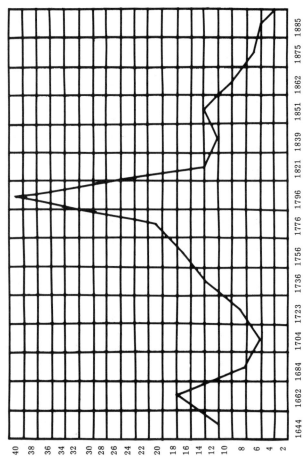

Number of
Tenures

Period

While these were the most difficult years to hold a governor-generalship for all the political-ethnic groups combined, there are some interesting contrasts among the groups themselves. For instance, one of the "safest" periods for Han Chinese or Manchu governors-general was 1736-76, precisely the time when the Chinese Bannerman/Mongol group experienced one of its highest casualty rates. Another contrast occurred between 1776 and 1838. This is the only period in which 50% or more Han Chinese tenures ended in either demotion or dismissal. Manchus, on the other hand, had a casualty rate of over 50%, not only for that period, but for the years 1662-83, 1851-61, and 1885-1900.

The contrast between rates of demotion and dismissal also merits attention. The rate of dismissal was higher in every period of the dynasty except the years 1662-83. While the percentage of tenures ending in either demotion or dismissal peaked in the years 1796-1820, thereafter the rate of demotion continued to fall. The percentage of dismissals fell in the 1820s and early 1830s but then increased, reaching its final peak in the 1880s. One might have expected a high percentage of demotions and dismissals in the years immediately following the succession of a new emperor, but this was not the case. Less than 10% of all demotions and dismissals took place in the first three years of a new reign.

A wide range of penalties could be imposed upon a governor-general. Dismissal might involve permanent exclusion from government employment. At the other extreme, an official might be dismissed and still retain his post. A governor-general subject to this penalty was deprived of his official salary during the period of dismissal. He could be fully restored to his position by the emperor if no serious administrative error was made during a four-year period.[9] Similarly, a governor-general could be demoted from one to three ranks and still retain his post. Full restoration was possible after three years and under the same conditions that prevailed for dismissal with the retention of post.[10] Officials could also be deprived of their salaries for periods of one month to two years.[11]

Most administrative penalties imposed upon Ch'ing governors-general were ultimately decided upon by the emperor himself and handed down in an imperial rescript. The information upon which these imperial decisions were based came to the court through a variety of avenues. Frequently the source was a censor or some other high-ranking official in the capital. At the other extreme, the governor-general himself might initiate his own punishment. This was frequently done when the faults were so obvious that they would almost certainly come to the emperor's attention. In these situations the governor-general would memorialize the throne, admitting his errors and requesting punishment in the hope that self-admission would lead to a lighter penalty. This did not always work.[12]

The court often obtained its information from the reports of imperial commissioners and other court officials sent to the provinces on special assignments, or from the reports of their "eyes and ears" planted in the provinces. The information provided in a governor-general's memorial to the throne was sometimes used as the basis for imposing a penalty upon him.[13] When a governor-general violated a specific regulation, the Board of Civil Appointments could report this to the emperor and recommend an appropriate penalty according to the regulations on administrative punishment for offences categorized according to the six boards.

Regular evaluation systems changed over the course of the dynasty. In 1654 the emperor Shun-chih decreed that all governors-general and governors should be jointly evaluated by the Board of Civil Appointments and the Censorate, but such evaluations could only be ordered by the emperor. The criteria, which were very clearly stated, included the quality of information contained in memorials, personal conduct, the degree to which imperial orders were executed, the extent to which power was used to recommend and impose penalties upon subordinates and the extent to which trials ordered by the emperor were effectively handled. The criteria also included success in flood control and grain transport, elimination of banditry, the search for and capture of fugitives from the eight banners, thoroughness in examining tax records, and speed in handling legal cases. All six boards were asked to compile specific information about each governor-general according to these criteria. The information was then forwarded to the Board of Civil Appointments and Censorate, which were responsible for editing it and producing a final performance evaluation. This evaluation was submitted to the emperor along with a recommendation regarding the appropriate reward or penalty.[14]

The results of these irregularly held evaluations could be anything from a temporary relief from duties to dismissal. It is not clear when this type of evaluation was discontinued. What appears to have been the last imperial edict ordering an evaluation of a governor-general in this manner was dated 1673.[15] We do know that it was slowly replaced by a system called *tzu-ch'en* (self-presentation), which was first introduced in 1656 and applied to all governors-general, governors, and metropolitan officials of rank 3 and above. Under the *tzu-ch'en* system, these officials were required to prepare a self-presentation record at designated intervals—every six years from 1656 to 1723, and every three years from 1723 to 1752. The record and a critical self-evaluation of it went to the emperor, who would then decide upon individual rewards or punishments.

With time, the system of self-presentation became little more than a bureaucratic ritual. Ironically, the worst problem was that officials, painfully conscious of their own vulnerability in a system of excessive bureaucratic taboos, became overly cautious, exaggerating their faults and minimizing, if even mentioning, their merits. As a rule, their reports would conclude with requests that they be dismissed. In 1752 the emperor Ch'ien-lung recognized the problem and decided to end the system, noting that:

> The presidents of the boards and the governors-general and
> governors all consider this "self-presentation" as nothing more than

a perfunctory routine. They always request dismissal with the full knowledge that the emperor will always want them to continue in their positions. . . . This hypocritical practice is quite meaningless . . . and should therefore be stopped.[16]

In 1759 the Ch'ien-lung emperor gave the evaluation responsibility back to the Board of Civil Appointments. Now, instead of the early Ch'ing system of irregular evaluations on the order of the emperor, the board was authorized to evaluate officials automatically every three years. This system appears to have remained in operation until the end of the dynasty.[17]

The causes of demotion and dismissal varied, and in themselves provide insight into the nature of government in imperial China. Although definitions may be somewhat arbitrary, the causes fall into two broad categories, the first concerned with lack of integrity on the part of the accused (for example, corruption, bribery, cowardice, discrepancies in accounts, failure to disclose a subordinate's transgressions, or submission of a false report), and the second involving general imcompetence (for example, military defeat, failure to suppress banditry and rebellion, or to prevent floods). The second category is most difficult to assess, for a great many of the causes given may not have been the direct or immediate responsibility of the incumbent governor-general, and in some cases appear to have represented nothing more than bad luck. For instance, to what degree can floods or the failings of subordinates be directly attributed to the man himself?

Across our entire sample, causes for dismissal were fairly evenly split between the two general categories (integrity, fifty-one dismissals; incompetence, fifty-eight dismissals). However, considerably more governor-general tenures ended in demotion due to incompetence (thirty-eight) than because of a lack of integrity (sixteen). Thus, lack of integrity was on the whole more severly punished than incompetence. In the causes for demotion there was no significant difference among the political-ethnic groups; all groups experienced demotion more often on the basis of incompetence than on lack of integrity. But in the case of the causes for dismissal, a striking contrast emerged. Almost twice as many Han Chinese were dismissed for incompetence than for lack of integrity (twenty-nine to seventeen), whereas the reverse was true for Manchus, who suffered eighteen dismissals for incompetence, and twenty-four dismissals for lack of integrity.

A frequent cause of demotion due to lack of integrity was related to a governor-general's responsibility for the transgressions or failures of a subordinate. The governor-general demoted might be accused of attempting to conceal a case, of falsifying a report about it, or of defending a protégé in trouble. More often, however, the demotion was simply the result of the subordinate's waywardness. This general cause accounted for almost all demotions for lack of integrity.

In the area of demotions due to incompetence, the most common causes were failure to suppress bandits or rebels, or to prevent floods and military defeat. These three shortcomings accounted for demotion in almost all the cases in our sample where anything more than a general remark about incompetence is given. Other causes were less frequent, but more interesting. For example, governors-general were demoted for reasons such as use of poor materials, delays in the transport of grain to troops, transmission of poor advice in memorials to the court, delays in forwarding a memorial, negligence, and failure to make an effort to rear horses.

Dismissals due to lack of integrity most often resulted from charges of direct personal corruption, often loosely defined, but sometimes including specific accusations such as "bribery." The second major cause was corruption on the part of a subordinate. Concealing information on matters such as local disturbances, banditry, or the transgressions of subordinates was also a common cause of dismissal. Frequently, implicit or explicit accusations of cowardice leading to military defeat were recorded. Other causes included disobeying orders and the abuse of subordinates or excessive leniency toward them. Incidental causes could be amusing. One governor-general was dismissed because he smoked opium. Another, officially cashiered because of a corrupt subordinate, was also accused of lusting after the subordinate's wives and reprimanded for allowing his servants to control his family affairs. At the outset of the dynasty one governor-general was dismissed because he entertained an envoy from the Ming prince, while another hapless governor-general in the late seventeenth century fell from power because he built a mansion when he was supposed to be in mourning for his mother. Toward the end of the dynasty a governor-general was dismissed after demonstrating a lack of respect to the Empress Dowager by photographing her funeral.

Close to 85% of dismissals due to incompetence were directly attributable to military defeat, failure to suppress rebels or bandits, or failure to prevent floods. In one or two cases governors-general were dismissed because they proved incapable of controlling their subordinates or servants, while one unfortunate Chinese Bannerman was cashiered because his seal was stolen.

Over the course of the dynasty, almost twice as many demotions and dismissals were for civil as for military causes. The majority resulting from military problems occurred in the nineteenth century, with a fairly even distribution of the remainder throughout the other periods.

One of the most interesting features of the whole pattern of demotion and dismissal is the strength of the concept of mutual responsibility in the Chinese bureaucracy. High officials were responsible for the conduct of their subordinates not only in theory, but in practice. Under Ch'ing rule the degree of punishment for misdeeds or shortcomings was in part detemined by the level of administrative responsibility. Governors and governors-general were held jointly responsible and shared the same penalty. For example, if a criminal escaped while being transported to the provincial capital for trial, the district magistrate responsible was dismissed, the prefect (his immediate superior) was demoted a full rank and transferred, the taotai within whose jurisdiction the escape occurred was demoted a full rank but retained in office, the provincial judicial commissioner forfeited a year's salary, and both the governor and governor-general forfeited six months' salary.[18] A very high number of Ch'ing governors-general either fell from office or were demoted (usually three full ranks) because they were held responsible for the errors of those beneath them.

The high rate of demotion and dismissal of governors-general also strongly suggests the "working of the Chinese system of jurisdictional or 'ritual' responsibility—one stayed in office by avoiding crises, not by creating them, for any untoward incident, preventable or not, was held against the official in charge of the situation."[19] Often recovery was rapid and complete, even from a sentence of exile. Yet, even when demotion or dismissal appeared as little more than a face-saving device for the court, for frequently the man was allowed to retain his post, it must have seriously inhibited individual initiative and the exercise of administrative imagination. It also may have encouraged officials to derive as much personal gain from their high positions as they could, before the likelihood of dismissal became reality. Like the basic ideology and administrative machinery of the Confucian state, the objective seems to have been the maintenance of social order and stability, not the active or imaginative pursuit of new national or regional policies.

Conclusions

The office of governor-general emerged in the Ming dynasty. The title was given solely to those high-ranking central government officials sent by the court on military assignments to the provinces. As broad regional coordination across several provinces became essential to the conduct of military affairs, the governor-generalship became an increasingly institutionalized office.

Governors-general also were appointed to supervise river conservancy and grain transport. In 1452 the first resident governor-general was appointed to encourage coordination between Kwangsi and Kwangtung in an effort to suppress a rebellion. The practice of appointing resident governors-general to oversee the affairs of more than one province became increasingly commonplace during the second half of the fifteenth century.

The granting to governors-general of concurrent titles in central government offices, in particular the Board of Wars, with other posts being added later, also began during this period and was continued by the Manchus.

In the early Ch'ing dynasty, the office of governor-general evolved into a highly institutionalized post at the top of the provincial administration. Strategic considerations sometimes led to changes in the jurisdictional boundaries of individual governor-generalships, but the general purpose and function of the office became reasonably stable at an early point in the dynasty.

The responsibilities of the office were enormous, although in many areas they were difficult to define precisely. As the highest ranking official resident outside Peking, a governor-general's far-reaching mandate was nothing less than the maintenance of peace, order, and good government within his jurisdiction. Remoteness from the capital and the vastness of the territory for which they were responsible combined to make the governor-generalship a powerful potential threat to the court. Clearly the alien Manchu rulers were extremely sensitive to this danger. In order to offset it, they developed a system of checks and balances which operated between the office of the governor-general and other high posts—especially that of governor. Indeed, the court appears to have deliberately avoided making clear and precise demarcations in the division of authority between the two offices. Nevertheless, as the highest ranking provincial official, the governor-general exercised great authority and the court was very careful to choose experienced, competent, and above all, loyal men for the post.

The political-ethnic composition of those who held the title, particularly in the early years of the dynasty, demonstrates the Manchu's concern with the question of loyalty. Initially, very few Han Chinese received such appointments and those who did were often given governor-generalships close to the imperial capital. By the K'ang-hsi period, however, the Manchu rulers' increased confidence and sense of security became reflected in the increasing numbers of Han Chinese who were appointed, and in the fact that they held the office for longer periods and were given posts in the more distant provinces.

Earlier, the court had relied heavily on Chinese Bannermen who spoke the language but were viewed as more loyal than Han Chinese. As time passed, however, the court grew disenchanted with this group. And as the Manchus' own experience in ruling China grew, they appointed increasing numbers of their own people to this and other provincial posts. The departure from past practice became particularly evident during the Ch'ien-lung reign. Later, from the early nineteenth century to the end of the dynasty, the majority or governors-general were Han Chinese.

Growing confidence in their ability and security, especially from the middle of the Ch'ien-lung reign to the late Tao-kuang period, appears to be indicated by the statistics. Governors-general in all groups were more frequently given second and subsequent appointments in the same, or other provinces. The total years of service in these appointments also increased in this period. Yet the court did not grow completely indifferent to questions of loyalty regarding their most senior provincial officials. Such an interpretation can be drawn from the fact that the length of individual tenures in one location, especially for Han Chinese in the same period, decreased substantially. Moreover, although most governors-general served at one time or another as governor, relatively few were appointed directly from that post to a governor-generalship in the same province. Throughout the dynasty, Han Chinese seldom received appointments as governor-general in the most distant provinces of Shen-kan, Yun-kwei, and Szechwan, where a very high percentage of appointees during the K'ang-hsi, Ch'ien-lung, and Chia-ch'ing reigns were Manchus. Indeed, it was only in the final century of Ch'ing rule that significant numbers of Han Chinese were appointed governor-general in these sensitive border areas.

The career patterns followed by the 504 men who served as governor-general in the Ch'ing dynasty varied according to political-ethnic group, regardless of whether they had the *chin-shih* degree or the period of the dynasty in which they held office. Minor variations in the offices held from initial career posting to appointment as governor-general were far too numerous to tabulate, but most fell into four or five general patterns.

With the exception of the nineteenth century, surprisingly few governors-general began their careers in the military. Although governors-general had important military responsibilities, less than one-quarter of all who held the office followed career patterns which included any significant degree of military experience. Fewer than 10% followed patterns defined as either predominantly or exclusively military. Indeed, the most common career pattern was one in which governors-general spent significant lengths of service in both general and provincial offices before appointment to their first governor-generalship.

Although experience in both Peking and the provinces was considered important, of the two, provincial service appears to have been viewed as the preferred background for an appointment as governor-general. The statistics also appear to confirm this interpretation by showing that the second most common career pattern centered upon movement through predominantly provincial posts, while the third relied upon exclusively provincial posts. Moreover, only slightly more than 11% of all governors-general were promoted either predominantly or exclusively from offices held in Peking. Also significant is the fact that as many as four out of five Ch'ing governors-general held a governship at some point prior to their first governor-general appointments. The conclusion that emerges quite clearly from the statistical analysis, therefore, is that a governor-generalship was regarded essentially as a civil post for which a combination of experience in both central and provincial government was desired, but for which long service in the provinces, rather than in Peking, was in fact the norm.

Almost two-thirds of the Han Chinese governors-general had the *chin-shih*. Nor surprisingly, less than one-third of the Manchus, and only 12.6% of the Chinese Bannermen had the empire's top degree. While it took many yearrs to acquire the degree, those with the *chin-shih* did not later make up the lost time by more rapid promotion than those without the degree. Once their careers were launched, the rate of progress appears to have been almost identical for the members of all groups. And, ironically, the minor variations which did exist indicate that Han Chinese without the *chin-shih* reached their first governor-generalship a little faster than Han Chinese who held the degree. What seems to have been more important than the degree in ensuring rapid promotion to a governor-generalship was following a career pattern of exclusively central posts. While most governors-general spent long careers in the provinces and capital, those who avoided provincial service entirely before being appointed to this post got to the top much more rapidly.

The lengthy process of acquiring the *chin-shih*, along with the long service in lower posts that most Ch'ing governors-general had experienced, meant that most were in their mid-fifties by the time they received their first appointment, and around sixty when their first tenure as governor-general ended. Because the majority of Han Chinese had the *chin-shih* degree, on the whole they were older when they recieved their initial appointment as governor-general than the members of the other groups. Therefore, the number of multiple postings to the office held by Han Chinese and the total length of service in the job was less than that of the other groups. Accordingly, relatively few governors-general—especially Han Chinese—went on to high posts in the capital. Of those who did not die in office, retire, or suffer demotion or dismissal, appointments to board presidencies, the Grand Council, and the

Grand Secretariat appear to have been the most common promotions enjoyed. A handful also went on to high military posts.

The office of governor-general was an extremely demanding one. Slightly over a quarter of all governor-general tenures ended in demotion, dismissal, or both. Han Chinese suffered the highest casualty rates (31.2%), when compared to the Manchus (24.2%) and the Chinese Bannermen/Mongols (18.8%). Across all groups, demotion or dismissal was higher in those governor-generalships closer to the capital and in those provinces such as Shen-kan and Hukuang where the incidence of rebellion and banditry were unusually high. Furthermore, an interesting contrast between the grain transport and river conservancy governor-generalships emerged from the statistics, which reveal that almost one in three officals in the river posts experienced demotion or dismissal, while only 16.5% of those in the grain posts suffered the same fate.

With the onslaught of Western imperialism in the nineteenth century and its impact on to the Liangkuang area, casualty rates there went up significantly. However, it was not during the middle and late nineteenth century that most demotions and dismissals occurred, but rather during the period from 1756 to 1820. More particularly, in the last twenty-five years of that period, close to 75% of all governor-general tenures ended in either demotion or dismissal.

The causes of demotion and dismissal have been divided into two broad categories in this study: lack of integrity and incompetence. The transgressions that led to dismissal could be quite evenly divided between the two categories. However, more than twice as many of the demotions resulted from incompetence than from lack of integrity. It follows then, that incompetence was not as severly punished as was the lack of integrity. Moreover, although the statistics do not reveal a significant difference among political-ethnic groups in terms of what type of failing led to demotion in each group, nearly twice as many Han Chinese as Manchus were dismissed on grounds of incompetence. Perhaps the most interesting finding in the analysis of the causes of both demotion and dismissal is how strong the concept of mutual responsibility was in Ch'ing government. A large number of governors-general were demoted or dismissed due to the misconduct or incompetence of their subordinates.

Admittedly, both the recovery of rank following demotion and the return to high office after dismissal were common. Yet the frequency with which these penalties were incurred underlines the difficulty of this office. It also suggests the extent to which Ch'ing government was based predominantly on the preservation of the status quo. Successful officials were those who stayed out of trouble, not those who took major initiatives or made interesting, individual contributions.

The 504 Ch'ing officials who successfully reached the top provincial post of governor-general usually did so near the end of their careers. For most of them the climb to high office was a long and arduous one in which competence, integrity, loyalty, and a certain amount of luck, were required. That so many suffered demotion or dismissal is perhaps the most graphic evidence that the governor-generalship was one of the most demanding jobs in Ch'ing government.

Appendix 1: Percentage of Complete Data by
Subject and Ethnic Group

| | | Percentage of Complete Data | | | |
| | Total | Han | | Chinese | |
Categories of Data	Sample	Chinese	Manchus	Bannermen	Mongols
Age of appointment and retirement	37.5	58.5	14.5	32.0	30.8
Years between first office and first appointment as governor-general	60.9	77.0	46.4	42.7	46.2
Years between award of last degree and appointment as governor-general	79.9	86.5	77.7	43.7	53.8
Degrees or other initial qualifications	92.4	95.0	93.4	90.3	84.6
First official post held	88.4	89.6	89.2	84.5	69.2
Total years experience in local posts prior to governor-generalship	62.7	66.7	62.7	56.3	46.2
Total years experience in central posts prior to governor-generalship	63.5	79.8	54.8	56.3	46.2
Post held immediately prior to first appointment as governor-general	90.1	89.2	91.6	90.3	84.6
Total years in high-ranking posts, provincial judge or above, before first appointment as governor-general	72.3	77.0	70.5	70.9	53.8
Appointments as governor and governor-general in same province	86.1	86.0	88.6	84.5	76.9
Demotions or dismissals	89.7	90.5	89.8	89.4	69.2
Causes of demotions and dismissals	84.3	84.7	84.3	85.4	69.2
Concurrent posts while governor-general	85.5	86.5	85.5	85.4	69.2
Reasons for leaving governor-generalship	96.2	97.3	96.4	94.2	92.3
Post held immediately after governor-generalship	86.3	86.9	86.1	87.4	69.2
Career pattern after governor-generalship	86.5	87.4	86.1	87.4	69.2
Time elapsed between last governor-generalship and appointment to Grand Council or Grand Secretariat	86.3	86.0	86.7	88.3	69.2
Never served as governor	86.3	86.5	88.0	85.4	69.2
Total years of service at rank 4B or above	60.7	64.0	59.0	58.3	46.2
Career pattern before appointment to first governor-generalship	86.9	87.8	86.8	87.4	69.2

Appendix 2: Memorials by Lin Tse-hsü and T'ao Chu

The following is a list of memorials found in Lin Tse-hsü's collected works *(Lin Wen-chung kung cheng-shu,* 37 chüan, reprint, 1963) and in T'ao Chu's collected works *(T'ao Wen-i kung ch'uan-chi,* 66 chüan, 1840). They were sent by Lin Tse-hsü while governor of Kiangsu, and T'ao Chu while governor-general of Liangkiang between July 1832 and December 1835. With one exception, these are regular memorials. The exception is a group of memorials sent by T'ao Chu regarding the salt administration for which he had sole responsibility. The memorials listed below demonstrate that beyond the one exception there were no clear lines of jurisdiction between the governors-general and governors in terms of the wide range of activities on which they had occasion to memorialize the throne. This point has been discussed in chapter 1 under the subsection "Powers and Responsibilities of Governors-general." The list does not include palace memorials, which differed in that they were secret and might address any matter.

They are identified by substance and by signatory, and, somewhat arbitrarily, have been placed in ten categories. When a memorial was drafted jointly, the officials normally referred to themselves as "we" and recorded their names together at the end. If a memorial was drafted by one person, but with the support or agreement of the other, the primary author would use "I" (with his name and title given in the body of the memorial), but would state at the end of the document that it was jointly drafted, then naming the other official. According to the laws of administrative punishments, the primary author of a memorial received a more severe penalty than his collaborator in the event that something went wrong.

1. Famine Relief

   a. Memorial seeking relief for the consequences of a flood in Kiangsu (joint memorial, with Lin serving as primary author).
   b. Report on the resettlement of refugees from a flood (Lin alone).
   c. Report of a poor harvest in Kiangsu, the result of natural disasters (Lin alone).
   d. Reply to an imperial request for a report on famine relief in Kiangsu (Lin alone).
   e. Report on the raising of funds for famine relief (Lin alone).
   f. Proposal for construction of a grain storage facility for future famine relief in Nanking (joint memorial, recorded in T'ao's collection).

2. Transport of Tribute Grain

   a. Report on the status of grain transport in Kiangsu (T'ao alone).
   b. Report on the quality of tribute rice produced in parts of Kiangsu (joint memorial, recorded in T'ao's collection).
   c. Report on disturbances caused by sailors on ships transporting tribute grains as they passed through Kiangsu (Lin alone).
   d. Report on the status of returning grain transport ships from the north (joint memorial, recorded in Lin's collection).
   e. Report on measures adopted to prevent sailors from causing disturbances (Lin alone).
   f. Report on assorted problems encountered in grain transport (joint memorial, recorded in Lin's collection).
   g. Request for permission to use silver ingots rather than foreign silver in the payment of expenses incurred in grain transport (joint memorial, with Lin as the primary author).

3. Civil Officials

   a. Request for permission to eliminate some sinecure positions in the local government (T'ao alone).

b. Secret evaluation of several provincial commissioners, taotai, and prefects, in response to an imperial request (Lin alone).

c. Request for permission to move the office of a district prison warden to another location (joint memorial, recorded in Tao's collection).

d. Request for permission to move the office of a second-class assistant district magistrate (joint memorial, recorded in Tao's collection).

4. Military Affairs

a. Plan for implementing an imperial order for the reduction of troops in the Green Battalion in three provinces (joint memorial, with T'ao the primary author; also signed by the governor-general of grain transport, the governor-general of water conservancy, and the governors of Kiangsu, Anhwei, and Kiangsi).

b. Request for permission to increase the number of troops stationed in a locality in Kiangsu (joint memorial, with T'ao the primary author).

c. Proposal to adopt rules and regulations governing naval forces in Kiangsu (joint memorial by T'ao, Lin, and the provincial commander-in-chief of Kiangsu, with T'ao the primary author).

5. Capturing Criminals

a. Report on the arrest of smugglers who escaped from prison (T'ao alone).

b. Report on the arrest and trial of salt smugglers (T'ao alone).

c. Report on the arrest and trial of local bandits (T'ao alone).

d. Report on the arrest and trial of bandits (joint memorial, with Lin the primary author).

6. River Works and Irrigation

a. Response to an imperial request, reporting that the sandbars along rivers in Kiangsu were not obstructing the flow of water into the canal (joint memorial, with T'ao the primary author).

b. Report on the results of an investigation ordered by the emperor into the problems of whether the flow of the Yellow River would affect the water level of the canal (joint memorial by T'ao, an imperial commissioner, and the governor-general of grain transport).

c. Report that the course of the Grand Canal need not be changed (joint memorial by T'ao, an imperial commissioner, and the governor-general of water conservancy).

d. Report on the inspection of a completed river works project (joint memorial, recorded in T'ao's collection).

e. Report on the inspection of a completed river works project (joint memorial, recorded in T'ao's collection).

f. Report on the inspection of a completed river works project (joint memorial, recorded in Lin's collection).

g. Report on the inspection of a completed river works project, also requesting administrative rewards for meritorious officials on the project (joint memorial, recorded in Lin's collection).

h. Request for permission to use funds in the provincial treasury for a water works project (joint memorial, recorded in T'ao's collection).

i. Request for permission to sell surplus grain originally collected as tribute for use in water works (joint memorial, recorded in T'ao's collection).

j. Report on funds used to buy rocks for the construction of river embankments in Chekiang (Lin alone).

k. Report on funds needed in Kiangsu for building river embankments (joint memorial, recorded in Lin's collection).

l. Report on the inspection of sites on a river works project (joint memorial, with Lin the primary author).

m. Proposal for repair of the canal (joint memorial, recorded in Lin's collection).

n. Report on the completion of a river embankment construction project (joint memorial, with Lin the primary author).

o. Report on the inspection of a completed river works project (joint memorial, with Lin the primary author).

p. Report on raising funds from officials and citizens for the repair of water works (joint memorial, with Lin the primary author).

q. Request for permission to use certain funds in the provincial treasury for the purpose of building river embankments in two districts in Kiangsu (joint memorial, by Lin and the governor-general of water conservancy).

7. Handling of Foreigners

a. Report on the activities of a British ship along the coast of Kiangsu and actions taken to send it away (joint memorial, with both T'ao and Lin as primary authors, cosigned by the provincial commander-in-chief).

b. Report on the return of the above ship, and the actions taken to chase it away (joint memorial, recorded in T'ao's collection).

8. Construction of Building

a. Request for permission to use the remains of a famine relief fund to construct a sacrificial temple in Nanking (T'ao alone).

b. Request for permission to use funds from the provincial treasury to repair the temple hall of a Ming emperor's tomb (joint memorial, with T'ao the primary author).

9. Examinations

a. Request for approval of regulations governing the reading of examination papers in the Kiangsu provincial examination (Lin alone).

10. Financial Matters

a. Report on the existence of a deficit resulting from the minting of copper coins (Lin alone).

b. Report on the results of an investigation concerning the prohibition of a shipment of foreign silver to Fukien and Kwangtung (joint memorial, recorded in Lin's collection).

c. Request for permission to cancel the collection of taxes owed by the people of Kiangsu before 1830 (joint memorial, with T'ao and Lin as primary authors, cosigned by the governor-general of grain transport and the governor-general of water conservancy).

d. Report on problems of local tax collection. In order to meet the deadline for delivery, the local government had to advance funds from its own treasury and was often unable to retrieve them (joint memorial, recorded in Lin's collection).

e. Request for permission to cancel collection of taxes as a result of unusual circumstances (joint memorial, recorded in Lin's collection).

f. Request for permission to cancel the collection of taxes as a result of unusual circumstances (joint memorial, recorded in Lin's collection).

g. Request for an the extension of time for the delivery of surplus funds from a levy on the operation of post stations (Lin alone).

h. Report on the results of an investigation ordered by the emperor to determine the situation that led to a rise in the value of silver (joint memorial, with Lin the primary author).

i. Request for postponement of tax collection due to a poor harvest (joint memorial, with Lin the primary author).

Appendix 3: Official Income of Governors-general

The official income of a governor-general was made up of several components. The basic annual salary *(feng-yin)*, was determined by rank, remained unchanged from 1647 to the end of the dynasty. For officials of rank 1A and 1B this basic salary was 180 taels; for ranks 2A and 2B it was 155 taels. In addition, between 1647 and 1670 an annual supplementary salary of 120 taels was given to all ranked provincial officials. The governors-general also received funds for miscellaneous administrative expenses. From 1647 to 1656 these funds amounted to 528 taels, and from 1656 onward they were 348 taels annually.[1]

The most substantial salary component was the *yang-lien yin* or fund to nourish honesty.[2] In principle the amount of *yang-lien yin* given to an official was determined by the complexity and difficulty inherent in his position. We have found no source that provides a general statement defining this principle, but the Ch'ing statutes do give sufficient specific examples for various positions that seem to suggest that this principle was applied routinely. For example, financial commissioner of Kiangsu is described as a position calling for nine thousand taels, a thousand more than the *yang-lien yin* of the financial commissioner in Nanking because "the former had more difficult matters to deal with." Similarly, the amount for the financial commissioner of Chihli was reduced to a sum equal to the amount for the same official in Kiangsu because "their workloads are the same." Ch'ing statutes stipulate that "Since the financial commissioners of Shantung, Honan, Fukien, Shensi, and Kwangtung have fewer problems with which to deal than the financial comissioners of Chihli and Kiangsu, their *yang-lien yin* should be reduced to eight thousand taels from ten thousand taels."[3] In the central government the *yang-lien yin* for the president of the Board of Rites was reduced in 1750 from ten thousand to five thousand taels because his portfolio was considered less complex than the portfolio of the president of the Board of Civil Appointments, who received ten thousand taels per annum.[4]

As a result of this practice of using the complexity and difficulty of the post to determine the amount of *yang-lien yin*, officials of lower rank sometimes received more funds than their superiors. For example, a prefect in Shantung could receive six thousand taels, twice the amount given to the provincial judge of Kweichow. Governors of Shantung, Shansi, and Honan—provinces which did not come under the jurisdiction of a governor-general—received more than some of the more highly ranked governors-general.[5]

Yang-lien yin of Governors and Governors-general 1734-1909

Jurisdictions	Taels per Annum	Jurisdictions	Taels per Annum
Governors-general		Honan	15,000
Yun-kwei	20,000	Kwangtung	13,000[b]
Shen-kan	20,000	Kiangsu	12,000
Liangkiang	18,000	Fukien	12,000
Chihli	15,000	Shensi	12,000
Hukuang	15,000	Kansu	12,000
Liangkuang	15,000	Anhwei	10,000
Min-che	13,000	Kiangsi	10,000
Szechwan	13,000	Chekiang	10,000
Grain transport	9,520	Hupei	10,000
River control	6,000[a]	Hunan	10,000
Governors		Yunnan	10,000
Shantung	15,000	Kweichow	10,000
Shansi	15,000	Kwangsi	10,000[c]

Source: HTSL, chüan 261.

Notes: a. In 1860 this was increased to 8,000 taels per annum.

      b. During the period 1734 to 1747 this was increased to 15,000 taels.

      c. Prior to 1747 this was 8,400 taels per annum.

Appendix 4: Examples of Regulations and Penalties for the
Conduct of Governors and Governors-general

The enormously complex nature of the tasks of a governor-general, who on the one hand was the "eyes and ears" of the emperor, and on the other the official chiefly responsible for the overall enforcement of the empire's laws and policies in the provinces, makes it extremely difficult to define his powers and responsibilities. This difficulty is reflected in the paucity of information on this subject even in the collected statutes of the Ch'ing dynasty. However, the researcher can learn something of the governor-general's powers and responsibilities implicitly from the regulations which define penalties for transgressions. The best source for this purpose is the 1892 edition of the *Ch'in-ting ch'ung-hsiu liu-pu ch'u-fen tse-li* [Imperially endorsed revised regulations on administrative punishments for offences categorized according to the six boards].[1] This book of regulations is prohibitive, punitive, and preventative in tone and purpose. It served to warn officials of the legitimate boundaries of their actions and the consequences of failing to conform to bureaucratic norms. By sifting through statements on what these officials were not permitted to do, and the consequences of failing to take a specific action or improperly fulfilling a certain responsibility, much may be learned about what was actually expected of them. One may, for example, acquire some notion of the conduct expected of a governor-general in reading that a demotion of three ranks is the penalty for failing to dispatch a certain routine report to a named board in the central government within a specified time and by an identified means of transmission.

It is clear from this that the governor-general was expected to work within a rigid bureaucratic protocol with precisely defined rules to follow even in the execution of routine business. In the 1892 edition of the *Ch'in-ting ch'ung-hsiu liu-pu ch'u-fen tse-li* there are a total of 299 regulations with specific and direct sanctions on governors and governors-general. Some of these regulations also cover such high provincial officials as financial commissioners and provincial judges. As a rule, the sample of these regulations given below excludes those of a more general nature. The regulations are found in all sections of the *Ch'in-ting ch'ung-hsiu liu-pu ch'u-fen tse-li* and are divided according to the jurisdiction of the six boards.

We may divide these regulations into six categories, according to the responsibilities they address. The first three are related to the role of the governors-general and governors as the "eyes and ears" of the court, namely, (1) impeachment, (2) evaluation and the recommendation of subordinate officials, and (3) reporting to the throne and the boards. Two additional categories (supervision and governance, and "other") deal with the role of these officials as the chief administrators in the provinces, and the sixth consists of regulations concerning their moral integrity. These categories have been determined by the presence in the regulations of certain common features, as follows:

1. Impeachment

   a. Failure to discover the misdemeanors of a subordinate and as a result failure to impeach him
   b. Intentional concealment of the misdemeanor of a subordinate and failure to lodge an impeachment
   c. Delay in processing an impeachment
   d. Failure to follow proper procedures for impeachment
   e. Impeachment of a subordinate with insufficient evidence
   f. Intentional or unintentional provision of incorrect information in an impeachment memorial.

2. Evaluation and Recommendation

   a. Bad judgement in the evaluation of subordinates
   b. Failure to recommend a meritorious subordinate

    c.   Recommendation of a subordinate before carefully checking his performance and ability

    d.   Willful distortion of the facts about a subordinate when recommending him

    e.   Recommendation of a subordinate for a position for which he is not qualified or suitable.

3.   Reports to the Throne and the Six Boards

    a.   Failure to report important events or failure to make routine reports

    b.   Submission of a report without first having carefully investigated the facts

    c.   Failure to include important information in reports

    d.   Submission of a false report in order to conceal one's own mistakes or the mistakes of one's subordinates

    e.   Delay in the submission of reports

    f.   Taking action without first reporting to the throne.

4.   Supervision and Governance

    a.   Failure to direct subordinates to carry out general policies or specific tasks

    b.   Failure to complete a task within a stipulated time

    c.   Failure to discover false information provided by subordinates

    d.   Failure to take appropriate action after receiving reports from subordinates

    e.   Negligence in taking preventive measures

    f.   Failure to investigate a situation before taking action

    g.   Failure to respond to the request of a subordinate

    h.   Overall administrative ineptness[2]

5.   Others

This category includes assorted regulations that deal primarily with transgressions of established rules.[3]

6.   Lack of Personal Integrity

This category includes acceptance of bribes, extortion for personal gain, solicitation of bribes or gifts, working for private gain under the pretense of public business, and forcing subordinates to cooperate in illicit activities.

The regulations translated below have been selected, not for their intrinsic importance, but because they are representative of our six categories and illustrate to a certain degree, the complexity of the responsibilities of a governor-general and the constraints placed upon him.

Although this study is not particularly concerned with the differentiation between "private" and "public" offenses, we have included this distinction in each case for the reference of others. Essentially, "private offenses" are of three general types: those related to the advancement of one's personal interest, major administrative errors, and intentional misdemeanors. "Public offenses" are administrative mistakes that demonstrate no intentional motive of self-interest, and are generally of less consequence.

In the following charts, the 299 regulations are statistically divided into "private" and "public" offenses. These are correlated with government jurisdiction (that is, the board under which they fall), with the form of penalty, and with our six categories.

These statistical breakdowns reveal a particularly interesting feature: they demonstrate that the most severe penalties were for "private offenses." Of the thirty-eight offenses punishable by dismissal, thirty-five are classified as "private." This percentage gradually decreases as the severity of the punishment is reduced. For example, none of the offenses punishable by forfeit of salary are classified as "private." A quarter of the 286 regulations that deal with administration involve failures in the category of impeachment. Furthermore, a surprisingly large percentage of these are "private offenses" as well. The opposite is true of the category of supervision and governance, in which less than 6% of the regulations involve "private offenses." As expected, all offenses related to a lack of personal integrity are considered "private."

Number of Private and Public Offenses and Type of Punishment Under Boards
By Government Jurisdiction

Boards	Dismissal	Demotion and Transfer	Demotion with Retention of Post	Forfeit of Salary	Total
Civil Appointments	20 (18- 2+)	46 (34- 12+)	17 (4- 13+)	22 (22+)	105 (56- 49+)
Revenue	5 (5-)	21 (18- 3+)	8 (8+)	20 (20+)	54 (23- 31+)
Rites	0	3 (2- 1+)	0	3 (3+)	6 (2- 4+)
War	9 (9-)	18 (10- 8+)	15 (15+)	18 (18+)	60 (19- 41+)
Punishments	2 (1- 1+)	12 (8- 4+)	10 (1- 9+)	39 (39+)	63 (10- 53+)
Works	2 (2-)	1 (1-)	4 (4+)	4 (4+)	11 (3- 8+)
TOTAL	38 (35- 3+)	101 (73- 28+)	54 (5- 49+)	106 (106+)	299 (113- 186+)

Number of Private and Public Offenses and Punishments Related to Duties and Conduct
By Types of Failures

Areas of Responsibility Where Failures Occur	Dismissal	Demotion and Transfer	Demotion with Retention of Post	Forfeit of Salary	Total
Administrative failure					
Impeachment	15 (14- 1+)	51 (49- 2+)	7 (3- 4+)	5 (5+)	78 (66- 12+)
Evaluation and recommendation	3 (2- 1+)	13 (6- 7+)	3 (2- 1+)	7 (7+)	26 (10- 16+)
Reporting to throne and six boards	5 (5-)	7 (4- 3+)	5 (5+)	4 (4+)	21 (9- 12+)
Supervision and governance	2 (1- 1+)	20 (7- 13+)	38 (38+)	85 (85+)	145 (8- 137+)
Other	1 (1-)	9 (6- 3+)	1 (1+)	5 (5+)	16 (7- 9+)
TOTAL	26 (23- 3+)	100 (72- 28+)	54 (5- 49+)	106 (106+)	286 (100- 186+)
Moral failure	12 (12-)	1 (1-)	0	0	13 (13-)
TOTAL	38 (35- 3+)	101 (73- 28+)	54 (5- 49+)	106 (106+)	299 (113- 186+)

Key: -   private offense;   +   public offense

Examples of Regulations and Penalties for Governors-general and Governors

If a governor-general or governor willfully distorts the facts about a subordinate when recommending him in a secret memorial, the governor-general or governor shall be demoted two classes and transferred, according to the regulation which applies to officials who wantonly recommend wicked persons to the throne. Private offense. The governor-general or governor should be exonerated from any responsibility if he is the one who later discovered the wrongdoings of that subordinate and initiated the impeachment proceedings.[4]

LPCFTL, chüan 4, p. 3b.

When an official is promoted and transferred as the result of a recommendation by a governor or a governor-general [under one of the two following circumstances], the name of the official and the name of the governor or governor-general who recommends him should be recorded by the Board of Civil Appointments so that in the future, when this official commits an offense, the governor or governor-general will also be held responsible:

1. [A circumstance in which] a governor or a governor-general memorializes the throne, pleading for approval of the promotion of a subordinate to a position for which he is not duly qualified in normal circumstances, and the emperor acts against the advice of the Board of Civil Appointments and on the basis of this special recommendation approves the promotion by issuing a special rescript.

2. [A circumstance in which] a recommendation was rejected by the emperor on the advice of the Board of Civil Appointments, but the governor or governor-general submits a specially prepared memorial pleading with the emperor to reconsider his decision because the official is urgently needed and uniquely qualified, and on the strength of this plea the emperor gives his approval, issued in a special rescript. . . . If in the future that official commits a private offense, one that is discovered by investigation, and if he is impeached by the superior official [the governor-general or the governor] who first recommended him, regardless of whether they were in the same province or in different provinces [at the time the offense was committed], the superior official shall not be punished. If a private offense is discovered and [results in] impeachment by other officials, the superior official [governor-general or governor] shall be punished. If it is an avaricious offense such as bribery, calling for a death penalty by decapitation or strangulation, the governor or governor-general who made the earlier recommendation shall be dismissed. . . . If the offense calls for a penalty of military service in a remote frontier garrison, the governor or governor-general shall be demoted three classes and transferred. . . . If the offense calls for a penalty of temporary banishment and flogging, the governor or governor-general shall be demoted two classes and transferred. . . . If the offense calls for dismissal, the governor or governor-general shall be demoted one class and transferred. . . . Public offense.

LPCFTL, chüan 4, p. 5a,b.

When an official holding a *fan-ch'üeh* [a troublesome and busy post] is transferred by the incumbent governor-general or governor back to a *chien-ch'üeh* [a simple and less burdensome position] because he is incapable of handling heavy responsibilities, the governor-general or governor who initially recommended the transfer of that official from a *chien-ch'üeh* to a *fan-ch'üeh* is to be demoted one class with retention of the post. Private offense. If an incumbent governor-general or governor, because he holds a grudge against his predecessor, intentionally acts overcritically toward an official his predecessor recommended, and unjustifiably transfers that official to a *chien-ch'üeh* . . . he shall be demoted three classes and transferred, according to the punishment for officials who harshly repress their subordinates. Private offense. If that man is indeed found to be incapable of handling the work of a *fan-ch'üeh* by officials other than the two governors-general or governors, the incumbent governor-general or governor, because of his tolerance of the mistakes of his predecessor, his procrastination, and his failure to impeach [his predecessor], shall be demoted two classes and transferred, according to the punishment for officials who practice favoritism. Private offense.

LPCFTL, chüan 4, p. 6a.

If a governor-general or governor, because of favoritism, engages in one of the following irregular appointment practices, he is to be demoted three classes and transferred. Private offense. If the official so recommended is indeed an appropriate candidate [promoted without selfish motivation], he shall forfeit nine months of his regular salary. Public offense.

1. [A situation in which] a [provincial] *pu-hsiian* position[5] is opened and the governor–general or the governor omits mentioning in his memorial the particular status of that position, proposing to fill it with someone he recommends; or simply filling it with someone he recommends, or simply filling it [without asking permission] by transferring one of his subordinates.

2. [A situation in which] the governor–general or governor, when requesting [permission] to fill a *liu-ch'üeh* position,[6] recommends someone whose status does not fit the requirements of that kind of position.

3. [A situation in which] when a *tiao-pu* position[7] is opened, the governor–general or governor fraudulently reports that there is no suitable candidate of appropriate rank, so that he can request the emperor's permission to fill that position by promoting an official of a lower rank.

4. [A situation in which] when a *t'i-pu* position[8] becomes available and the governor–general or governor recommends that the emperor fill it by promoting an official whose rank is much lower than that of the position, or fill it by promoting someone low on the promotion order list.

LPCFTL, chüan 4, p. 4a.

When a governor or governor–general memorializes [the throne] to impeach an avaricious and immoral or fatuous subordinate, he should clearly state [the following]: the name of the superior official who in a memorial originally recommended the guilty official; whether this superior official has previously exposed the misdeed of the guilty official and impeached him; and whether the superior official is currently in the same province (if he is not, the province to which he has moved should also be provided). If any of this information is missing, the Board of Civil Appointments should immediately investigate the matter. The governor or governor–general who fails to provide complete information should be demoted one class, with retention of duties, if the official is impeached for avariciousness and immorality. He should be fined one year's regular salary if the official is impeached for fatuousness. Public offense. The governor or governor–general should be dismissed if he is found to have unjustly sheltered and connived with the superior official who made the original recommendation. He should also be dismissed if it was he who made that original recommendation, and, in order to hide his former mistake, failed to [immediately] expose and impeach his subordinate. Private offense.

LPCFTL, chüan 4, p. 6a.

When an upright, honest, and benevolent official is demoted or dismissed due to some mistake made while carrying out his public duties, the governor–general or governor is permitted to memorialize [the throne] requesting permission to retain him in his post. However, if it is later demonstrated that the official thus retained has in fact always been a wicked and devious person, the governor–general or governor [who recommended him] shall be demoted two classes and transferred. Private offense.

LPCFTL, chüan 4, p. 8b.

When it is proven in a trial that a governor has been corrupt, the governor–general who failed to impeach him, shall be demoted three classes and transferred, regardless of whether the two have their yamen in the same city. The same applies to a governor who fails to impeach an avaricious governor–general. Private offense.

LPCFTL, chuan 4, p. 11b.

If a governor or governor–general, in an impeachment [memorial] to the throne, unjustly accuses an honest and upright official of being avaricious and morally inferior, the governor or governor–general should be dismissed. If the accusation is fabricated by a provincial commissioner, a taotai, a prefect, or a grain or salt intendant, this individual shall be dismissed. The governor or governor–general should be demoted three classes and transferred. All private offenses.

LPCFTL, chüan 4, p. 12b.

When a governor-general or a governor wrongly impeaches a subordinate because he has a grudge against that official, and when the more serious accusations in the impeachment have been proved in a trial to be totally unfounded, the governor-general or governor shall be dismissed. Private offense.

LPCFTL, chüan 4, p. 13a.

In accordance with the established regulations, when the magistrate of a district or a department is evaluated [in the triennial evaluation] as outstanding and distinctive, and consequently recommended [for promotion] by the prefect and taotai, the recommendation and its claims should be carefully scrutinized by the provincial financial commissioner and the provincial judge, under the direction of the governor-general and the governor. The result should then be reported to the throne in a memorial . . . . In cases in which the governor-general and others used their power to coerce the taotai and prefect into making the recommendation, the taotai and the prefect may expose this directly to the Board of Civil Appointments or the Censorate: the governor-general, the governor, and the two provincial commissioners shall all be dismissed. Private offense.

LPCFTL, chüan 6, p. 3b.

If a governor-general or governor wishes to leave office for the purpose of mourning a parent, he must not simply leave the seal of his office with the acting official and depart. He should select a temporary provincial commissioner to look after his official correspondence and should wait with reverence for the arrival of the edict [permitting him to depart]. If the said official does not abide by this established regulation, he shall be punished with dismissal for violating the imperial order. Private offense.

LPCFTL, chüan 8, p. 1a.

The dates for the reporting of provincial financial accounts to the throne shall be recorded and checked by the Board of Revenue and the Board of Works. If a report [by the provincial authorities to the emperor] is three years or less overdue, the governor-general and the governor shall be spared the responsibility. If it is between three and four years overdue, the governor-general and the governor shall be fined one year's salary . . . . If it is between six and seven years overdue, the governor-general and the governor shall be demoted one class and transferred . . . if it is nine years or more overdue, the governor-general and the governor shall be dismissed. Public offense.

LPCFTL, chüan 10, p. 8b.

The governor-general and governor are the highest provincial officials. If it is discovered that people in their provinces are forced to leave their homes to wander about in other places, leading miserable lives, neglecting their land, and failing to perform their labor service and pay their land taxes, or if there is generally no governance at all, the said governor-general and governor shall be dismissed. Private offense.

LPCFTL, chüan 14, p. 6b.

The governor-general and governor will be demoted by two classes and transferred if they fail to impeach a provincial judicial commissioner or taotai who in the trying of cases does not make his own decision, leaving such judgments completely in the hands of clerks who may then do evil things and easily conceal them from their superior. Public offense.

LPCFTL, chüan 14, p. 7a.

When a governor-general or governor from another province, any superior official of the same province, or an imperial commissioner travels through the territory of a local official, that official is permitted to greet or see off the travelling official within a distance of not more than two   from the seat of his jurisdiction . . . . The governor-general, governor, or other great official [mentioned above] shall be demoted by one class if he knows that a local official has violated this regulation and does not report it. He shall be dismissed, arrested, and tried criminally if he orders a local official to greet or see him off [when he travels through the territory of that official]. Private offense.

LPCFTL, chüan 15, p. 4b.

If a governor-general or governor uses his private servant as the gate porter of his yamen, he shall be dismissed. Private offense.

LPCFTL, chüan 15, p. 5a.

If a governor-general, governor, financial commissioner, or provincial judge orders his subordinate officials, clerks, or runners to enter or leave his yamen by the side gates, he shall be dismissed. Private offense.

LPCFTL chüan 15, p. 5b.

If a governor-general, governor, financial commissioner, or provincial judge dispatches his domestic staff to travel extensively in various *chou* and *hsien* [departments and districts] under the pretense of conducting an inquiry or investigation, he shall be dismissed. Private offense.

LPCFTL, chuan 15, p. 5b.

When the purchasing clerk in the office of a magistrate of a district in which a provincial capital is situated is asked to purchase materials needed in the yamen of a governor-general, a governor, a financial commissioner, or a provincial judge, the official [who orders this] shall be dismissed. Private offense.

LPCFTL, chüan 15, p. 5b.

Any governor-general, governor, financial commissioner, provincial judge, or taotai who uses various excuses to solicit irregular contributions from his subordinates during the year of "great reckoning" shall be dismissed, arrested, and brought to trial. Private offense.

LPCFTL, chüan 15, p. 5b.

A governor-general or governor is to be dismissed if he fails to impeach a high minister or a censor whose male children have presumed upon the position and influence of their elders and forced local officials to connive in their illicit activities. [Type of offense not given.]

LPCFTL, chüan 15, p. 9a.

A governor-general, governor, financial commissioner, or provincial judge shall be dismissed if, without a good and legitimate reason, he hires a *mu-fu* [private secretary] who worked for his predecesor in the same capacity and as a result makes it possible for this person to occupy continuously the same position in the same yamen. Private offense.

LPCFTL, chüan 15, p. 9b.

If a department or district magistrate, when collecting taxes, arbitrarily increases the amount of the *huo-hao* [meltage fee] or levies extra taxes [beyond the quota] without proper authorization, he is to be dismissed . . . . After this [misconduct] is exposed and reported, the governor-general or governor shall be dismissed if he fails to impeach the offending official in a memorial. Private offense.

LPCFTL, chüan 25, p. 13b.

When the incumbent financial commissioner is leaving his post or preparing annual financial reports for the throne, the governor and the governor-general, if stationed in the same city, should go personally to the provincial treasury to check its contents against the account book. They then should sign a statement and report the result to the emperor. Also, on arrival at a new post and at the end of every year, the governor-general and the governor should go personally to the provincial treasury to carry out the same inspection. If, evidence is found of embezzlement, such as shifting funds without authorization or other malpractices, the governor-general or governor should immediately impeach the guilty official in a memorial. If the governor-general or governor is found guilty of collaborating with his subordinate by sheltering and concealing the misdeeds, he shall be dismissed also. Private offense.

LPCFTL, chüan 7, p. 1a.

When a governor-general or govenor receives a report from a subordinate about the results of a natural disaster [in an area under his jurisdiction], and does not immediately report it in a memorial transmitted to the court by a most urgent courier service, he shall be dismissed. Private offense.

LPCFTL, chüan 24, p. 1a.

When a governor-general or governor coerces the financial commissioner into illegally shifting funds from one expenditure account to another, or into misappropriating funds, the financial commissioner is permitted to report this in a memorial to the throne. The governor-general or governor shall be dismissed and arrested for questioning. Private offense.

LPCFTL, chüan 27, p. 1a.

A governor-general or governor who allows a foreign tributary ship to leave without first memorializing the throne and asking for imperial instructions shall be dismissed. Private offense.

LPCFTL, chüan 35, p. 9a.

Provincial officials ordered to transmit funds to another province for military provisions should divide the funds into five parts. Half should be dispatched every year in April and the balance delivered in September. If the governor-general or governor falsely reports to the throne that the delivery has been completed, when in fact it has not, he shall be dismissed. Private offense.

LPCFTL, chüan 37, p. 3a.

If, after learning from the officials responsible for supervision and execution of a repair project on a warship that the project cannot be completed by the deadline, a governor-general or governor fraudently reports to the throne that the project was completed on time, he shall be dismissed. Private offense.

LPCFTL, chüan 38, p. 2b.

If a governor-general or governor conceals the misdeeds of a high-ranking military officer and does not impeach him when that officer allows his troops to burn the houses of law-abiding people, pillage their properties, and take their children captive, that governor-general or governor shall be dismissed. Private offense.

LPCFTL, chüan 37, p. 6a.

The financial commissioner or the salt or grain intendant is to be dismissed, if without first reporting to the governor-general and the governor he proceeds on his own authority to spend tax funds originally budgeted for military expenditures (such as building military camps or ships, and making helmets, armor, weapons, and equipment) for other purposes, and, furthermore, presumptuously enters these [unauthorized] expenditures into the annual financial reports presented by the governor-general and governor to the throne. Private offense. The governor-general or governor who presented this report shall be demoted four classes and transferred. Public offense. If a governor-general or governor is told [by the financial commissioner or the intendant] about the proposal to shift funds, and instead of memorializing the throne [asking for approval], the governor-general or governor gives permission without proper authorization, he shall be dismissed and ordered to pay restitution. Private offense. The financial commissioner or the intendant is not to be punished.

LPCFTL, chüan 38, p. 1a.

The trial of a case ordered by the emperor in a special rescript should be concluded within two months, and the trial of a case referred by a board or other capital offices should be concluded in four months, all dating from the arrival of the culprit at the court. These trials should be conducted personally by the governor-general or governor within the prescribed time. If he is unable to conclude the trial within the scheduled period because the necessary witnesses cannot be procured, or because he must absent himself to attend to important official business, he may be permitted to have an extension. The length of this extension is determined by the established regulations. For a trial ordered by the emperor, the request for an extension should be sent to the Grand Council. In other cases it should be sent to the office that originally referred the case. On the day of the conclusion of the trial, the governor-general or the governor should state very clearly in the palace memorial or dispatch the dates of the original prescribed period and the duration of the extension. A copy [should be sent] to the Board of Civil Appointments for further verification. If the governor-general or governor delays the trial or exceeds the prescribed time limit without a proper reason for a period of one month or less, he shall be fined three months' salary. If the delay is between one and three months, he shall be fined one year's salary. For a delay between three and six months, the punishment shall be a demotion of one class and transfer. If it is over six months, he shall be dismissed. Public offense.

LPCFTL, chüan 48, p. 12a.

When a governor-general or governor impeaches a subordinate, he must provide a detailed and factual account of the misdeeds of that subordinate in the impeachment memorial and also give reasons for the impeachment. If he does not do so and only gives an equivocal explanation, he is to be demoted one class with retention of duties. Private offense.

LPCFTL, chüan 4, p. 12b.

When a governor-general or governor recommends a subordinate as being outstanding and distinctive, he should state in his dispatch to the Board of Civil Appointments that the recommended official is not in arrears in the collection of principal taxes for his current term of office. If it is found that an official, after leaving his post as the result of a promotion or transfer, did not collect the full budgeted amount of principal taxes in his last office, the governor-general or governor [who earlier recommended him as outstanding], is to be demoted three classes and transferred. Public offense. However, if this [problem of arrears in collecting principal taxes] is discovered and reported in an impeachment memorial by the same governor-general or governor, that governor-general or governor is exonerated from any responsibility.

LPCFTL, chüan 6, p. 3a.

A governor-general or governor is not permitted, under any pretext except that of meeting an urgent local need, to transfer an intendant, prefect, subprefect, or magistrate of an independent department, department, or district, to another post in an acting capacity. Should he find it necessary to arrange for such a transfer, he should give the reasons. [Furthermore], he should send a seasonal report to the Board of Civil Appointments within the prescribed time, giving the total number of such transfers made during that period. If there is a delay [in submitting the report], he shall receive a more severe punishment. When a department or district magistrate's position is vacant, and the governor-general or governor wishes to propose the appointment of an assistant magistrate as the acting official in that position, he should immediately send the request in the form of a dispatch to the Board of Civil Appointments with a detailed explanation. If, after checking the request, the Board of Civil Appointments find violations of the established regulations, not only will the request be rejected, but the governor-general or governor will forfeit nine month's regular salary. Public offense.

LPCFTL, chüan 7, p. 10b.

If the annual provincial total of appointments of assistant magistrates appointed as acting department or district magistrates exceeds 20% of that province's total number of officials holding substantive positions as assistant magistrates, [i.e., excluding those holding honorary positions], the Board of Civil Appointments should immediately impeach the governor-general, the governor, and the two commissioners, all of whom are to be demoted two classes and transferred. Public offense.

LPCFTL, chüan 7, p. 10b.

The director of grain transport is responsible for the administration of all aspects of work dealing with tribute grain in all provinces. If, in any year, 5% or more of the total tribute grain is not delivered, the director of the grain transport will forfeit one year's regular salary. Public offense. If this continues for three consecutive years, the director is to be demoted one class and retained to supervise the collection of tribute grain while bearing the record of [this] misdeed. When the arrears are fully collected and delivered, he shall be reinstated. [Type of offense not given.]

LPCFTL, chüan 18, p. 7b.

When a department or district magistrate intentionally does not report or otherwise conceals the truth about the outbreak of a locust plague in his territory, he is to be dismissed and arrested for questioning. Private offense. If the prefect or the magistrate of an independent department, with jurisdiction over that locality, fails to investigate and report [the misdeeds of the magistrate of that department or district indicated above], he is to be dismissed. If the governor-general, governor, either of the two commissioners, or the salt and grain intendant fails to investigate the truth and impeach those responsible, he is to be demoted three classes and transferred. Private offense.

LPCFTL, chüan 24, p. 4b.

When a deficit in tax funds in a department or district treasury office is discovered and reported by the prefect or the magistrate of an independent department, the commissioner or the intendant who receives this report should in turn submit the information to his superior, the governor or the governor–general. If the commissioner or the intendant refuses to report this to his superior, or the governor or governor–general, after receiving the report fails to lodge an impeachment, the prefect or the magistrate of the independent department is permitted to report this directly to the Board of Revenue or the Censorate. The official [the commissioner or the intendant] who refuses to transmit the report or the official [the governor or governor–general] who does not lodge an impeachment is to be demoted three classes and transferred. Private offense. A restitution payment [to cover the deficit] is to be paid by all who have committed the offense.

LPCFTL, chüan 27, p. 2a.

When a governor–general or governor impeaches a department or district magistrate who is responsible for a deficit in tax funds, he should first carry out an investigation and than state in his impeachment memorial whether or not the immediate superior [of that department or district magistrate] ought to share in the restitution payment. If he fails to specify this in the memorial, he is to be demoted three classes and transferred. Public offense.

LPCFTL, chüan 27, p. 9a.

After *kung-sheng* [tribute students] are selected, by examinations held in the provinces, they are sent to the Board of Rites to be examined further by imperially appointed great officials and are ranked accordingly. If the provincial director of education, the governor, and the governor–general cannot carry out the selection in a fair manner, but show favoritism which results in the selection of students extremely inferior in writing, low in moral conduct, or mediocre in ability, they are to be demoted three classes and transferred. Private offense. If the writing of a *kung-sheng* contains serious errors, the sort that should not have been made by a person of that status, the officials [who first selected him] are to be demoted one class and transferred. Public offense.

LPCFTL, chüan 30, p. 3a.

If a superior official uses his position to force a department or district postal officer to buy horses from him [for courier service] at an abnormally high price, he is to be demoted two classes and transferred. Private offense. The governor–general or the governor who fails to investigate and lodge an impeachment is to forfeit one year's salary. Public offense.

LPCFTL, chüan 35, 1a.

A governor–general or governor should immediately report the arrival of a tributary envoy in a memorial via military postal service. He then should assign high-ranking civil and military officials to look after the envoy, escorting him to the capital and confining his activities to the normal realm of propriety. At the same time he should notify other governors–general and governors so that they can assign high-ranking officials to receive the envoy's delegation when it arrives in their areas of jurisdiction and give it protection . . . . The governor–general or governor who fails to assign high-ranking officials to escort, receive, or protect the envoy, shall be demoted two classes with retention of duties. Public offense.

LPCFTL, chüan 35, 9a.

If provincial officials repeatedly ignore instructions from the Board of Revenue to transfer an earmarked contingency fund [held in the treasury] for the purpose of acquiring certain military provisions [for troops in another province], the financial commissioner, if found by the governor–general or governor deliberately to have hindered the transfer of the fund, is to be dismissed according to the regulation for officials who blemish their post. If the governor–general or governor deliberately conceals the misdeed and does not lodge an impeachment, he shall be demoted three classes and transferred. Private offense.

LPCFTL, chüan 37, 3b.

When a department or district magistrate on some pretext or other and with the intention of soliciting bribes refuses to accept a shipment of rice, beans, or hay purchased from and delivered by the people [for the use of troops], or when the same knavish obstruction is carried out between the superior official and his subordinates, he [the official] shall be dismissed, arrested, and criminally tried. Private offense. If the victim goes to the governor–general or governor to bring an accusation [against that corrupt official] and the governor–general or governor refuses to receive it and lodge an impeachment, the governor–general or governor shall also be dismissed. Private offense. If the governor–general or governor was unaware of this extortion prior to its exposure by a censor in an impeachment or by others, the governor-general or governor shall be demoted four classes and transferred. Public offense.

LPCFTL, chüan 37, 5a.

When a provincial commander-in-chief or a brigadier general is found negligent in training the troops under his direct command, the Board of War shall deliberate on the proper punishment. If the troops under the direct command of the governor-general or the governor are found to be lax in training, the said governor-general or governor is to be demoted one class with retention of duties. Public offense.

LPCFTL, chüan 37, 1a.

When the position of a sergeant [rank 9B], ensign [rank 8A], or color-sergeant [rank 9A] is vacant, it should be filled by someone selected and promoted from the rank and file. If the governor-general or governor fills that position with a nonmilitary person, he is to be demoted three classes and transferred. Private offense.

LPCFTL, chüan 37, 2a.

A department or district magistrate is to be dismissed if he fails to report a case of robbery, or if he fraudulently describes a case of armed robbery as theft. Private offense. A governor-general, governor, or other official who collaborates in concealing the truth shall be demoted three classes and transferred. Private offense. If it is [merely] the failure to investigate and uncover the truth . . . the governor-general or governor shall forfeit one year's salary if the robbery occurred in the same city as his office. He shall forfeit six months' salary if the robbery occurred in a city within one hundred *li* of his office. If it occurred in a city more than one hundred *li* from his office, he shall forfeit three months' salary. Public offense.

LPCFTL, chüan 41, 13a.

The governor-general of Chihli has control over the entire province and is responsible for ensuring the security of the military district. When trees in the imperial mausoleum area are stolen, the penalty for the governor-general's negligence shall be proportionately less than the punishment of the provincial commander-in-chief. If the provincial commander-in-chief is to be dismissed, the governor-general shall be demoted one class and transferred. If the former is to be demoted and transferred, the latter shall be demoted one class with retention of duties. If the former is to be demoted with retention of duties, the latter is to forfeit one year's salary. If the former is to forfeit one year's salary, the latter shall forfeit six months' salary. Public offense.

LPCFTL, chüan 42, 1a.

When a governor-general or governor lodges an impeachment against a subordinate in which he requests that the subordinate be dismissed and tried criminally, he should, in the case of an official above the position of a prefect or an intendant, [and immediately after submitting the impeachment memorial] summon the witness to the provincial capital and conclude the trial within two months of the day he receives the dispatch from the Board of Punishment [giving him permission to carry out the trial]. In trying an official below the position of a first class subprefect, he should conclude the trial within two months of the day he gathered all the witnesses [in the provincial capital. This process] should be started immediately after the submission of his impeachment memorial. If there is a delay in concluding the trial, he shall be punished according to the regulation concerning delays in trials by a provincial judicial commissioner.* Public offense.

LPCFTL, chüan 47, 2b.

*If the trial extends beyond the prescribed time limit by one month or less, the provincial judicial commissioner shall forfeit three months' salary. If the delay is more than one month and less than six months, he shall forfeit one year's salary. If the delay is between six months and one year, the fine is two years's salary. If the delay is longer than one year, he is to be demoted one class with retention of duties. Public offense.

LPCFTL, chüan 47, 2a.

If after the [provincial] autumn assizes are held, there are fewer than five instances in which the Board of Punishments has reclassified cases from deferred execution [*huan-chüeh*] to capital punishment [*ch'ing-shih*], the provincial officials are exonerated from responsibility. If there are more than five cases of incorrect classification, the governor, the judicial commissioner, and those governors-general who are also concurrently governor of a province [this refers to the governors-general of Chihli, Kansu, and Szechwan] shall be demoted one class and transferred. If more than ten cases are involved, these officials shall be demoted one class and transferred. The demotion of one class is to be added for every five cases of incorrect classification. [Type of offense not given.]

LPCFTL, chuan 48, 1b.

If a sentence proposed by the provincial authorities [mistakenly] places a case in the category of "deserving capital punishment," [and this sentence] is later changed by the Board of Punishments to the category of "deferred execution," [the three provincial officials mentioned above] shall be demoted one class for each case of incorrect classification, and transferred.[9] [Type of offense not given.]

LPCFTL, chüan 48, 1b.

If it is found in the autumn assizes, that the sentence in a case is lighter than it should have been, the governor-general (if he has jurisdiction over two or three provinces), the provincial financial commissioner, and the intendant (the cosignatories of the sentencing document) are to be demoted one class with retention of duties. This demotion is to be applied regardless of the number of cases involved . . . . If a sentence is found to be heavier than it should have been, the above officials shall be demoted one class with retention of duties. This demotion is to be applied in every case of a wrongful sentence. [Type of offense not given.]

LPCFTL, chüan 48 1b.

If a major criminal escapes from a jail administered by the provincial judicial commissioner and the [subsequent] investigation shows that the criminal bribed [a jail officer to set him free], the governor-general and governor shall be demoted one class and transferred. Public offense. If the escape resulted from accidental negligence [by jail officers], the governor-general and the governor are to be demoted one class with retention of duties. Public offense.

LPCFTL, chüan 49, 5a.

River works officials should give a one-year guarantee on the dykes they build along the Yellow River, and a three-year guarantee on dykes along the Canal. If a dyke on the Yellow River or the Canal is breached by a flood within half a year and a year, respectively [of the completion of construction], those first- and second-class subprefects, department magistrates, and district magistrates who are directly responsible for construction and maintenance of the dyke shall be dismissed. The intendant is to be demoted four classes and transferred. The governor-general of water conservancy is to be demoted three classes with retention of duties. Public offense. If a dyke along the Yellow River or the Canal breaks within half a year or a year, respectively, of the completion of construction [before the guarantee period expires], the subprefects and magistrates shall be dismissed. The intendant is to be demoted three classes and transferred. The Governor-general of water conservancy is to be demoted two classes with retention of duties. Public offense. If a dyke is broken by a flood after the guarantee period expires, the officials responsible for the construction of the dyke are to be exonerated from any responsibility. The two river subprefects [kuan-ho and fang-shou] shall be dismissed, but retained to make repairs while bearing the record of a misdeed. The intendant is to be demoted two classes and transferred, but retained to supervise the repairs. When the work is completed, he shall be reinstated. The Governor-general of water conservancy is to be demoted one class with retention of duties. Public offense.

LPCFTL, chüan 51, 1a.

Notes

Introduction

1. Hsieh Pao-chao, *The Government of China, 1644-1911*.

2. John K. Fairbank, "The Manchu-Chinese Dyarchy in the late 1840s and 1850s," *Far Eastern Quarterly* 12 (May 1953): 265-78.

3. Franz Michael, "Military Organization and Power Structure of China During the Taiping Rebellion," *Pacific Historical Review* 18 (November 1949): 469-83. Ssu-yü Teng, *The Nien Army and Their Guerrilla Warfare, 1851-1868*.

4 Robert M. Marsh, *The Mandarins: The Circulation of Elites in China, 1600-1900*. Among the works of Ping-ti Ho, two at least touch upon material dealt with here. See especially his *The Ladder of Success in Imperial China: Aspects of Social Mobility, 1368-1911*.

5. In the Ch'ing civil service, positions were divided into nine ranks. Each rank was subdivided with designations which in Western languages are normally given as "A" for the higher and "B" for the lower designation. Thus the highest rank was 1A and the lowest 9B. Officials who received their first appointment through provincial and palace examinations usually started at rank 8 (for most *chü-jen* degree holders) or rank 7 (for *chinshih* degree holders). Those who held a rank of 3B or higher were designated as high officials. As Pao-chao Hsieh points out in his *Government of China* (p. 117), most promotions and demotions were of half a rank. "Without a special edict of the emperor, half a rank at a time was the common promotion or demotion; one full rank at a time would immediately become the gossip of the mandarin circle." For a list of ranks and the official titles under each rank, see HTSL, chüan 17, 18. For an English translation of these titles and their ranks, see Adam Y. C. Lui, *The Hanlin Academy*, pp. 175-82.

6. Fu Tsung-mao, *Ch'ing-tai tu-fu chih-tu* [The institution of governor-general and governor in the Ch'ing dynasty].

7. Lawrence D. Kessler, "Ethnic Composition of Provincial Leadership During the Ch'ing Dynasty," *Journal of Asian Studies* 28 (May 1969): 489-511.

8. For a comprehensive list of Ch'ing dynasty collected writings by names of authors, see Nishimura Gensho, *Nihon genson Shinjin bunshu mokuroku* [Catalog of individual collected works of Ch'ing authors found in Japanese libraries]. Another useful catalogue is Wang Ch'ung-min, *Ch'ing-tai wen-chi p'ien-mu fen-lei so-yin* [Classified index to essays contained in individual collected works by Ch'ing authors].

9. For an interesting example of this, see Thomas Metzger, *The Internal Organization of Ch'ing Bureaucracy*.

10. The difference in totals and ethnic breakdowns between our study and Kessler's is:

	Chu/Saywell	Kessler
Total Sample	504	554
Han	222	238
Manchu	166	187
Chinese Bannerman	103	115
Mongol	13	14

11. The dynasty is divided into seventeen consecutive periods varying in length from eleven to twenty-four years. Period of tenure in an office refers to the number of years a governor-general held that office. See Table 2.1.

12. The twenty categories of information referred to are listed in appendix 1, with percentage of data available on the entire sample and political-ethnic breakdown charted for each.

Chapter 1

1. *Yeh-ho pien* [Personal observations and reading notes of Shen Te-fu] (1869 ed.), chüan 22, p.1.

2. Ibid., 2-3.

3. Charles O. Hucker, "Governmental Organization of the Ming Dynasty," *Harvard Journal of Asiatic Studies* 21 (1958): 39.

4. *Ch'un-ming meng-yü-lu* [Miscellaneous notes on the capital city and the central administration in the Ming dynasty], chüan 48, p.24.

5. *Yeh-ho pien* (1869 ed.), chüan 22, p. 1.

6. *Ming-shih* [History of the Ming dynasty], chüan 73, p. 759.

7. Ibid.

8. *Yeh-ho pien* (1869 ed.), chüan 22, pp. 2-3. Censors were officials whose primary duty was to carry out investigations and impeachments of fellow officials. At times they were also required to remonstrate with the sovereign and the imperial family.

9. THL, Ch'ien-lung, chüan 28, p. 43.

10. THL, Shun-chih, chüan 31, p. 2.

11. SL, Yung-cheng, chüan 65, p. 4.

12. SL, Yung-cheng, chüan 69, pp. 14-15, and chüan 59, p. 15.

13. THL, Yung-cheng, chüan 25, p. 8.

14. Most of these changes took place during the Shun-chih and K'ang-hsi reigns. The dates when the last changes occurred are as follows:

Chihli	1724	Szechwan	1760
Liangkuang	1734	Min-che	1738
Hukuang	1688	Liangkiang	1682
Yun-kwei	1747	Northeastern	
Shen-kan	1760	provinces	1907

15. HT (1733 ed.), chüan 8, p. 2.

16. HTSL, chüan 23.

17. Ibid, chüan 20.

18. HT (1899 ed.), chüan 6, p. 4. See also Tao-chang Chiang, "Salt Industry of China: 1644-1911," especially pages 48-56; and Thomas Metzger, "T'ao Chu's Reform of the Huai-pei Salt Monopoly, 1831-1833," *Papers on China* 16 (1962): 1-39.

19. HT (1899 ed.), chüan 6, p. 4; *Ch'ing-shih kao* [Draft history of the Ch'ing dynasty], Chih-kuan chih 3, p. 6. There were occasions when a provincial governor-general was concurrently a river governor-general. From 1749 to 1795, the governor-general of Chihli was concurrently governor-general of the northern section of the Yellow River, a position eliminated in 1795 when its responsibilities were fully absorbed by the Chihli governor-general as a part of his regular responsibilities. From 1803 to 1805, the governor-general of Liangkiang was concurrently governor-general of the southern section of the Yellow River.

20. *Ch'ing-shih kao*, Chih-kuan chih 3, p. 4. See also Masataku Banno, *China and the West, 1858-1861: The Origins of the Tsungli Yamen*, 233-35.

21. CHWHTK, chüan 139, pp. 8993, 9004.

22. Ibid., chüan 115, p. 8740; chüan 132, pp. 8917-18.

23. Ibid., chüan 118, p. 8781.

24. Pao-chao Hsieh, *Government of China*, 291.

25. SL, Shun-chih, chüan 111, pp. 23-4.

26. SL, Yung-cheng, chüan 3, pp. 1-4.

27. Ibid.

28. Ibid., 4-8.

29. The works used are those of T'ao Chu, Lin Tse-hsü, Chang Po-hsing, T'ang Pin, Sung Lo, Chang K'ai-sung, and Ts'en Yü-ying, as follows: *T'ao Wen-i kung ch'üan-chi* [Complete works of T'ao Chu]; *Lin Wen-chung kung cheng-shu* [Official writings of Lin Tse-hsü]; *Cheng-i-t'ang chi* [Collected works of Chang Po-hsing]; *T'ang-tzu i-shu* [Collected works of the late T'ang Pin]; *Hsi-p'i lei-kao* [Classified writings of Sung Lo]; *Fu Tien tsou-shu* [Memorials of Chang Kai-sung submitted during his tenure as the governor of Yunnan]; and *Ts'en Hsiang-ch'in kung i-chi* [Collected works of the late Ts'en Yü-ying].

30. *Lin Wen-chung kung cheng-shu*, chüan 1, p. 3.

31. *T'ao Wen-i kung ch'üan-chi*, chüan 4, p. 31.

32. *T'ao Ch'in-su kung tsou-i i-kao* [Memorials of the late T'ao Mo], chüan 11, p. 2.

33. *Chao Kung-i kung sheng-kao* [Collected writings of Chao Shen-ch'iao], chüan 1, p. 17.

34. Some topics of consultation mentioned in the memorials surveyed were irrigation (see *T'ao Wen-i kung*, chüan 28, pp. 10-23, 54); the raising of funds for famine relief (see *Lin Wen-chung kung*, chia-chi, Chiang-su tsou-kao, chüan 2, p. 25); construction of river embankments (see ibid., chüan 7, p. 9); provincial finances (see ibid., chüan 8, p. 14); grain transport (see *T'ao Wen-i kung*, chüan 7, p. 52); collection of likin taxes (see *Fu Tien tsou-shu*, chüan 1, p. 15); selection of officials (see ibid., p. 19); border defense (see ibid., chüan 2, p. 20); transfer of military officers during a military operation and the recruitment of troops (see *Ts'en Hsiang-ch'in kung*, chüan 1, pp. 14-15); investigation of accounts in the provincial treasury (see *T'ao Wen-i, Kung* chüan 6, p. 7); the redeployment of troops (see ibid., chüan 22, p. 1, 6); plans for the capture of bandits (see ibid., chüan 24, p. 24); and plans to arrest salt smugglers (see ibid., chüan 25, p. 39). For examples of the text of an exchange of views between a governor-general and a governor, see *Yü Ch'ing-tuan kung cheng-shu* [Official papers of Yü Ch'eng-lung], chuan 7, pp. 6-7 (governor-general to governor); and *Chao Kung-i kung*, chüan 5, pp. 22-23, 34-36 (governor-governor-general).

35. *T'ao Wen-i kung*, chüan 15, pp. 21-32, and chüan 18, pp. 1-5. Another example was the frequent consultation between, and joint memorials from, the governor-general of Liang-kiang, the director-general of grain transport, and the director-general of the South Canal on issues related to water conservancy in central Kiangsu. Robert Alan Hackmann, "The Politics of Regional Development: Water Conservancy in Central Kiangsu Province," 30.

36. *Cheng-i-t'ang chi*, nien-p'u, shang chüan, p. 37.

37. Ibid., 40.

38. *Hsi-p'i lei-kao*, chüan 1, shang, pp. 55, 61, 62, 66, 74.

39. J. Y. Wong, *Yeh Ming-ch'en: Viceroy of Liang Kuang, 1852-58*, 38.

40. Ibid., 39.

41. Ibid., 40.

42. Ibid., 41.

43. Daniel Bays, "The Nature of Provincial Authority in Late Ch'ing Times: Chang Chih-tung in Canton, 1884-1889," *Modern Asian Studies* 4, no. 4 (1970): 329.

44. Ibid.

45. Quoted in Kenneth Folsom, *Friends, Guests and Colleagues: The Mu-fu System in the Late Ch'ing Period*, 71.

46. *Huang-ch'ao chang-ku hui-pien* [A compilation of unofficial materials on Ch'ing institutional history], Nei-pien, chüan 5, p. 15.

47. THL, Ch'ien-lung reign, chüan 99, p. 18.

48. According to Ch'ing statutes, only the emperor had the power to select and appoint the *cheng-yin kuan* (chief officials) of some of the most important circuits and prefectures. For a list of these positions, see HT (1899 ed.), chuan 8. Similarly, certain local positions were filled only by officials selected by the Board of Civil Appointments. In both cases, the number of positions involved was relatively small. See Fu Tsung-mao, "Ch'ing-tai wen-kuan ch'üeh-fen chih yen-chiu" [A study of categories of official positions in the Ch'ing civil administration], *Cheng-chih ta-hsüeh hsüeh-pao* 21 (May 1970): 169-70.

49. In a memorial composed during the K'ang-hsi reign, "Special Recommendations Regarding the Financial Commissioner," the governor-general of Liangkiang (Yü Ch'eng-lung) and the governor of Kiangsu jointly recommended the appointment of a financial commissioner to Kiangsu, acknowledging in the memorial that their action was not permitted by the regulations. See *Yü Ch'ing-tuan kung*, chüan 6, pp. 22-27. In 1722 an imperial edict condemned governors-general and governors for too frequently recommending officials to become financial and judicial commissioners. See CWHTK, chüan 55, p. 5375.

50. Metzger, *Internal Organization*, 40-41.

51. Ibid., 299.

52. CWHTK, chüan 56, p. 5382; chüan 57, pp. 5387, 5389.

53. *Ts'en Hsiang-ch'in kung*, tsou-kao section, chüan 8, p. 32. The phrase "assignment of responsibility to a single office or official" is the translation for *"chuan-tse,"* given in Metzger, *Internal Organization*, 123.

54. HTSL, chüan 80.

55. *Yü Ch'ing-tuan kung*, chüan 4, pp. 38-39.

56. For example, if a *t'an-k'u* (avaricious and cruel) official was wrongly recommended as *chuo-i* (outstanding and distinctive), the governor-general and governor were demoted two ranks and transferred, regardless of who initiated the recommendation. The same punishment was imposed if an official was wrongly accused during the "great reckoning" of committing one of the "eight proscriptions" (see note 71). The governor-general and governor were severely punished if they failed to recommend, or plotted to stop the recommendation of, an official who should have been graded "outstanding and distinctive." HTSL, chüan 80.

57. SL, Ch'ien-lung, chüan 171, pp. 9-10. The emperor criticized the governors-general and governors for writing only "casual" and "vague" assessments of minor officials such as the assistant district magistrates and postmasters.

58. THL, K'ang-hsi, chüan 5, p. 7; HCCSWHP, chüan 13, p.24.

59. HCCSWHP, chüan 13, p. 63.

60. See Kwang-ching Liu, "The Limits of Regional Power in the Late Ch'ing Period: A Reappraisal," *Ch'ing-hua hsüeh-pao* 10, no. 2, (July 1974): 208-09. Also Tung-tsu Ch'ü, *Local Government in China Under the Ch'ing*, 33, 44, 111.

61. Governors-general had their own staffs of privately appointed advisers and assistants known individually as *mu-yu* and collectively as the *mu-fu*. Of military origin, the *mu-fu* system was particularly powerful during periods of weak central government and thus represented a force of decentralization. See the excellent study by Kenneth Folsom, *Friends, Guests and Colleagues, 35-36. In the Ch'ing period most provincial officials from magistrate to governor-general had their own mu-fu*. A number of forces during this period made officials increasingly dependent upon them as the proliferation of official regulations and statutes led to the need for greater staff expertise. In the nineteenth century, in particular, senior provincial leaders on the coast of China who found their bureaucracies incapable of dealing with Westerners and Western ideas turned increasingly to the more pragmatic and specialized *mu-yu*. This was especially true of tax and legal *mu-yu* and those who specialized in the preparation of documents and memorials (Ibid., 51-52). In part, the *mu-fu* system reflected the increasing professionalization of Ch'ing government. It also represented a challenge to central control.

"Personal loyalty replaced private hiring as the basis of the *mu-fu* system, and because of their more pervasive nature, such loyalties made the system a greater corrosive of central authority" (Ibid., 151). Recognizing this, Ch'ing emperors "singled out for praise" those officials who served without the aid of *mu-yu* (Ibid., 55).

62. Liu, "Limits of the Regional Power," 222.

63. Ibid., 222.

64. Derk Bodde and Clarence Morris, *Law in Imperial China*, 115.

65. HT (1733 ed.), chüan 193, p.21.

66. Ibid., pp. 115-16.

67. Ibid., p. 119.

68. Ch'ü, *Local Government*, 125-26.

69. HT (1899 ed.), chüan 56.

70. Bodde and Morris, *Law in Imperial China*, 120.

71. The eight proscriptions *(pa-fa)* were reduced to six during the Chia-ch'ing period and are listed in the *Ta Ch'ing hui-tien* as follows:

1.	improper in conduct	4.	incapable
2.	tardy, weak and incompetent	5.	aged
3.	shifty and hasty	6.	in poor health

See HT (1899 ed.), chüan 11; I-tu Zen Sun, *Ch'ing Administrative Terms*, p.44.

72. HTSL, chüan 81.

73. For example, when a governor-general or governor, as a result of his own investigation, charged a district magistrate with bribery, the prefect, whose office was in the same town as that of the magistrate, was demoted three ranks and transferred, and the circuit intendant was demoted two ranks and transferred. Ibid., chüan 82.

74. Metzger, *Internal Organization*, 299.

75. There was an exception to this general practice. If an official in Chekiang, Kiangsi, Kwangsi, or Kweichou was impeached by the governor of that province, he most likely would be interrogated by the governor as well. This was done to avoid any possible delay caused by the length of time it would take to travel between that province and the one in which the governor-general was stationed. The results of such an interrogation would be sent to the governor-general, and, if he approved, he and the governor would submit a joint memorial to the throne. THL, Yung-cheng, chüan 7, p. 10.

76. THL, Ch'ien-lung, chüan 99, p. 18.

77. SL, Shun-chih, chüan 105, p. 20.

78. THL, K'ang-hsi, chüan 9, p. 9.

79. HTSL, chüan 82.

80. CHWHTK, chüan 132, pp. 8916-17. An early eighteenth-century case involving Chang Po-hsing, governor of Kiangsu, and Ke-li, governor-general of Liangkiang, provides an interesting example of this unusual procedure. Governor-general Ke-li, a Manchu, was appointed to his post in 1708, one year before the Han governor received his appointment. By 1711 their differences came to a head on the occasion of a provincial *chü-jen* examination. It was rumored at the time that two district magistrates and a deputy chief examiner were accepting bribes from candidates. The chief examiner memorialized the throne seeking the impeachment of these officials and requesting punishment for himself. The president of the Board of Revenue was sent to the province as an imperial commissioner to investigate the matter. After several months of calling witnesses and hearing testimony in which both the governor-general and governor participated, no decision was reached.

In the first month of 1712, the governor began impeachment proceedings against the governor-general with a *shu* (memorial) which contained two main accusations: (1) the governor-general was harboring corrupt officials and persecuting those who were unwilling to collaborate with him (details were provided); and (2) when the governor-general heard the rumors of officials taking bribes from candidates, he extorted half a million taels of silver form the chief examiner in exchange for offering to help him escape responsibility. In the ensuing investigation, evidence surfaced that the governor-general knew of the bribes when they took place and threatened witnesses during the investigation. The governor's memorial further accused the governor-general of deceiving the emperor and resisting the imperial order to investigate, and recommended his immediate dismissal and prosecution. In closing, the governor informed the court that he had notified the governor-general of the initiation of impeachment proceedings (*Cheng-i-t'ang chi*, shang, chüan 1 pp. 24-36).

In the meantime, informed of these actions, the governor-general launched impeachment proceedings against the governor in a memorial listing seven accusations that in fact arrived at the court before the governor's document. In the second month of 1712 both officials were relieved of their duties pending the outcome of an imperial inquiry undertaken by the president of the Board of Revenue (SL, K'ang-hsi, chüan 249, pp. 8-9). At the same time the emperor secretly ordered two of his bond servants, Li Hsü, then a textile commissioner at Soochow, and Ts'ao Yin, a textile commissioner at Nanking, to investigate and report to him the truth behind the bribery charges, the reputation of the governor-general and governor, the public reaction to the case, and the progress of the inquiries. In the next several months the emperor received eighteen secret palace memorials from the two informants. See Silas Hsiu-liang Wu, *Communication and Imperial Control in China*, 142-48; and Jonathan Spence, *Ts'ao Yin and the K'ang-hsi Emperor: Bondservant and Master*, 240-54. For the memorials of Li Hsü, see *Li Hsü tsou-che* [Memorials of Li Hsü], numbers, 127, 129, 131, 133, 135, 137, 141, 142, 151, 158, and 160. For memorials from Ts'ao Yin, see *Kung-chung tang K'ang-hsi ch'ao tsou-che* [Secret palace memorials of the K'ang-hsi period], vol. 3, pp. 555-60, 577-79, 606-12, 646-50, 669-72.

These reports concluded that neither set of accusations was well founded, that the governor had a favorable reputation, and that the governor-general was better known for his competence than his integrity. The conflict between the two top officials was attributed primarily to differences in temperament and poor advice received from their subordinates.

The official imperial inquiry was conducted separately for each official and in August 1712 a report was sent to the emperor with no conclusive recommendation. Two more board presidents were sent to assist the imperial commissioner and two months later another report recommended dismissal of the governor and exoneration of the governor-general. The emperor was displeased with this recommendation and rebuked those who sent it for having confused "right and wrong." The matter was referred to the Assembly of Nine Ministers and Censors for deliberation. In November the emperor made the final decision himself, accusing both officials of accepting slanderous rumors as truth and initiating impeachment proceedings against each other without cause. Because the governor had always been known as an upright official, he was dismissed, though with the retention of his post. In fact, five months later he was fully restored to his position and his punishment removed. The governor-general was dismissed. See *Cheng-i-t'ang chi*, nien-p'u, shang, 46-60; SL, K'ang-hsi, chüan 251, pp. 15, 20; and *Ch'ing-shih kao*, chüan 266, pp. 5-6.

81. In the beginning of the dynasty there were two financial commissioners (one senior, one junior) for each province, except Chihli and Kansu, which had none at all. In 1667 the number in each province was reduced to one. Chihli got its first financial commissioner in 1724 and Kansu in 1884. After 1760 the only province to have two financial commissioners was Kiangsu (HTSL, chüan 24). For the functions of the financial commissioner, see *Ch'ing-ch'ao t'ung-tien* [Institutional history of the Ch'ing dynasty], chüan 34, p. 2209; and Hsiao I-shang, *Ch'ing-tai t'ung-shih* [A general history of the Ch'ing period] 1: 490.

82. I-tu Zen Sun, "The Board of Revenue in Nineteenth-century China," *Harvard Journal of Asiatic Studies* 24(1962-63): 192-94. See also Liu, "Limits of Regional Power," 209.

83. HT (1899 ed.), chüan 82. See also Silas Wu, "Memorial System of the Ch'ing Dynasty," *Harvard Journal of Asiatic Studies* 27(1967): 61, n.49. This practice was not followed strictly by all financial commissioners. Fan I-ping, a censor, pointed out in a memorial in 1760 that some financial commissioners often showed the draft of a memorial to the governor-general or governor, and only with their approval submitted it to the throne. This was done to avoid arousing the suspicions of superiors who might take revenge later (Memorial from the Grand Council archives, quoted by Fu in *Ch'ing-tai tu-fu*, 176).

84. Sun, "Board of Revenue," 192-94.

85. Ibid., 211; P'eng Yü-hsin, "Ch'ing-mo chung-yang yü ko sheng ts'ai-cheng kuan-hsi" [The fiscal relationship between the central government and provinces during the late Ch'ing], *Chung-kuo chin-tai-shih lun-ts'ung* [Collection of articles on modern Chinese history] edited by Wu Hsiang-hsiang, 2d ser., 5: 3-4.

86. The estimates for the following year were always submitted by the governor-general and governor in the winter months. They contained a separate volume for the provincial Green Standard Army. HT (1899 ed.), chüan 19. For a fuller discussion of these operation, see P'eng, "Ch'ing-mo chung-yang," 4-6. A partial translation of regulations from Ch'ing statutes concerning these operations can be found in Silas Hsiu-liang Wu, "The Memorial System of the Ch'ing Dynasty," *Harvard Journal of Asiatic Studies* 27(1967): 18-22.

87. Sun, "Board of Revenue," 208; *Ch'in-ting hu-pu tse-li* [Imperially endorsed (compilation of) regulations of the Board of Revenue], chüan 9.

88. CWHTK, chüan 40, p. 5228; HTSL, chüan 183.

89. For an excellent study of land tax surcharges in the Ch'ing dynasty, see chapter 3 of Wang Yeh-chien, *Land Taxation in Imperial China, 1750-1911*.

90. Before 1724, the meltage fee (silver lost in the process of melting) was collected as a kind of *kuei-fei* (customary fee) to be kept by the local government for the official and personal expenses of the district magistrates. After 1724, this fee was legitimized and kept in the provincial treasury for the use of the provincial and local governments. Wang Yeh-chien, "Ch'ing Yung-cheng shih-ch'i (1723-35) ti ts'ai-cheng kai-ke," [Fiscal reform during the Yung-cheng reign (1723-35)], *Bulletin, Institute of History and Philology* (Academia Sinica) 33 (1961): 47-76.

91. Wang, *Land Taxation*, 34-35.

92. HTSL, chüan 170.

93. Wang, *Land Taxation*, 10, 16.

94. Recorded cases exist in which provincial customs duties were used by the governor-general and governor without obtaining the consent of the central government. However, these actions were officially condemned and did not occur frequently enough to be considered a threat to the financial authority of the central government. Sun, "Board of Revenue," 194-96, 220.

95. Liu, "Limits of Regional Power," 211.

96. Ibid., 211

97. Ibid., 212

98. Ibid., 219-20.

99. Lo Erh-kang, "Ch'ing-chi ping wei chiang-yu ti ch'i-yüan" [The origin of personal armies in the late Ch'ing period], *Chung-kuo chin-tai shih lun-ts'ung*, [Collection of articles on modern Chinese history], edited by Wu Hsiang-hsiang, 2d ser., 5 (1963): 89.

100. HTSL, chüan 255, 258; Fu, *Ch'ing-tai tu-fu*, 85-6, 139.

101. *Ch'in-ting kung-pu tse-li* [Imperially endorsed (compilation of) regulations of the Board of Works], chüan 27, p. 5.

102. Fu, *Ch'ing-tai tu-fu*, 94-5.

103. HT (1899 ed.), chüan 47.

104. HTSL, chüan 568.

105. Ibid., chüan 614; CWHTK, chüan 59, p. 5408.

106. HTSL, chüan 567, 614.

107. SL, Yung-cheng, chüan 3, pp. 2-3.

108. SL, Shun-chih, chüan 21, pp. 8, 23.

109. THL, K'ang-hsi, chüan 2, p. 2.

110. Ibid., chüan 13, p. 11.

111. HTSL, chüan 23.

112. *Ch'ing-shih kao*, chih-kuan, chüan 3, pp. 6-8.

113. SL, Yung-cheng, chüan 96, pp. 4-5; HTSL, chüan 577.

114. For a detailed account of the sizes of these various detachments, see HTSL, chüan 546-55; see also Ralph L. Powell, *The Rise of Chinese Military Power, 1895-1912*, 15.

115. For a concise yet illuminating discussion of this practice, see HCCSWP, chüan 78, pp. 5-8 (comments by Hsüeh Fu-ch'eng). For specific examples, see Fu, *Ch'ing-tai tu-fu, 177-78.*

116. For an excellent brief summary of one example of this, see Wong, *Yeh Ming-ch'en*, 70-73. As imperial commissioner, Yeh exercised considerable authority over the banner forces, including the right of inspection, the dismissal of officers, and in battle, the right to command the banners as well as the Green Standard Army, mercenaries, and the militia. For example, during the Arrow War one brigadier general asked Yeh (as well as the Tartar general) for reinforcements.

117. See, for example, Stanley Spector, *Li Hung-chang and the Huai Army;* Powell, *Rise of Military Power;* Franz Michael, "Military Organization and Power Structure of China During the Taiping Rebellion," *Pacific Historical Review* 18 (November 1949): 469-83, and Philip A. Kuhn, *Rebellion and its Enemies in Late Imperial China: Militarization and Social Structure, 1796-1864.*

118. Liu, "Limits of Regional Power," 210.

119. Ibid., 219.

120. Ibid., 209.

121. Ibid., 213.

122. Metzger, *Internal Organization*, 176.

123. See chapter 4.

Chapter 2

1. HTSL, chüan 23.

2. See chapter 2, section on appointments by reign and ethnic group.

3. For the powers and functions of these two assemblies, see Wu, *Communication and Imperial Control*, 100-101; and Fu Tsung-mao, "Ch'ing-ch'u i-cheng t'i-chih chih yen-chiu" [A study of early Ch'ing decision-making procedures], *Cheng-chih ta-hsüeh hsüeh-pao* 2 (1965): 245-53. For an example of the Assembly of Deliberative Princes and Ministers being asked to nominate candidates, see SL, Shun-chih, chüan 117. Since the nomination was made collectively by members of the assembly, it was normally referred to as *hui-t'ui*, a short form of *hui-t'ung t'ui-chü*, literally a "joint nomination." It sometimes was referred to as *t'ing-t'ui* or "court nomination." See SL, Shun-chih, chüan 79, p. 13.

4. Chang Chih-an, "Ming-tai t'ing-t'ui chih yen-chiu" [A study of the Ming system of selecting high officials by joint action of court officials], *Cheng-chih ta-hsüeh hsüeh-pao* 29 (1974): 203-26.

5. In a 1649 memorial, Hung Ch'eng-ch'ou, a grand secretary at that time, stated, "There were precedents [before] for appointing officials by the method of *hui-t'ui"* (SL,

Shun-chih, chüan 42, p. 9). It is not clear from the text whether the word "before" refers to the *hui-t'ui* system of the Ming or to a few unrecorded cases in the very early years of the Shun-chih reign.

6. SL, K'ang-hsi, chüan 35, p. 14. See also a memorial by the censor Hsü Hsing in *Huang-Ch'ing tsou-i* [Collected memorials of the Ch'ing dynasty], chüan 13, pp. 38-39. For an example of the emperor's rejection of the list, see the biographies of T'ang Ping, in *Ch'ing-shih lieh-chuan*, chuan 8, p. 5, and of Ma Ku in *Ch'ing-shih-kao*, lieh-chuan, chüan 60, p. 9.

7. SL, Shun-chih, chüan 71, pp. 17-19; and chüan 86, p. 4.

8. Ibid., chüan 79, p. 13; chüan 100, p. 16 (a memorial dated 1656 by the censor Wang Yüan-hsi).

9. Wu, *Communication and Imperial Control*, 18-19; THL, K'ang-hsi, chüan 36, p. 2.

10. CWHTK, chüan 55, p. 5371.

11. See a memorial by P'an Lei in CSWP, chüan 13, pp. 16-17; THL, K'ang-hsi, chüan 41, p. 4.

12. HT (1733 ed.), chüan 12, p. 4; CWHTK, chüan 55, p. 5371.

13. Fu Tsung-mao, *Ch'ing-tai chün-chi-ch'u tsu-chih chi chih-chang chih yen-chiu* [A study of the organization and functions of the Grand Council in the Ch'ing period], 407-08, 440-42, note 216. Fu discovered four *k'ai-lieh* lists in the Grand Council archives now in the Palace Museum in Taiwan. The number of candidates in each of the four lists numbered 20,57, 19, and 16.

14. For a fuller description, see HT (1899 ed.), chüan 7, 8; HTSL, chüan 51; and Hsü Tao-lin, "Ch'ing-tai k'ao-shih yü jen-kuan chih-tu" [The examination system and bureaucratic appointments in the Ch'ing period], in *Chung-kuo cheng-chih ssu-hsiang yü chih-tu-shih lun-chi* [Collected articles on the history of Chinese political thought and institutions], 3: 13.

15. In all four *k'ai-lieh* lists cited in footnote 13, the names within groups are arranged strictly in the following order: grand secretary, president of a board (in order of civil appointments, revenue, rites, war, punishment, and the Censorate), senior vice-presidents of the boards, and junior vice-presidents of the boards.

16. THL, Chia-ch'ing, chüan 12, p. 15.

17. This system applied only to the following appointments: grand secretary, president or vice-president of the boards, chancellors of the Hanlin Academy, governor-general, governor, financial commissioner, judicial commissioner, provincial director of education, adjutant general, lieutenant general and deputy lieutenant general of the Manchu garrisons, commandants of the vanguard division, provincial commander-in-chief, brigadier general, and special commisssioners such as the chief examiner of the metropolitan examination. See HT (1899 ed.), chüan 3, 8.

18. For excellent discussions of the role of the Grand Council and the use of secret palace memorials, see Pei Huang, *Autocracy at Work: A Study of the Yung-cheng Period*, 113-61; and Wu, *Communication and Imperial Control*. In the Yung-cheng reign, a network of secret memorialists was established that spread throughout the empire. These memorialists, some of whom held positions as low as prefect, were directly responsible to the emperor, and did not know each other. They regularly sent detailed reports on the performance of other officials regardless of rank and position, and on conditions they observed in any part of the empire. The emperor diligently read these secret memorials, checking one against another and frequently making extensive comments on them.

19. See *Huang-ch'ao ch'ing-shih wen san-pien* [Collected writings on statecraft of the Ch'ing dynasty, 3rd series], chüan 22, p. 15, for the Yung-cheng emperor's comments on Li Wei's memorial of 1724. Cases exemplifying this policy can be found easily in Ch'ing sources, for example, THL, Yung-cheng, chüan 5, p. 19, for the appointment of Li Wei-chün as the governor-general of Chihli in 1724; THL, Yung-cheng, chüan 25, p. 8, for the appointment of Hao Yü-lin as governor-general of Liangkiang in 1734; and *Pei-chuan chi* [Collection

of memorial inscriptions], chüan 70, p. 22, for the appointment of Huang T'ing-kuei as governor-general of Szechwan in 1731.

20. In this edict, the emperor decreed that

> The governor-general and governor set examples for all the provincial officials and are immensely important. However, I am often deeply distressed at not being able to find a suitable candidate for such a position when it becomes vacant. . . . Henceforth, officials in the capital from subchancellor of the grand secretary and vice-president of a board up, and provincial officials from judicial commissioner and financial commissioner up, should by means of secret memorials nominate one person, naming the post for which he is recommended as governor-general or governor, and stating the reasons clearly. In doing so, one should not take into consideration differences between Han and Manchu, seniority, or other qualifications. Even district magistrates or prefects, whose rank is obviously low, can be nominated in the memorials if they genuinely possess true knowledge and in the opinion of the nominator can fulfill competently the duties of governor-general or governor. (SL, Yung-cheng, chüan 80, p. 17.)

See also chapter 3, below. Our analysis of career patterns does indicate interesting and significant aberrations in appointment policy during the Yung-cheng period.

21. Liu Chia-chü, "Ch'ing-ch'u Han-chün pa-ch'i ti chao-chien" [The creation of the eight Chinese banners in the early Ch'ing], Ta-lu tsa-chih 34, nos. 11, 12 (1967): 13-18, 17-19. See also SL, T'ai-tsung, chüan 14, p. 10. For biographies of some early leaders of the Chinese Bannermen, see Hummel, Eminment Chinese of the Ch'ing Period. Included are biographies of Ning Wan-wo (pp. 231-32), Fan Wen-ch'eng (pp. 592-93), and T'ung Yang-hsing (pp. 797-98).

22. Fang Chao-ying, "A Technique for Estimating the Numerical Strength of the Early Manchu Military Forces," Harvard Journal of Asiatic Studies 13 (June 1950): 206-7.

23. Oxnam, Ruling from Horseback, 59, 71, n. 12.

24. Li Kuo-ch'i, et. al., "Ch'ing-tai chi-ts'eng ti-fang-kuan jen-shih shan-ti hsien-hsiang chih liang-hua fen-hsi," Taiwan Shih-fan ta-hsüeh li-shih hsüeh-pao 2 (February 1974): 349-55.

25. The table below gives the percentages of Chinese Bannermen and Han Chinese holding positions as provincial financial commissioner and judicial commissioner during the reign of Shun-chih and the period following Chia-ch'ing.

Position	Period	Percentage Chinese Bannermen	Percentage Han Chinese
Financial Commissioner	1661-68	40.90	59.10
	1796-1908	2.24	75.06
Judicial Commisssioner	1661-68	44.50	55.50
	1796-1908	3.36	74.16

Oxnam, Ruling from Horseback, 214-15; and Wei Hsiu-mei, "Ts'ung liang ti kuan-ch'a t'an-t'ao Ch'ing-chi pu-cheng-shih jen-shih ti-shan hsien-hsiang" [A quantitive analysis of the careers of provincial financial commissioners of the late Ch'ing period], Bulletin, Institute of Modern History (Academia Sinica) 2 (1971): 505-33. See also Wei Hsiu-mei, "Tsung liang ti kuan-ch'a t'an-t'ao Ch'ing-chi an -ch'a-shih ti jen-shih shan-ti" [A quantitative analysis of the careers of provincial judicial commissioners of the late Ch'ing period], ibid., 3, pt. 2 (1972): 475-95.

26. Oxnam, Ruling from Horseback, 92-93.

27. Lawrence D. Kessler, K'ang-hsi and the Consolidation of Ch'ing Rule, 1661-1684, 18.

28. For an example of Han Chinese criticism of the Manchus' heavy reliance upon Chinese Bannermen for top provincial positions, see the memorial of Wei I-chieh quoted in *Ch'ing-shih* [History of the Ch'ing dynasty], chüan 263, p. 3889.

29. Kessler, "Chinese Scholars and the Early Manchu State," *Harvard Journal of Asiatic Studies* 31 (1971): 197.

30. Before the K'ang-hsi reign, Chinese Bannermen were eligible for *Han-ch'üeh* (posts filled by Han Chinese) as well as *Han-chün-ch'üeh* (posts filled by Chinese Bannermen) in the central government. The only ministry from which they were excluded was the Board of Justice. Of the *Han-chun-ch'üeh* in the central government, the most notable were subchancellor reader, assistant reader, and secretaries of the Grand Secretariat; department directors, second-class secretaries of the boards; and secretary of the Court of Judicatories and Revision. These Chinese Bannerman appointments were posts with identical titles for both Han Chinese and Manchus. However, starting at the end of the seventeenth century, there was a gradual trend toward reducing appointments of Chinese Bannermen to special posts in the central government. For example, the number of Chinese Bannermen serving as department directors in the Board of Rites fell from eight in 1644 to none in 1727; in the Board of Civil Appointment from two to none; in the Board of War from two to none; in the Board of Punishments from four to none; and in the boards of works and revenue from two to none. See HTSL, chüan 20.

31. THL, K'ang-hsi, chüan 34, pp. 8-9.

32. Ibid., chüan 40, p. 3.

33. HCCSWP, chüan 7, pp. 12-13.

34. THL, K'ang-hsi, chüan 67, p. 2.

35. Kessler, "Ethnic Composition," 497, table 2.

36. Ibid.

37. For a discussion of *P'eng-tang-lun*, see David Nivison, "Ho-shen and His Accusers: Ideology and Political Behaviour in the Eighteenth Century," in *Confucianism in Action*, 224-28.

38. SL, Yung-cheng, chüan 44, pp. 21-23.

39. In an edict of 1726, the emperor commented,

> Chinese Bannermen always like to collude with each other, circulating secret messages among themselves and giving each other undue protection regardless of whether they are in the province or in the capital [and] whether they have known each other before or not. . . . After a long while, they form cliques and become a great threat to the nation. (SL, Yung-cheng, chüan 42, pp. 15-16).

In 1730 the emperor again lamented the lack of talent among the Chinese Bannermen.

> When our dynasty was first founded, the Chinese Bannermen were all brave and competent. Now that the nation has been at peace for a long period, the Chinese Bannermen like to pursue an easy and comfortable life, showing no interest in military careers and desiring only civil positions. Very few of them can reach the position of provincial commander-in-chief or brigadier general. I have great difficulty finding suitable candidates for the position of lieutenant general or deputy lieutenant general for the Eight Chinese Banners. (SL, Yung-cheng, chüan 99, pp. 6-7.)

40. CWHTK, chüan 56, p. 5381.

41. SL, Yung-cheng, chüan 112, p. 27; for another example see chüan 100, p. 6.

42. Kessler, "Ethnic Composition," p. 497.

43. *Huang-Ch'ing tsou-i*, chüan 54, p. 32.

44. Hsiao I-shan, *Ch'ing-tai t'ung-shih* 2: 21; Fu Tsung-mao, *Ch'ing-chih lun-wen-chi* [Collected papers on Ch'ing institutions] 2: 283.

45. The following is based on Fu, *Ch'ing-tai tu-fu,* 167–68.

Governors and Governors-general in Each Ethnic/Political Group by Reign:
Numbers and Percent of Total

Group	Shun-chih	K'ang-hsi	Yung-cheng	Ch'ien-lung	Chia-ch'ing	Tao-kuang	Hsien-feng	T'ung-chih	Kuang-hsü	Hsüan-t'ung
Han Chinese	23 (47.90%)	41 (42.70%)	29 (51.80%)	67 (48.20%)	38 (71.70%)	34 (73.90%)	31 (73.80%)	35 (87.50%)	24 (68.50%)	2 (33.30%)
Manchus	1 (2.08%)	24 (25.00%)	18 (32.10%)	60 (43.16%)	9 (17.00%)	11 (23.90%)	10 (23.80%)	5 (12.50%)	9 (25.70%)	3 (50.00%)
Mongols				4 (2.80%)	3 (5.65%)	1 (2.20%)			1 (2.90%)	
Chinese Bannermen	24 (50.02%)	31 (32.30%)	9 (16.10%)	8 (5.84%)	3 (5.65%)		1 (2.40%)		1 (2.90%)	1 (16.70%)
Bannermen Subtotal	25 (53.10%)	55 (57.30%)	27 (48.10%)	72 (51.80%)	15 (28.30%)	12 (26.10%)	11 (22.20%)	5 (12.50%)	11 (31.50%)	4 (66.70%)
TOTAL	48 (100%)	96 (100%)	56 (100%)	139 (100%)	53 (100%)	46 (100%)	42 (100%)	40 (100%)	35 (100%)	6 (100%)

46. Fu, *Ch'ing-chih lun-wen chi* 2: 261.

47. *Ta Ch'ing shih-ch'ao sheng-hsün* [Sacred instructions from ten Ch'ing emperors], Kao-tsung sheng-hsün, chüan 59, p. 6.

48. Li Kuo-ch'i, et. al., "Ch'ing-tai chi-ts'eng ti-fang-kuan jen-shih shan-ti hsien-hsiang chih liang-hua fen-hsi" [A qualitative analysis of the careers of prefects and magistrates in the Ch'ing dynasty], *Taiwan shih-fan ta-hsüeh li-shih hsüeh-pao* 2 (February 1974): 349, 355, charts A-1, A-4.

49. Ibid., 349.

50. Kessler, "Ethnic Composition," p. 497.

51. See, for example, ibid., 496.

52. See chapter 3.

53. It is interesting to note that the highest national figure of reappointment to the same post was for river governor-generalships. See chapter 4.

54. The highest incidence of reappointment to the same location for all governors-general occurred between 1776 and 1795. After 1826 no Chinese Bannermen or Mongols, and after 1842 no Manchus, received second postings to the same location.

55. Thirty-two percent of all Yun-kwei and Liangkuang governors-general were governors in these areas previously. In Yun-kwei, 22% were appointed directly from governor to governor-general and in Liangkuang this figure was 18%. In Shen-kan, 30% had been governors in the same area at some point and 17% were appointed directly from governor to governor-general. One rather strange figure emerged for Chihli. While 22% of the area's governors-general served as governor of Chihli at some point, 19% moved directly from governor to governor-general. In 1724 the governorship of Chihli was abolished and the province was subsequently ruled by a governor-general alone. These figures correspond to the analysis done by Fu Tsung-mao. His study shows the following number of tenures by men who had served as governors in one of the provinces covered by their governor-generalships.

Yun-kwei	27	Min-che	21
Hukuang	27	Liangkiang	22
Liangkuang	23	Shen-kan	12

See Fu, *Ch'ing-chih lun-wen chi* 2: 288.

56. See chapter 2.

57. LPTL, Ch'üan-hsüan Han-kuan, chüan 8, 14-15.

58. SL, Yung-cheng, chüan 42, p. 15.

59. HT (1733 ed.), chüan 8, p. 2, and chüan 5, p. 1.

60. THL, K'ang-hsi, chüan 96, p.5.

61. Hsiao, *Ch'ing-tai t'ung-shih* 2: 24, as quoted and translated in Kessler, "Ethnic Composition," 493.

62. Kessler, "Ethnic Composition," 493.

Chapter 3

1. Shang, *Ch'ing-tai k'o-chü*, pp. 204-10.

2. Average age of successful *chin-shih* candidates according to Chang Chung-li, *The Chinese Gentry*, 122, table 10.

Year of exam	Average age of successful *chin-shih* candidates
1835	36
1868	34
1894	33

Another study gives 35 as the average age in the 1829 examination. See John R. Watt, *The District Magistrate in Late Imperial China*, 33.

3. Ch'en Wen-shih, "Ch'ing-tai ti Pi-t'ieh-shih" [Bithesi or Manchu clerks in the Ch'ing period], *Shih-huo* n. 5. 4, no. 3 (June 1974): 72.

4. SL, Shun-chih, chüan 106, pp. 24-25.

5. CWHTK, chüan 48, p. 5307.

6. SL, Yung-cheng, chüan 22, pp. 21-22.

7. *Ta-Ch'ing shih-ch'ao*, Ch'ien-lung, chüan 31, pp. 12-13.

8. THL, Ch'ien-lung, chüan 41, p. 24.

9. CWHTK, chüan 78, p. 5582.

10. Ibid.

11. Fang Chao-ying and Tu Lien-che, *Tseng-chiao Ch'ing-ch'ao chin-shih t'i-ming pei-lu* [Lists of the *chin-shih* degree during the Ch'ing dynasty, re-edited and appended with an index], 105-28.

12. Shang Yen-liu, *Ch'ing-tai k'o-chü k'ao-shih shu-lu* [A descriptive account of the civil service examination under the Ch'ing], 52-53.

13. CWHTK, chüan 55, p. 5376, and chüan 48, p. 5307.

14. HTSL, chüan 17; *Ch'ing-shih kao*, hsüan-chü chih, 5.

15. *T'ing-yü ts'ung-t'an* [Miscellaneous accounts of various aspects of Ch'ing government], chüan 1, p. 18; chüan 8, p. 160.

16. *Ch'ing-shih kao*, hsüan-chü chih, 5.

17. CWHTK, chüan 79, pp. 5585-8.

18. *Shang-yü nei-ko*, dated 19 August 1727, quoted in Kuan Tung-kuei, "Man-tsu ju-kuan ch'ien ti wen-hua fa-chang tui t'a-men hou-lai Han-hua ti ying-hsiang" [The influence of Manchu cultural developments prior to 1644 on their subsequent sinicization] *Bulletin, Institute of History and Philology* (Academia Sinica) 40, pt. 1 (1968).

19. Ch'en Wen-shih, "Ch'ing tai ti pi-t'ieh-shih," p. 73.

20. Since the same man may have held more than one governor-generalship in any given period, or during more than one period, these percentages do not represent the number of men with *chin-shih* degrees, but rather the number of governor-general tenures. They provide a more accurate reflection of the extent to which the post at any given time was in the hands of men with the degree.

21. The average annual number of *chin-shih* degrees granted in different reigns are as follows.

Reign	Number of *chin-shih*
Shun-chih	174.8
Yung-cheng	125.0
Chia-ch'ing	117.5
Hsien-feng	104.6
Kuang-hsu	113.6
K'ang-hsi	69.4
Ch'ien-lung	92.8
Tao-kuang	112.8
T'ung-chih	132.3

Figures are from Ho, *Ladder of Success*, 189.

22. SL, Yung-cheng, chüan 87, pp. 28-33.

23. For a detailed discussion of the differences between these terms, see Ho, *Ladder of Success*, chapter 1.

24. *Pa-ch'i t'ung-chih* [Comprehensive history of the eight banners] (1799 ed.), chüan 95; Shang, *Ch'ing-tai k'o-chü,* 213-14; and Nancy Evans, "The Banner-school Background of the Canton T'ung-wen Kuan" *Papers on China* (Harvard University), 22(A) (May 1969): 90-92.

25. See, for example, the careers of P'eng Yü-lin, governor-general of Liangkiang, and Yang Yüeh-pin, governor-general of Shen-kan. Hummel, *Eminent Chinese,* 617-20.

26. HCCSWP, chüan 7, p. 13.

27. Ho, *Ladder of Success,* 149-53; LPTL, chüan-hsüan Han-kuan, chüan 4, pp. 35-41.

28. Li, et. al., "Ch'ing-tai chi-ts'eng," 365-71.

29. *Ch'ing-shih-kao,* chih-kuan chih, p. 2; SL, Yung-cheng, chüan 3, pp. 2-3; THL, Yung-cheng, chüan 2, p. 1.

30. Eighty percent of Han Chinese and 55% of Manchus and Chinese Bannermen/Mongols had extensive experience in provincial posts.

31. Of Han Chinese governors-general 36.6% took this route; 25.3% of the Chinese Bannerman/Mongol group did the same.

32. These figures might be a little low because they exclude the career pattern in which an official had significant lengths of service in three of the following: provincial, central, military, or imperial posts.

33. See note 32.

34. Li, et. al., *Ch'ing-tai chi-ts'eng ti-fan-kuan jen-shih shan-ti hsien-hsiang chih liang-hua fen-hsi* [A quantitative analysis of the careers of prefects and magistrates in the Ch'ing dynasty], 2: 872-73, 882-83, 892-93, 902-3.

35. In a recent study on the Hanlin Academy, Adam Lui found that the annual average number of Hanlin members (including unranked student members and senior members above rank 4B) for the period from 1644 to 1795 is 126. If the unranked students and senior members above rank 4B are excluded, the average number of Hanlin members between ranks 4B and 7B in any given year of this period was approximately eighty. See Adam Lui, *The Hanlin Academy: Training Ground for the Ambitious, 1644-1850,* pp. 12-15.

36. The total number of middle and low level positions in the central government which were available to Han Chinese was far fewer than the total number of positions of equivalent rank in just three of the provinces, as the following table demonstrates.

Rank of Position	No. of Positions in the Central Government*	No. of Postitions in the Provinces of Chihli, Shangtung, and Kiangsu
4A	6	17
4B	9	28
5A	72	73
5B	74	29
6A	73	32
6B	8	14
7A	8	283
Totals:	250	476

*Includes only those positions available to Han Chinese.
Source: HTSL, chüan 19-22, 25, 26, 28, 29.

37. Ibid.

38. CWHTK, chüan 60, p. 5415.

39. HCCSWHP, chüan 16, p. 9.

40. LPTL, chapters on "ch'üan-hsuan Han-kuan p'in-chi k'ao." For example, department directors and assistant department directors were eligible for appointments as prefect;

metropolitan censors could become circuit intendants; and department magistrates could be promoted to assistant department directorships in the central government.

41. In the regulations of the Board of Civil Appointments the order of promotion between ranks and positions is clearly spelled out. It usually reads as follows:

Rank X   Position/Title A   Should be filled by [people presently holding] positions B, C, D, or E.

As it turned out, if position A was in the central government, position B could in no case be a provincial title. In fact, if the provincial title was included, it always came at the end of the list.

42. The number of student members was not fixed by either number or percentage. The 23% suggested here is a figure based on the statistics given by Fang and Tu in *Tseng-chiao Ch'ing-ch'ao*, which gives the total number of *chin-shih* recipients during the dynasty as 26,747, and the total number of student members in the Hanlin Academy as 6,065.

43. HTSL, chüan 72.

44. Positions in the central government available to Han Chinese upon acquiring the *chin-shih* degree.

A. Secretaries of the Six Boards:

Civil Appointment	7
Revenue	14
War	5
Punishments	18
Works	8
Rites	4
TOTAL	56
B. Secretaries of the Grand Secretariat	28
C. Directors of Studies, Imperial Academy of Learning	6
GRAND TOTAL	90

HTSL, chüan 19, 20, 23.

45. For the methods of selecting *chü-jen* degree holders for official appointments see Shang, *Ch'ing-tai k'o-chü*, 94-6. See also HTSL, chüan 73. Regarding positions for which *chü-jen* were qualified, see LPTL, chapters entitled "ch'üan-hsüan Han-kuan p'in-chi k'ao," chüan 2, 3, and 4.

46. LPTL, chüan 4.

47. SL, Yung-cheng, chüan 12, p. 17; CWHTK, chüan 55, p. 5368. See also Chung, "Hanlin Academy," 118.

48. The percentage of those who began in military posts and then followed exclusively military careers are:

Han Chinese	40.0
Manchus	21.7
Chinese Bannermen/Mongols	16.7

If we add those who remained in predominantly military careers, the percentages are:

Han Chinese	60.0
Manchus	34.8
Chinese Bannermen/Mongols	45.8

49. This policy of retaining a clear distinction between military and civil careers may be exemplified anecdotally. During the reign of Ch'ien-lung, a military officer in a memorial to the throne addressed himself as a "humble scholar from Honan," which later provoked

the emperor to declare in an edict, "How on earth does Li Ch'üan, a military officer, dare address himself as a scholar. . . ? This edict should be made known to others as well." (HTSL, chüan 577.)

50. Toward the middle of the nineteenth century it became less unusual for military officers to be transferred to civil posts. This could be done either by special recommendation or by the purchase of a civil official title. However, among civil officials there was strong resentment of this practice. For an example, see a memorial of Chiang Ch'i-ling, a metropolitan prefect, dated 1862 (HCCSWHP, chüan 13, pp. 32-3).

51. For a detailed discussion of the military responsibilities of governors and governors-general, see Fu, Ch'ing-tai tu-fu, pp. 94-102. See also HTSL, chüan 51.

52. For regulations related to the transfer of bannermen military officers to civil posts, see LPTL, section on Ch'üan-hsüan Man-chou kuan-yüan tse-li, chüan 1, pp. 8-9; chüan 2, p. 63; and chüan 3, p. 20. See also Pa-ch'i t'ung-chih, chüan 52, p. 13; chüan 51, pp. 38-40. For civil officials transferred to military posts, see LPTL, section on Ch'üan-hsüan Man-chou kuan-yüan tse-li, chüan 4, p. 12. and Pa-ch'i t'ung-chi, chüan 51, p. 38.

53. The only other post in which more than 10% of the governors-general had predominantly central service careers was Szechwan (13%).

54. See LPTL, Ch'üan-hsüan Han-kuan tse-li, chüan 2, p. 28, and chüan 1, p. 4.

55. The sum of the figures for positions below and above provincial judge normally do not match the figure for total provincial service due to variations in the amount of data. For example, in some cases we do not have data for total length of service, but only for time spent above or (less often) below the rank of provincial judge.

56. Wei Hsiu-mei, "Ts'ung liang ti kuan-ch'a t'an-t'ao Ch'ing-chi an-ch'a-shih ti jen-shih shan-ti," 480-82; Wei Hsiu-mei, "Ts'ung liang ti kuan ch'a t'an-t'ao Ch'ing-chi pu-cheng-shih chih jen-shih ti-shan hsien-hsiang," 512-16; Li et. al., "Ch'ing-tai chi-ts'eng," 349-55.

57. Consider, for example, the career of Hu Lin-i who in only two years rose from prefect to acting governor of Hupeh. See also material on the careers of Peng Yü-lin and Yang Yüeh-pin (Hummel, Eminent Chinese, pp. 333-335).

58. See chapter 2.

59. These figures should be considered reasonably reliable, as they are based on only those men for whom actual birthdates are known. This was more than one-third of our sample or a total of 189 governors-general. However, they are undoubtedly more reliable for Han Chinese for whom the percentage of actual birthdates recorded was 58.5%, than for Chinese bannerman (32.03%), Mongols (30.76%), and in particular Manchus (14.45%).

The age for Han Chinese was compared with estimated ages based on a calculation of the probable date of birth for those who had the chin-shih, assuming they were 31 years of age when they attained the degree. The average age of attaining the chin-shih was calculated by combining the averages from all governors-general in this study with all Chinese chin-shih degree holders listed in Hummel, Eminent Chinese. Based on this, the average age of attainment of the chin-shih among Han Chinese was 30.6 years and for Manchus, 25.5 years. Rounding these figures to 31 and 26, and making second estimates of age at first appointment as governor-general, we now have data for 48.4% of our sample and the age for Han Chinese becomes 56.7 years. This differs from our first estimate by only six months. Unfortunately, there was not enough additional information on Manchu chin-shih degree holders to estimate their age of appointment on this basis. See chapter 4 for a more complete discussion of the age of appointment to a governor-generalship as one criterion of success, as well as other criteria such as rates of demotion and dismissal. These factors are correlated with career patterns taken, degrees held, and first appointments.

60. See Li, et. al., "Ch'ing-tai chi-ts'eng," 319.

61. See chapter 4.

62. CWHTK, chüan 61, p. 5425, and chüan 62, pp. 5431-3.

63. Adam Y. C. Lui, "The Ch'ing Civil Service: Promotions, Demotions, Transfers, Leaves, Dismissals and Retirements," *Journal of Oriental Studies* 8, 2 (July 1970): 344-45.

Chapter 4

1. See CWHTK, chüan 61, pp. 5425-26; chüan 62, pp. 5429, 5431-33.

2. CWHTK, chüan 62, p. 5433.

3. The following is a table showing the number of years between first career appointment and first appointment as governor-general, categorized by career pattern.

Career Pattern	Years between first appointment and first governor-generalship
Exclusively central posts	17.00
Significant military and provincial	24.16
Significant posts in at least three areas	24.20
Predominantly central posts	24.25
Exclusively provincial posts	25.33
Predominantly provincial posts	25.82
Significant provincial and central	27.08

Note: "Significant" means at least one major appointment and normally several years in more than one position. "Predominant" means a majority of posts and time.

4. Degrees held by governors-general according to their native province

Province	Total Governors-general	Chin-shih and Chü-jen	Chü-jen Only	Neither Degree
Anhwei	16	8	2	6
Kiangsi	12	11	1	0
Honan	13	9	0	4
Hupeh	10	6	0	4
Hunan	23	13	0	10
Northeast Provinces[*]	17	7	0	10
Shensi	9	6	0	3
Kansu	3	2	0	1
Shansi	12	5	1	6
Chihli	11	10	0	1
Shantung	19	13	3	3
Kiangsu	27	20	3	4
Chekiang	20	14	1	5
Fukien	8	7	1	0
Kwangtung	9	7	0	2
Kwangsi	3	1	1	1
Szechwan	6	3	2	1
Yunnan	1	1	0	0
Kweichow	6	4	1	1

[*]Liaoning, Chilin, Heilung chiang.

5. Wei, "Ts'ung liang ti . . . pu-cheng-shih," 518; Wei, "Ts'ung liang ti . . . an-ch'a-shih," 484; Li, et. al., "Ch'ing-tai chi-ts'eng," 319.

6. The average length of tenure for political-ethnic groups in the various governor-generalships posts was as follows.

Province	Han Chinese	Manchu	Chinese Bannerman/ Mongol	National Average
Chihli	3.83	3.61	2.22	3.41
Liangkiang	3.25	2.91	3.16	3.04
Shenkan	3.46	2.70	2.57	2.82
Szechwan	2.60	2.91	2.77	2.76
Min-che	2.90	2.36	3.10	2.86
Hukuang	2.53	2.05	2.69	2.38
Liangkuang	2.53	2.08	4.14	2.85
Yun-kwei	2.62	2.78	3.70	2.95
Grain	2.13	2.88	3.41	2.56
River	2.77	3.04	3.43	3.00

7. This relationship between length of tenure and frequency of demotion or dismissal was found only in these two governor-generalships. The provincial post with the second highest average length of tenure, Liangkiang, was by far the safest province in which to serve as governor-general in terms of the risk of demotion or dismissal.

8. See Hsiao I-shan, *Ch'ing-tai t'ung shih*, 2: 287-93.

9. LPCFTL, chüan 2, p. 10a, 12a.

10. Ibid., chüan 2, p. 12a.

11. On the general question of the administrative punishment of Ch'ing officials, see Metzger, *Internal Organization*, chapter 4.

12. See, for example, the case of T'ao Chu, governor-general of Liangkiang in 1832, who initiated the process and was slapped with a demotion of four classes. Metzger, *Internal Organization*, 369.

13. For examples of this, see THL, Shun-chih, chüan 23, p. 2, and Yung-cheng, chüan 6, p. 12.

14. HT (1733 ed.), chüan 15, p. 31, HTSL, chüan 78; CWHTK, chüan 59, p. 5405.

15. THL, K'ang-hsi, chüan 13, p. 3.

16. HTSL, chüan 78.

17. See LPCFTL, chüan 5, pp. 1-2.

18. *Ch'in-ting li-pu ch'u-fen tse-li* [Imperially endorsed (compilation of) regulations of the Board of Civil Appointments on administrative punishment] (1843 ed.), chuan 46, p. 22. Throughout the two editions (1843 and 1892) of the *ch'u-fen tse-li* (regulations on administrative punishment) the governors-general and governors shared identical penalties for the transgressions of their subordinates with two exceptions: in the 1843 edition in the section on the collection of taxes *(ts'ui-cheng)*, in the chapter on the Board of Revenue (chüan 25, pp. 6-26), and in the section dealing with the Autumn Assizes in part of the chapter on trials (chüan 48, pp. 2-3, 7). In both of these cases only governors and those governors-general who were concurrently governors were mentioned (i.e., the governors of Chihli, Szechwan, and Shen-kan). These explicit references emphasize the fact that in all other situations joint responsibility was assumed.

19. Fairbank, "Manchu-Chinese Dyarchy," p. 272.

Appendix 3

1. HTSL, chüan 251.

2. For the origin and source of the funds, see Ch'ü, *Local Government Under the Ch'ing*, 215, n. 36; and 219, n. 73.

3. HTSL, chüan 262.

4. Ibid., chüan 260.

5. Ibid., chüan 261-62.

Appendix 4

1. Imperially endorsed [compilation of] revised regulations on administrative punishment for offenses, categorized according to the six boards.

2. For an example of this, see our translation of LPCFTL, chüan 14, p. 6b.

3. For examples of this, see our translation of LPCFTL, chüan 8, p. 1a; chüan 15, p. 4b; chüan 7, p. 10b; and chüan 37, p. 2a.

4. An edict that precedes this regulation, dated November 1, 1820, pronounces:

> Should any governor-general or governor have a subordinate, be he a provincial commissioner, taotai, prefect, department or district magistrate, or a military officer, who is extraordinary in both ability and virtue, and is also very conscientious in his duties, the governor-general or the governor should write a detailed and truthful evaluation of that official and especially recommend him to the emperor in a secret memorial. If that official commits a public offense in the future, the governor-general or governor [who recommended him] should be exonerated from any responsibility. [On the other hand], if he breaks the law and commits a private offense, the one who recommended him is to be held personally responsible. If the subordinate official is corrupt and breaks the law, confuses right and wrong, or is too old and muddle-headed to carry out his duties, the governor-general or governor should impeach him, based on the facts, and should not allow him to hold the position without doing a stroke of work because that would harm the people. (LPCFTL, chüan 4, p.3b.)

5. A pu-hsüan position was to be filled by someone selected and recommended by the Board of Civil Appointments.

6. A liu-ch'üeh position was originally to be filled by a Board of Civil Appointments appointee, but at the request of the governor-general or the governor it could tentatively be filled by an official who was recently reinstated, had just returned from a sick leave or mourning observance, or was earlier commissioned by the emperor to carry out a specific mission in that province.

7. A tiao-pu position was to be filled by an official of the same rank as that of the position to which he is transferred.

8. A t'i-pu position was to be filled by a candidate recommended by the governor-general or the governor subject to the approval of the emperor. For details concerning the different types of positions, see Fu, "Ch'ing-tai wen-kuan," 121-75.

9. For information concerning the classification of punishments, see Bodde, Law in Imperial China, 134-43.

an-ch'a-shih 按察使

cha-wei 札委

Chang Chih-tung 張之洞

Chang K'ai-sung 張凱嵩

Chang Po-hsing 張伯行

Chao Shen-ch'iao 趙申喬

cheng-ch'ih pien-kuan 整飭邊關

cheng-yin kuan 正印官

chi-ch'a 稽察

Chiang Ch'i-ling 蔣琦齡

chiang-nan ho-tao tsung-tu

江南河道總督

chieh-chih 節制

chieh-chih t'ung-sheng ping-ma

節制通省兵馬

chieh-pao 揭報

chien-ch'üeh 簡缺

Chien-kuan chiang-chun shih wu

兼管將軍事務

chien-sheng 監生

ch'ien-tsung 千總

chih 制

chin-shih 進士

Ch'in Ch'eng-en 秦承恩

Ching-an 景安

ch'ing-shih 情實

chuo-i 卓異

chou 州

Ch'u Fang-ch'ing 儲方慶

chü-jen 舉人

chuan-tse 專責

ch'üan-hsüan Han-kuan p'in-chi k'ao

銓選漢官品級考

Ch'uan-shen 川陝

chün-cheng 軍政

fan-ch'üeh 繁缺

fan-i hui-shih 翻譯會試

Fan Wen-ch'eng 范文程

fang-shou 防守

feng-yin 俸銀

fu-chiang 副將

fu-chih liu-min 撫治流民

Fu-i ch'üan-shu 賦役全書

Han-ch'üeh 漢缺

Han-chün-ch'üeh 漢軍缺

Hanlin 翰林

han-shang 函商

hao-hsien 耗羨

Hao Yü-lin 郝玉麟

Ho Shen 和珅

ho-tung ho-tao tsung-tu

河東河道總督

hsieh-en che 謝恩摺

hsien 縣

hsin-yin 薪銀

hsiu-ts'ai 秀才

Hsü Kuang-chin 徐廣縉

Hsüeh Fu-ch'eng 薛福成

hsün-fu 巡撫

Hu Lin-i 胡林翼

huan-chüeh 緩決

Huang T'ing-kuei 黃廷桂

Hukuang 湖廣

hui-shang 會商

hui-t'ui 會推

hui-t'ui-pen 會推本

hui-t'ung t'ui-chu 會同推舉

Hung Ch'eng-ch'ou 洪承疇

huo-hao 火耗

i-chien hsiang-t'ung 意見相同

i-hsü 議敘

k'ai-lieh 開列

Kao Ch'i-chuo 高其倬

131

Ke-li 嗑禮

kuan-ho 管河

kuan-hsueh 官學

kuei-fei 規費

kung-sheng 貢生

Li Chih-fang 李之芳

Li Ch'üan 李銓

Li Feng-han 李奉翰

Li Hsü 李煦

Li Hung-chang 李鴻章

Li Wei 李衛

Li Wei-chün 李維鈞

Liangkiang 兩江

Liangkuang 兩廣

Lin Tse-hsü 林則徐

liu-ch'üeh 留缺

liu-ch'u 留處

liu-fa 六法

Lu-ch'uan 麓川

Man-Han i-chia 滿漢一家

Man-Han i-t'i hsiang-shih
滿漢一體相使

Miao 苗

mien-shang 面商

Min-che 閩浙

mu-fu 幕府

mu-yu 幕友

Nan-yang t'ung-shang ta-ch'en
南洋通商大臣

nien-p'u 年譜

Ning Wan-wo 甯完我

pa-fa 八法

pa-tsung 把總

pai-shou wei lang, shih-nien pu-tiao
白首為郎，十年不調

P'an Lei 潘耒

Pei-yang t'ung-shang ta-ch'en
北洋通商大臣

pen-sheng t'i-tiao 本省提調

P'eng-tang lun 朋黨論

P'eng Yü-lin 彭玉麐

pi-t'ieh-shih 筆帖式

Pi Yüan 畢沅

po-hsüeh-hung-tz'u 博學鴻詞

Po Kuei 柏貴

pu-cheng-shih 布政使

pu-hsüan 部選

san-ssu 三司

Shen-kan 陝甘

sheng-yüan 生員

shou-pei 守備

shu 疏

shu-chi-shih 庶吉士

shu-li 署理

sui-ts'ai shih-yung, liang-neng shou-chih
隨才使用，量能授職

Sun Lo 孫犖

ta-chi 大計

t'an-k'u 貪酷

T'ang Pin 湯斌

tao-jen che 到任摺

taotai 道台

T'ao Chu 陶澍

T'ao Mo 陶模

t'e-chien 特簡

t'e-chien kuan 特簡官

t'e-ts'an 特參

t'i-piao 提標

t'i-pu 題補

t'i-tu 提督

t'i-tu chün-wu 提督軍務

T'ien Wen-ching 田文鏡

t'ing-t'ui 廷推

t'ou-ch'eng 投誠

tsan-li chün-wu 贊理軍務

Ts'ao Yin 曹寅

ts'ao-yin tsung-tu 漕運總督

Ts'en Yü-ying 岑毓英

Tseng Kuo-fan 曾國藩

tsou-che 奏摺

ts'ui-cheng 催徵
tsung-chih 總制
tsung-li ho-tao 總理河道
tsung-ping 總兵
tsung-tu 總督
tsung-tu chun-wu 總督軍務
tu-fu 督撫
tu-piao 督標
tung-ku 冬估
t'ung-pen 通本
T'ung Yang-hsing 佟養性
tzu-ch'en 自陳

Wang Chi 王驥
Wang Ching-ch'i 汪景祺
Wei I-chieh 魏裔介
wen-chi 文集

wen-wu fen-t'u 文武分途
Wu San-kuei 吳三桂
yang-lien yin 養廉銀
Yang Yüeh-pin 楊岳斌
Yeh Ming-ch'en 葉名琛
yen-chiang 嚴疆
yin 陰
yin-sheng 蔭生
ying-kai 應改
ying-sheng 應升
ying-tiao 應調
Yü K'o 毓科
yü-pao 預保
yüeh-hsüan 月選
Yün-kwei 雲貴
yung-ying 勇營

Bibliography

I. Primary Sources

It should be noted that only those collected writings *(wen-chi)* used extensively are listed below. Collected writings used in a more incidental way, for acquiring or checking biographical details, are too numerous to include here.

Chao Kung-i kung sheng-kao 趙恭毅公賸稿 [Collected writings of Chao Shen-ch'iao]. By Chao Shen-ch'iao 趙申喬 . 8 chüan. N.p.: Che-chiang shu-chü, 1892.

Cheng-i-t'ang chi 正誼堂集 [Collected works of Chang Po-hsing]. By Chang Po-hsing 張伯行 . 6 chüan. San-hsien cheng-shu series. 1879. Reprint. Taipei: Hsüeh-sheng, 1976.

Ch'in-ting ch'ung-hsiu liu-pu ch'u-fen tse-li 欽定重修六部處分則例 [Imperially endorsed (compilation of) revised regulations on administrative punishment for offences, categorized according to the six boards]. 1892. Reprint. Taipei, Wen-hai, n.d.

Ch'in-ting hu-pu ts'ao-yün ch'üan-shu 欽定戶部漕運全書 [The Board of Revenue's imperially endorsed (compilation of) the complete book on the tribute grain transport]. 1766. Reprint. Taipei: Ch'eng-wen, 1969.

Ch'in-ting hu-pu tse-li 欽定戶部則例 [Imperially endorsed (compilation of) regulations of the Board of Revenue]. 1865. Reprint. Taipei: Ch'eng-wen, 1968.

Ch'in-ting kung-pu tse-li 欽定工部則例 [Imperially endorsed (compilation of) regulations of the Board of Works]. 1884. Reprint. Taipei: Ch'eng-wen, 1966.

Ch'in-ting li-pu ch'u-fen tse-li 欽定吏部處分則例 [Imperially endorsed (compilation of) regulations of the Board of Civil Appointments on administrative punishment]. 52 chüan. 1843. Reprint. Taipei: Ch'eng-wen, 1966.

Ch'in-ting li-pu tse-li 欽定禮部則例 [Imperially endorsed (compilation of) regulations of the Board of Rites]. 1841. Reprint. Taipei: Ch'eng-wen, 1966.

Ch'in-ting li-pu tse-li 欽定吏部則例 [Imperially endorsed (compilation of) regulations of the Board of Civil Appointments]. 1843. Reprint. Taipei: Ch'eng-wen, 1969.

Ch'ing-ch'ao hsü wen-hsien t'ung-k'ao 清朝續文獻通考 [Encyclopaedia of the historical records of the Ch'ing dynasty, continued]. Compiled by Liu Chin-tsao 劉錦藻 . Shih-t'ung edition. Shanghai: Shang-wu, 1935.

Ch'ing-ch'ao t'ung-tien 清朝通典 [Institutional history of the Ch'ing dynasty]. Shih-t'ung edition. Shanghai: Shang-wu, 1935.

Ch'ing-ch'ao wen-hsien t'ung-k'ao 清朝文獻通考 [Encyclopaedia of the historical records of the Ch'ing dynasty]. Shih-t'ung edition. Shanghai: Shang-wu, 1935.

Ch'ing-shih 清史 [History of the Ch'ing dynasty]. Compiled by Ch'ing-shih pien-tsuan wei-yüan-hui 清史編纂委員會 [Committee on the Compilation of the History of the Ch'ing Dynasty]. 8 vols. Taipei: Kuo-fang yen-chiu-yüan,1961.

Ch'ing-shih-kao 清史稿 [Draft history of the Ch'ing dynasty]. Compiled by Chao Erh-hsün 趙爾巽 , et. al. 536 chüan. Peking: Ch'ing-shih kuan, 1927-28.

Ch'ing-shih lieh-chuan 清史列傳 [Collected biographies of the Ch'ing period]. Shanghai: Chung-hua, 1928.

Ch'ing-tai cheng-hsien lei-pien 清代徵獻類編 [Classified historical records of the Ch'ing dynasty]. Compiled by Yen Mao-kung 嚴懋功 . 29 chüan. Wu-hsi: Min-sheng, 1931.

Ch'un-ming meng-yü lu 春明夢餘錄 [Miscellaneous notes about the capital city and the central administration in the Ming dynasty]. By Sun Ch'eng-tse 孫承澤. Nan-hai: Ku-hsiang-chai, 1881.

Chung-hsing chiang-shuai lieh-chuan 中興將帥列傳 [Unofficial biographies of military commanders of the Restoration period]. Compiled by Chu K'ung-chang 朱孔彰. Ssu-pu pei-yao edition. Shanghai: Chung-hua, 1934.

Fu Tien tsou-shu 撫滇奏疏 [Memorials (of Chang K'ai-sung) submitted during his tenure as the governor of Yunnan]. By Chang K'ai-sung 張凱嵩. 4 chüan. 1893. Reprint. Taipei: Wen-hai, 1968.

Han ming-ch'en chuan 漢名臣傳 [Biographies of eminent Chinese of the Ch'ing dynasty]. Compiled by Kuo-shih Kuan 國史舘 [Bureau of Ch'ing History]. Peking: Jung-chin shu-fang, n.d.

Hsi-p'i lei-kao 西陂類稿 [Classified writings of Sung Lo]. By Sung Lo 宋犖. 3 chüan. San-hsien cheng-shu series. 1879. Reprint. Taipei: Hsüeh-sheng, 1976.

Hsiao-t'ing tsa-lu 嘯亭雜錄 [Miscellaneous notes of Chao-lien]. By Chao-lien 昭槤 Chiu-ssu-t'ang edition. 1880. Reprint. Taipei: Wen-hai, 1966.

Hsü pei-chuan chi 續碑傳集 [Collection of memorial inscriptions, continued]. Compiled by Miao Ch'üan-sun 繆荃孫. Ssu-k'u shan-pen ts'ung-shu ed. N.p.: Chiang-ch'u pien-i shu-chü, 1910.

Hsüeh Fu-ch'eng ch'üan-chi 薛福成全集 [Complete works of Hsüeh Fu-ch'eng]. By Hsueh Fu-ch'eng 薛福成. 4 chüan. 1897. Reprint. Taipei: Kuang-wen, 1963.

Huang-ch'ao chang-ku hui-pien 皇朝掌故彙編 [A compilation of unofficial materials on Ch'ing institutional history]. Compiled by Chang Shou-yung 張壽鏞. 100 chüan. 1902. Reprint. Taipei: Wen-hai, 1964.

Huang-ch'ao ching-shih wen-pien 皇朝經世文編 [Collected writings on statecraft of the Ch'ing dynasty]. Compiled by Ho Ch'ang-ling 賀長齡 120 chüan. N.p.: 1836.

Huang-ch'ao ching-shih wen hsü-pien 皇朝經世文續編 [Collected writings on statecraft of the Ch'ing dynasty, continued]. Compiled by Sheng K'ang 盛康. 120 chüan. Wu-chin, Kiangsu: Sheng-shih ssu-pu-lou, 1897.

Huang-ch'ao ching-shih wen san-pien 皇朝經世文三編 [Collected writings on statecraft of the Ch'ing dynasty, third series]. Compiled by Ch'en Chung-i 陳忠倚. 80 chüan. Shanghai: Shanghai shu-chü, 1902.

Huang-Ch'ing tsou-i 皇清奏議 [Collected memorials of the Ch'ing dynasty]. 1936. Reprint. Taipei: Wen-hai, 1967.

Kung-chung tang K'ang-hsi ch'ao tsou-che 宮中檔康熙朝奏摺 [Secret palace memorials of the K'ang-hsi period]. Compiled by Ku-kung po-wu-yüan 故宮博物院 [Palace Museum]. Taipei: Ku-kung po-wu-yüan, 1976-77.

Kung-chung tang Kuang-hsü ch'ao tsou-che 宮中檔光緒朝奏摺 [Secret palace memorials of the Kuang-hsü period]. Compiled by Ku-kung po-wu-yüan 故宮博物院 [Palace Museum]. 26 vols. Taipei: Ku-kung po-wu-yüan, 1973-75.

Kuo-ch'ao ch'i-hsien lei-cheng ch'u-pien 國朝耆獻類徵初編 [Classified biographical records of venerable persons of the Ch'ing dynasty]. Edited by Li Huan 李桓. N.p.: 1884.

Kuo-ch'ao hsien-cheng shih-lüeh 國朝先正事略 [Biographies of some eminent officials of the Ch'ing dynasty]. By Li Yüan-tu 李元度. 60 chüan. N.p.: 1866.

Kuo Shih-lang tsou-shu 郭侍郎奏疏 [Memorials of Ko Sung-t'ao]. By Kuo Sung-t'ao 郭嵩燾. 12 chuan. 1892. Taipei: Wen-hai, 1967.

Kuo-shih lieh-chuan 國史列傳 [Official biographies of eminent Chinese of the Ch'ing dynasty]. Originally published by Tung-fang Hsüeh-hui. Reprint. Taipei: Wen-hai, 1974.

Li Hsü tsou-che 李煦奏摺 [Memorials of Li Hsü]. By Li Hsü 李煦. Peking: Chung-hua, 1976.

Liao-hai ts'ung-shu 遼海叢書 [Collectanea of writings dealing with the history of the Liao-tung region]. Compiled by Chin Yü-fu 金毓黻. Liao-hai shu-she edition. 1931-34. Reprint. Taipei: I-wen, 1971(?).

Lin Wen-chung kung cheng-shu 林文忠公政書 [Official writings of Lin Tse-hsü]. By Lin Tse-hsü 林則徐. 37 chüan. Reprint. Taipei: Te-chih, 1963.

Man-chou ming-ch'en chuan 滿洲名臣傳 [Biographies of eminent Manchu officials of the Ch'ing dynasty]. Compiled by Kuo-shih kuan 國史館 [Bureau of Ch'ing History]. 48 chüan. Peking: Jung-chin shu-fang, n.d.

Ming-shih 明史 [History of the Ming dynasty]. 6 vols. Taipei: Kuo-fang yen-chiu-yüan, 1962.

Pa-ch'i t'ung-chih 八旗通志 [Comprehensive history of the eight banners]. 342 chüan. 1799. Reprint. Taipei: Hsüeh-sheng, 1968.

Pei-chuan chi 碑傳集 [Supplement to collection of memorial inscriptions]. Compiled by Ch'ien I-chi 錢儀吉. Taipei: Wen-hai, 1973.

Pei-chuan chi pu 碑傳集補 [Collection of memorial inscriptions]. Compiled by Ming Erh-ch'ang 閔爾昌 1893. Reprint. Ssu-k'u shan-pen ts'ung-shu edition. N.p.: 1923.

Shih-ch'ü yü-chi 石渠餘紀 [Personal notes on Ch'ing governmental affairs]. By Wang Ch'ing-yün 王慶雲. N.p.: 1898.

Ta-Ch'ing hui-tien 大清會典 [Collected statutes of the Ch'ing dynasty]. 250 chüan. N.p.: 1733. Also, 100 chüan. N.p.: 1899.

Ta-Ch'ing hui-tien shih-li 大清會典事例 [Collected statutes of the Ch'ing dynasty with cases and precedents]. 1,220 chüan. N.p.: 1899.

Ta-Ch'ing li-ch'ao shih-lu 大清歷朝實錄 [Veritable records of successive reigns of the Ch'ing dynasty]. 4,485 chüan. 1937-38. Reprint. Taipei: Hua-wen, 1964.

Ta-Ch'ing shih-ch'ao sheng-hsün 大清十朝聖訓 [Sacred instructions from ten Ch'ing emperors]. N.p.: 1875-1908(?).

T'ang-tzu i-shu 湯子遺書 [Collected works of the late T'ang Pin]. By T'ang Pin 湯斌. 5 chüan. San-hsien cheng-shu series. 1879. Reprint. Taipei: Hsüeh-sheng, 1976.

T'ao Ch'in-su kung tsou-i i-kao 陶勤肅公奏議遺稿 [Memorials of the late T'ao Mo]. By T'ao Mo 陶模. 12 chüan. 1924. Reprint. Taipei: Wen-hai, 1970.

T'ao Wen-i kung ch'üan-chi 陶文毅公全集 [Complete works of T'ao Chu]. By T'ao Chu 陶澍. 66 chüan. N.p.: 1840.

T'ing-yü ts'ung-t'an 聽雨叢談 [Miscellaneous accounts of various aspects of the Ch'ing government]. By Fu-ke 福格. 1856. Reprint. Taipei: Wen-hai, 1971.

(Shih-i-ch'ao) Tung-hua lu (十一朝) 東華錄 [The Tung-hua records of eleven Ch'ing reigns]. Compiled by Wang Hsien-ch'ien 王先謙. Shanghai: Kuang-po-sung-chai, 1884.

Ts'en Hsiang-ch'in kung i-chi 岑襄勤公遺集 [Collected works of the late Ts'en Yü-ying]. By Ts'en Yü-ying 岑毓英. 30 chüan. Wu-ch'ang: Tu-liang kuan-shu, 1897..

Wei Wen-i-kung tsou-i 魏文毅公奏議 [Memorials of Wei I-chieh]. By Wei I-chieh 魏裔介. Shanghai: Shang-wu, 1936.

Yeh-ho pien 野獲編 [Personal observations and reading notes of Shen Te-fu]. By Shen Te-fu 沈德符. 30 chüan. N.p.: Fu-li shan-fang, 1869.

Yü Ch'ing-tuan kung cheng-shu 于清端公政書 [Official papers of Yü Ch'eng-lung]. By Yü Cheng-lung 于成龍. 8 chüan. Reprint. Taipei: Wen-hai, 1976.

II. Secondary Sources

Adshead, S. A. M. "Vice-regal government in Szechwan in the Kuang-hsü period (1875-1909)." *Papers on Far Eastern History* (The Australian National University) 4 (1971): 41-52.

Banno, Masataku. *China and the West, 1858-1861: the Origins of the Tsungli Yamen.* Cambridge: Harvard University Press, 1964.

Bays, Daniel. "The Nature of Provincial Authority in Late Ch'ing Times: Chang Chih-tung in Canton, 1884-1889." *Modern Asian Studies* 4, no. 4 (1970): 325-47.

_____. *China Enters the Twentieth Century: Chang Chih-tung and the Issues of a New Age, 1895-1909.* Ann Arbor: University of Michigan Press, 1978.

Bodde, Derk, and Clarence Morris. *Law in Imperial China.* Cambridge: Harvard University Press, 1967.

Boorman, Howard L., and Richard C. Howard. *Biographical Dictionary of Republican China.* 4 vols. Vol. 5 index, 1979. New York: Columbia University Press, 1969-71.

Brunnert, H. S., and V. V. Hagelstrom. *Present Day Political Organization of China.* Revised by N. Th. Kolessoff and translated by A. Beltchenko. Shanghai: 1912. Reprint. Taipei: n.p., n.d.

Chang Che-lang. 張哲郎 . *Ch'ing-tai ti ts'ao-yün* 清代的漕運 [Tribute grain transport in the Ch'ing dynasty]. Taipei: Chia-hsin, 1969.

Chang Chih-an 張治安 . "Ming-tai t'ing-t'ui chih yen-chiu" 明代廷推之研究 [A study of the Ming system of selecting high officials by the joint action of court officials]. *Cheng-chih ta-hsüeh hsüeh-pao* 政治大學學報. 29 (1974): 203-26.

Chang Chung-li. *The Chinese Gentry.* Seattle: University of Washington Press, 1955.

Ch'en Nai-ch'ien 陳乃乾 . *Ch'ing-tai pei-chuan wen t'ung-chien* 清代碑傳文通檢 [Index to memorial inscriptions of the Ch'ing period]. Peking: Chung-hua, 1959.

Ch'en Wen-shih 陳文石 . "Ch'ing-tai ti pi-t'ieh-shih" 清代的筆帖式 [Bithesi or Manchu clerks in the Ch'ing period]. *Shih-huo* 食貨 . New series 4, no. 3 (June 1974): 65-76.

Cheng Chao-ching 鄭肇經 . *Chung-kuo shui-li shih* 中國水利史 [History of water conservancy in China]. Ch'ang-sha: Shang-wu, 1939.

Chia Ching-te 賈景德 . *Hsiu-ts'ai chü-jen chin-shih* 秀才舉人進士 [The first, second, and the third degree holders in the Ch'ing dynasty]. Hong Kong: Lien-sheng, 1956.

Chiang Tao-chang. "Salt Industry of China: 1644-1911." Ph.D. diss., University of Hawaii, 1975.

Ch'ien Shih-fu 錢實甫 . *Ch'ing-chi chung-yao chih-kuan nien-piao* 清季重要職官年表 [Chronological tables of important offices of the late Ch'ing period]. Peking: Chung-hua, 1959.

Chu P'ei-lien 朱沛蓮 . *Ch'ing-tai ting-chia lu* 清代鼎甲錄 [Records of the highest ranking graduates of the Ch'ing palace examinations]. Taipei: Chung-hua, 1968.

Ch'ü Tung-tsu. *Local Government in China Under the Ch'ing.* Cambridge: Harvard University Press, 1962.

Chung, A. L. Y. "The Hanlin Academy in the Early Ch'ing Period: 1644-1795." *Journal of the Royal Asiatic Society--Hong Kong Branch* 6 (1966): 100-119.

Evans, Nancy, "The Banner-School Background of the Canton T'ung-wen Kuan." *Papers on China* 22(A) (May, 1969): 89-103.

Fairbank, John K., ed. *Cambridge History of China.* Vols. 10 and 11, *Late Ch'ing, 1800-1911.* Liu Kwang-ching, co-editor (volume 11). Cambridge: Cambridge University Press, 1978, 1980.

Fairbank, John K. "The Manchu-Chinese Dyarchy in the Late 1840s and 1850s." *Far Eastern Quarterly* 12 (May, 1953): 265-78.

Fang Chao-ying. "A Technique for Estimating the Numerical Strength of the Early Manchu Military Forces." *Harvard Journal of Asiatic Studies* 13 (June, 1950): 192-215.

Fang Chao-ying 房兆楹 , and Tu Lien-che 杜連喆 . *Tseng-chiao Ch'ing-ch'ao chin-shih t'i-ming pei-lu* 增校清朝進士題名碑錄 [Lists of holders of the *chin-shih* degree during the Ch'ing dynasty, enlarged, re-edited, and appended with an index]. Peking: Yenching University, 1941.

Feuerwerker, Albert; Rhoads Murphey; and Mary C. Wright; eds. *Approaches to Modern Chinese History*. Berkeley: University of California Press, 1967.

Folsom, Kenneth. *Friends, Guests and Colleagues: the Mu-fu System in the Late Ch'ing Period*. Berkeley: University of California Press, 1968.

Fu Tsung-mao 傅宗懋. *Ch'ing-chih lun-wen chi* 清制論文集 [Collected papers on Ch'ing institutions]. Taipei: Shang-wu, 1977.

_____. "Ch'ing-ch'u i-cheng t'i-chih chih yen-chiu" 清初議政體制之研究 [A study of early Ch'ing decision-making procedures]. *Cheng-chih ta-hsüeh hsüeh-pao* 政治大學學報 11 (1965), 245-94.

_____. "Ch'ing-ch'u t'ung-chih hsing-t'ai chih yen-hua" 清初統治形態之演化 [Changes of forms of political control in the early Ch'ing dynasty]. *Cheng-chih ta-hsüeh hsüeh-pao* 政治大學學報 9 (1964): 339-79.

_____. *Ch'ing-tai Chün-chi-ch'u tsu-chih chi chih-chang chih yen-chiu* 清代軍機處組織及其職掌之研究 [A study of the organization and functions of the Grand Council in the Ch'ing period]. Taipei: Chia-hsin, 1967.

_____. *Ch'ing-tai tu-fu chih-tu* 清代督撫制度 [The institution of the governors-general and governors in the Ch'ing dynasty]. Taiwan: National Cheng-chih University, 1963.

_____. "Ch'ing-tai wen-kuan ch'üeh-fen chih yen-chiu" 清代文官缺分之研究 [A study of categories of official postitions in the Ch'ing civil administration]. *Cheng-chih ta-hsüeh hsüeh-pao* 政治大學學報 21 (May, 1970): 151-75.

Hackmann, Robert Alan. "The Politics of Regional Development: Water Conservancy in Central Kiangsu Province." Ph.D. diss., University of Michigan, 1979.

Hinton, Harold. *Grain Tribute System of China: 1845-1911*. Cambridge: Harvard University Center for East Asian Studies, 1956.

Ho Ping-ti. *The Ladder of Success in Imperial China: Aspects of Social Mobility, 1368-1911*. New York: Columbia University Press, 1962.

Hsiao, I-shan 蕭一山. *Ch'ing-tai t'ung-shih* 清代通史 [A general history of the Ch'ing period]. Revised edition. 5 vols. Taipei: Shang-wu, 1962-63.

Hsieh Pao-chao, *The Government of China: 1644-1911*. Baltimore: Johns Hopkins Press, 1925.

Hsü Ta-ling 許大齡. *Ch'ing-tai chüan-na chih-tu* 清代捐納制度 [The system of purchasing official titles during the Ch'ing dynasty]. Peking: Harvard-Yenching Institute, 1950.

Hsü Tao-lin 徐道隣. "Ch'ing-tai k'ao-shih yü jen-kuan chih-tu" 清代考試與任官制度 [The examination system and bureaucratic appointments in the Ch'ing period]. In *Chung-kuo cheng-chih ssu-hsiang yü chih-tu shih lun-chi* 中國政治思想與制度史論集 [Collected articles on the history of Chinese political thought and institutions]. Edited by Chang Ch'i-yün 張其昀. Vol. 3, 1-22. Taipei: Chung-hua wen-hua ch'u-pan shih-yeh, 1961.

Hu Ch'ang-tu, "The Yellow River Administration in the Ch'ing Dynasty," *Far Eastern Quarterly* 14, no. 4 (August, 1955): 505-513.

Huang Pei, "Aspects of Ch'ing Autocracy: An Institutional Study, 1644-1735." *Ch'ing-hua hsüeh-pao* 清華學報 new series 6, nos. 1-2 (December, 1967): 105-148.

_____. *Autocracy at Work: A Study of the Yung-cheng Period*. Bloomington: Indiana University Press, 1974.

_____. "Yung-cheng shih-tai ti mi-tsou chih-tu" 雍正時代的密奏制度 [Secret-report system during the Yung-cheng reign]. *Ch'ing-hua hsüeh-pao* 清華學報 new series 3, no.1 (May, 1962): 17-52.

Hucker, Charles O. ed., *Chinese Government in Ming Times*. New York: Columbia University Press, 1969.

_____. "Governmental Organization of the Ming Dynasty." *Harvard Journal of Asiatic Studies* 21 (1958): 1-66.

Hummel, A. W. ed., *Eminent Chinese of the Ch'ing Period*. Washington, D.C.: Government Printing Office, 1943-44. 2 vols. Reprint. Taipei: Ch'eng-wen, 1964.

Kahn, Harold. *Monarchy in the Emperor's Eyes: Image and Reality in the Ch'ien-lung Reign*. Cambridge: Harvard University Press, 1971.

Kessler, Lawrence D., "Chinese Scholars and the Early Manchu State." *Harvard Journal of Asiatic Studies* 31 (1971): 179-200.

_____. "Ethnic Composition of Provincial Leadership During the Ch'ing Dynasty." *Journal of Asian Studies* 28 (May 1969): 489-511.

_____. *K'ang-hsi and the Consolidation of Ch'ing Rule, 1661-1684*. Chicago: University of Chicago Press, 1976.

Kindai Chūgoku kenkyū iinkai 近代中國研究委員會 [Committee on Research into Modern China]. *Keisei bumpen sō-mokuroku* 經世文編總目錄 [Comprehensive index to various collections of writings on statecraft]. 3 vols. Tokyo: n.p., 1956.

Kuan Tung-kuei 管東貴 . "Ju-kuan ch'ien Man-tsu ping-shu yu jen-k'ou wen-t'i ti t'an-t'ao" 入關前滿族兵數與人口問題的探討 [A study of the numbers of Manchu troops and the size of Manchu population prior to 1644]. *Bulletin, Institute of History and Philology* (Academia Sinica) 41, pt. 2 (1969): 179-94.

_____. "Man-tsu ju-kuan ch'ien ti wen-hua fa-chang tui t'a-men hou-lai Han-hua ti yin-hsiang" 滿族入關前的文化發展對他們後來漢化的影響 [The influence of the cultural development of the Manchus prior to 1644 on their subsequent sinicization]. *Bulletin, Institute of History and Philology* (Academia Sinica) 40, pt. 1 (1968): 255-80.

Kuhn, Philip A. *Rebellion and its Enemies in Late Imperial China: Militarization and Social Structures 1796-1864*. Cambridge, Harvard University Press, 1970.

Li Kuang-t'ao 李光濤 . "Ch'ing-shih-kao Shun-chih ch'ao chiang-ch'en piao ting-wu" 清史禍順治朝疆臣表訂誤 [Correction of errors found in the "Lists of governors-general and governors during the Shun-chih reign," a section of the draft history of the Ch'ing dynasty]. *Bulletin, Institute of History and Philology* (Academia Sinica) 24 (1953): 135-44.

Li Kuo-ch'i 李國祁 . "Ming-Ch'ing liang-tai ti-fang hsing-cheng chih-tu chung tao ti kung-neng chi ch'i yen-pien" 明清兩代地方行政制度中道的功能及其演變 [The functions and evolution of the office of intendant in the Ming and Ch'ing local administrations]. *Bulletin, Institute of Modern History* (Academia Sinica) 3, pt. 1 (1972): 139-88.

Li Kuo-ch'i, 李國祁 Chou T'ien-sheng 周天生 , and Hsu Hung-i 許弘義. *Ch'ing-tai chi-ts'eng ti-fang-kuan jen-shih shan-ti hsien-hsiang chih liang-hua fen-hsi* 清代基層地方官人事嬗遞現象之量化分析 [A quantitative analysis of the careers of prefects and magistrates in the Ch'ing dynasty]. 3 vols. Taipei: National Science Council, 1975.

_____. "Ch'ing-tai chi-ts'eng ti-fang-kuan jen-shih shan-ti hsien-hsiang chih liang-hua fen-hsi" 清代基層地方官人事嬗遞現象之量化分析 [A quantitative analysis of the careers of prefects and magistrates in the Ch'ing dynasty]. *Taiwan Shih-fan ta-hsueh li-shih hsueh-pao* 台灣師範大學歷史學報 2 (February 1974): 301-84.

Li Tsung-t'ung 李宗侗 . "Ch'ing-tai chung-yang cheng-ch'üan hsing-t'ai ti yen-pien" 清代中央政權形態的演變 [Changes in the forms of political control in the central government during the Ch'ing dynasty]. *Bulletin, Institute of History and Philology* (Academia Sinica) 31, no. 1 (March 1967): 79-158.

Liu Chia-chü 劉家駒 . "Ch'ing-ch'u Han-chün pa-ch'i ti chao-chien" 清初漢軍八旗的肇建 [The creation of the eight Chinese banners in the early Ch'ing]. Pt. 1,2. *Ta-lu tsa-chih* 大陸雜誌 34, no. 11 (1967): 13-18, no. 12 (1967): 17-19.

Liu Kwang-ching. "Li Hung-chang in Chihli: the Emergence of a Policy, 1870-1875," in Albert Feuerwerker, Rhoads Murphey, and Mary C. Wright, eds. *Approaches to Modern Chinese History*, 68-104. Berkeley: University of California Press, 1967.

_____. "The Limits of Regional Power in the Late Ch'ing Period: a Reappraisal." *Ch'ing-hua hsüeh-pao* 清華學報 10, no. 2 (July 1974): 207-223.

Lo Erh-kang 羅爾綱. "Ch'ing-chi ping wei chiang-yu ti ch'i-yüan" 清季兵為將有的起源 [The original of personal armies in the late Ch'ing period]. in *Chung-kuo chin-tai-shih lun-ts'ung* 中國近代史論叢 [Collection of articles on modern Chinese history]. Edited by Wu Hsiang-hsiang 吳相相. 2d series, vol. 5, 85-100. Taipei: Cheng-chung, 1963.

Lui Adam Y. C. *The Hanlin Academy.* Hamden, Connecticut: Shoe String Press, 1981.

_____. "The Ch'ing Civil Service: Promotions, Demotions, Transfers, Leaves, Dismissals and Retirements." *Journal of Oriental Studies* 8, no. 2 (July 1970): 333-56.

_____. "The Practical Training of Government Officials Under the Early Ch'ing, 1644-1795," *Asia Major* new series, 16 (January 1971): 82-95.

Ma Ch'i-hua 馬其華. "Ch'ing Shih-tsung chi ch'i chih-shu" 清世宗及其治術 [Emperor Yung-cheng and his method of governing]. *Tung-fang tsa-chih* 東方雜誌. 1, no. 7 (1968): 82-91.

Ma Feng-ch'en 馬奉琛. *Ch'ing-tai hsing-cheng chih-tu yen-chiu ts'an-k'ao shu-mu* 清代 行政制度研究參考書目 [Bibliography of research materials on the Ch'ing administrative system]. Peking: Peking University, 1935.

Marsh, Robert M., *The Mandarins: The Circulations of Elites in China, 1600-1900.* Glencoe, Ill.: Free Press, 1961.

Meng Sen 孟森. "Pa-ch'i chih-tu k'ao-shih" 八旗制度考實 [A critical study of the eight banner system]. *Bulletin, Institute of History and Philology* (Academia Sinica) 6, no. 3 (1936): 343-412.

Meng Ssu-ming. *The Tsungli-Yamen: Its Organization and Functions.* Cambridge: Harvard University Press, East Asian Research Center, 1962.

Meskill, John. "A Conferral of the Degree of Chin-shih," *Monumenta Serica* 23 (1964): 351-71.

Metzger, Thomas. *The Internal Organization of Ch'ing Bureaucracy.* Cambridge: Harvard University Press, 1973.

_____. "T'ao Chu's Reform of the Huai-pei Salt Monopoly, 1831-1833." *Papers on China* 16 (1962): 1-39.

Michael, Franz, "Military Organization and Power Structure of China During the Taiping Rebellion." *Pacific Historical Review* 18 (November 1949): 469-83.

_____. *The Origin of Manchu Rule in China.* New York: Octagon Books, 1965.

Nishimura Genshō 西村元照. *Nihon genson Shinjin bunshu mokuroku* 日本現存清人文集目錄 [Catalogue of individual collected works of Ch'ing authors found in Japanese libraries]. Kyoto: Toyoshi Kenkyu Kai, 1972.

Nivison, David. "Ho-shen and His Accusers: Ideology and Political Behaviour in the Eighteenth Century." In *Confucianism in Action,* edited by David Nivison and Arthur Wright, 209-43. Stanford: Stanford University Press, 1959.

Oxnam, Robert B.. "Policies and Institutions of the Oboi Regency, 1661-1669." *Journal of Asian Studies* 32, no. 2 (February 1973): 265-86.

_____. *Ruling from Horseback.* Chicago: University of Chicago Press, 1975.

P'eng, Yü-hsin 彭雨新. "Ch'ing-mo Chung-yang yü ko sheng ts'ai-cheng kuan-hsi" [The fiscal relationship between central government and the provinces during the late Ch'ing]. In *Chung-kuo chin-tai-shih lun-ts'ung* 中國近代史論叢 [Collection of articles on modern Chinese history], edited by Wu Hsiang-hsiang 吳相相. 2d series, vol. 5, 3-46. Taipei: Cheng-chung, 1963.

Powell, Ralph L. *The Rise of Chinese Military Power, 1895-1912.* Princeton: Princeton University Press, 1955.

Saeki Tomi 佐伯富. *Ch'ing-tai Yung-cheng ch'ao ti yang-lien-yin yen-chiu* 清代雍正朝的養廉銀研究 [A study of the "fund to nourish honesty" during the Yung-cheng reign]. Translated from Japanese by Cheng Liang-shen 鄭樑生. Taipei: Shang-wu, 1976.

Shang Yen-liu 商衍鎏. *Ch'ing-tai k'o-chü k'ao-shih shu-lu* 清代科舉考試述錄 [A descriptive account of the civil service examination under the Ch'ing]. Peking: San-lien, 1958.

Shen Nai-cheng 沈乃正. "Ch'ing-mo chih Tu-fu chi-ch'üan" 清末之督撫集權 [The accumulation of power of governors-general and governors towards the end of the Ch'ing dynasty]. *She-hui k'o-hsüeh* 社會科學 2, no. 2 (January 1937): 311-42.

Shinkoku gyōseiho 清國行政法 [Administrative laws of the Ch'ing state]. Compiled by Rinji Taiwan Kyūkan chōsakai 臨時臺灣舊慣調查會 [Commission of the Taiwan government-general for the study of old Chinese customs]. 5 vols. Tokyo: n.p., 1905-1911.

Skinner, G. William, and Winston Hsieh. *Modern Chinese Society: An Analytical Bibliography*. 3 vols. Stanford: Stanford University Press, 1973.

Spector, Stanley. *Li Hung-chang and the Huai Army*. Seattle: University of Washington Press, 1964.

Spence, Jonathon. "The Seven Ages of K'ang-hsi, 1654-1722." *Journal of Asian Studies* 26, no. 2 (February 1967): 205-11.

_____. *Ts'ao Yin and the K'ang-hsi Emperor: Bondservant and Master*. New Haven: Yale Unviersity Press, 1966.

Sun, I-tu Zen. "The Board of Revenue in Nineteenth-Century China." *Harvard Journal of Asiatic Studies* 24 (1962-63): 175-227.

_____. *Ch'ing Administrative Terms*. Cambridge: Harvard University Press, 1961.

T'ao Hsi-sheng 陶希聖. *Ming-Ch'ing cheng-chih chih-tu* 明清政治制度 [Political system of the Ming and Ch'ing dynasty]. Taipei: Shang-wu, 1967.

Teng Ch'ing-p'ing 鄧青平. "Ch'ing Yung-cheng nien-chien (1723-1735), ti wen-kuan yang-lien chih-tu" 清雍正年間(1723-1735)的文官養廉制度 [The system of providing a "fund to nourish honesty" for civil officials during the Yung-cheng reign (1723-1735]. *Hsin-ya hsüeh-pao* 新亞學報 10, no. 1, pt. 2 (July 1973): 249-336.

Teng Ssu-yü 鄧嗣禹. *Chung-kuo k'ao-shih chih-tu shih* 中國考試制度史 [The history of the examination system in China]. Taipei: Hsueh-sheng, 1967.

_____. *The Nien Army and Their Guerrilla Warfare, 1851-1868*. Paris: Mouton, 1961.

Toyo Bunko Mambun Rōtō Kenkyūkai 東洋文庫滿文老檔研究會 [Society for the study of early Manchu documents held in the Toyo Bunko]. *Hakki tsūshi retsuden sakuin* 八旗通志列人專索引 [Index to the biographies in the general history of the eight banners]. Tokyo: Toyo Bunko, 1965.

Tu Lien-che 杜連詰, and Fang Chao-ying 房兆楹. *San-shih-san chung Ch'ing-tai chuan-chi tsung-ho yin-te* 三十三種清代傳記綜合引得 [Index to thirty-three collections of Ch'ing dynasty biographies]. Peking: Yenching University Library, 1932.

Van der Sprenkel, Sybille M. *Legal Institutions in Manchu China*. London: University of London Press, 1966.

Wakeman, Frederick, Jr., "High Ch'ing: 1683-1839." In *Modern East Asia*, edited by James B. Crowley, 1-28. New York: Harcourt, Brace and World, 1970.

Wang Ch'ung-min 王重民. *Ch'ing-tai wen-chi p'ien-mu fen-lei so-yin* 清代文集篇目分類索引 [Classified index to essays contained in individual collected works of Ch'ing authors]. Taipei: Kuo-feng, 1965.

Wang Erh-min 王爾敏. "Nan-pei yang ta-ch'en chih chien-chih chi ch'i ch'üan-li chih k'uo-chang" 南北洋大臣之建置及其權力之擴張 [The establishment of the offices of the superintendents of trade for southern and for northern ports and the expansion of their power]. *Ta-lu tsa-chih* 大陸雜誌 20, no. 5 (March 1960): 152-59.

Wang Yeh-chien 王業鍵. "Ch'ing Yung-cheng shih-ch'i (1723-35) ti ts'ai-cheng kai-ke" 清雍正時期(1723-35)的財政改革 [Fiscal reform during the Yung-cheng reign (1723-35)]. *Bulletin, Institute of History and Philology*, (Academia Sinica) 33 (1961): 47-76.

_____. *Land Taxation in Imperial China, 1750-1911*. Cambridge: Harvard University Press, 1973.

Watt, John R. *The District Magistrate in Late Imperial China*. New York: Columbia University Press, 1972.

Wei Hsiu-mei 魏秀梅. *Ch'ing-chi chih-kuan piao* 清季職官表 [Offices and personnel in the late Ch'ing period]. 2 vols. Taipei: Institute of Modern History, Academia Sinica, 1977.

———. "Ts'ung liang ti kuan-ch'a t'an-t'ao Ch'ing-chi an-cha-shih ti jen-shih shan-ti" 從量的觀察探討清季按察使的人事嬗遞 [A quantitative analysis of the careers of provincial judicial commissioners of the late Ch'ing period]. *Bulletin, Institute of Modern History* (Academia Sinica) 3, pt. 2 (1972): 475-95.

———. "Ts'ung liang ti Kuan-ch'a t'an-t'ao Ch'ing-chi pu-cheng-shih chih jen-shih ti-shan hsien-hsiang" 從量的觀察探討清季布政使之人事遞嬗現象 [A quantitative analysis of the careers of provincial financial commissioners of the late Ch'ing period]. *Bulletin, Institute of Modern History* (Academia Sinica) 2 (1971): 505-533.

———. "Ts'ung liang ti kuan-ch'a t'an-t'ao Ch'ing-chi tu-fu jen-shih shan-ti" 從量的觀察探討清季督撫人事嬗遞 [A quantitative analysis of the careers of governers-general and governors of the Ch'ing period]. *Bulletin, Institute of Modern History* (Academia Sinica) 4, pt. 1 (1973): 259-91.

Wong, J. Y. *Yeh Ming-ch'en: Viceroy of Liang Kuang, 1852-1858*. Cambridge: Cambridge University Press, 1976.

Wu, Silas Hsiu-liang, "The Memorial System of the Ch'ing Dynasty." *Harvard Journal of Asiatic Studies* 27 (1967): 7-75.

———. *Communication and Imperial Control in China*. Cambridge: Harvard University Press, 1970.

———. *Passage to Power: K'ang-hsi and His Heir Apparent, 1661-1722*. Cambridge: Harvard University Press, 1979.

MICHIGAN MONOGRAPHS IN CHINESE STUDIES

No. 3. *Two Studies in Chinese Literature*, by Li Chi and Dale Johnson.
Early Communist China: Two Studies, by Ronald Suleski and Daniel Bays.

No. 5. *The Chinese Economy, ca. 1870-1911*, by Albert Feuerwerker.

No. 7. *The Treaty Ports and China's Modernization: What Went Wrong?*, by Rhoads Murphey.

No. 8. *Two Twelfth Century Texts on Chinese Painting*, by Robert J. Maeda.

No. 10. *Educated Youth and the Cultural Revolution in China*, by Martin Singer.

No. 11. *Premodern China: A Bibliographical Introduction*, by Chun-shu Chang.

No. 12. *Two Studies on Ming History*, by Charles O. Hucker.

No. 13. *Nineteenth-Century China: Five Imperialist Perspectives*, selected by Dilip Basu and edited by Rhoads Murphey.

No. 14. *Modern China, 1840-1972: An Introduction to Sources and Research Aids*, by Andrew J. Nathan.

No. 15. *Women in China: Studies in Social Change and Feminism*, edited by Marilyn B. Young.

No. 17. *China's Allocation of Fixed Capital Investment, 1952-1957*, by Chu-yuan Cheng.

No. 18. *Health, Conflict, and the Chinese Political System*, by David M. Lampton.

No. 19. *Chinese and Japanese Music-Dramas*, edited by J. I. Crump and William P. Malm.

No. 21. *Rebellion in Nineteenth-Century China*, by Albert Feuerwerker.

No. 22. *Between Two Plenums: China's Intraleadership Conflict, 1959-1962*, by Ellis Joffe.

No. 23. *"Proletarian Hegemony" in the Chinese Revolution and the Canton Commune of 1927*, by S. Bernard Thomas.

No. 24. *Chinese Communist Materials at the Bureau of Investigation Archives, Taiwan*, by Peter Donovan, Carl E. Dorris, and Lawrence R. Sullivan.

No. 25. *Shanghai's Old-Style Banks (Ch'ien-chuang), 1800-1935*, by Andrea Lee McElderry.

No. 26. *The Sian Incident: A Pivotal Point in Modern Chinese History*, by Tien-wei Wu.

No. 27. *State and Society in Eighteenth-Century China: The Ch'ing Empire in Its Glory*, by Albert Feuerwerker.

No. 28. *Intellectual Ferment for Political Reforms in Taiwan, 1971-1973*, by Mab Huang.

No. 29. *The Foreign Establishment in China in the Early Twentieth Century*, by Albert Feuerwerker.

No. 30. *A Translation of Lao Tzu's Tao Te Ching and Wang Pi's Commentary*, by Paul J. Lin.

No. 31. *Economic Trends in the Republic of China, 1912-1949*, by Albert Feuerwerker.

No. 33. *Central Documents and Politburo Politics in China*, by Kenneth Lieberthal.

No. 34. *The Ming Dynasty: Its Origins and Evolving Institutions*, by Charles O. Hucker.

No. 35. *Double Jeopardy: A Critique of Seven Yuan Courtroom Dramas*, by Ching-hsi Perng.

No. 36. *Chinese Domestic Politics and Foreign Policy in the 1970s*, by Allen S. Whiting.

No. 37. *Shanghai, 1925: Urban Nationalism and the Defense of Foreign Privilege*, by Nicholas R. Clifford.

No. 38. *Voices from Afar: Modern Chinese Writers on Oppressed Peoples and Their Literature*, by Irene Eber.

No. 39. *Mao Zedong's "Talks at the Yan'an Conference on Literature and Art": A Translation of the 1943 Text with Commentary*, by Bonnie S. McDougall.

No. 40. *Yuarn Music Dramas: Studies in Prosody and Structure and a Complete Catalogue of Northern Arias in the Dramatic Style,* by Dale R. Johnson.

No. 41. *Proclaiming Harmony,* translated by William O. Hennessey.

No. 42. *A Song for One or Two: Music and the Concept of Art in Early China,* by Kenneth DeWoskin.

No. 43. *The Economic Development of Manchuria: The Rise of a Frontier Economy,* by Kang Chao.

No. 44. *A Bibliography of Chinese-Language Materials on the People's Communes,* by Wei-i Ma.

No. 45. *Chinese Social and Economic History from the Song to 1900,* edited by Albert Feuerwerker.

No. 46. *China's Universities: Post-Mao Enrollment Policies and Their Impact on the Structure of Secondary Education,* by Suzanne Pepper.

No. 47. *Songs from Xanadu,* by J. I. Crump.

No. 48. *Social Organization in South China, 1911-1949: The Case of The Kuan Lineage of K'ai-p'ing County,* by Yuen-fong Woon.

No. 49. *Labor and the Chinese Revolution,* by S. Bernard Thomas (cloth only).

No. 50. *Soviet Studies of Premodern China: Assessments of Recent Scholarship,* edited by Gilbert Rozman.

No. 51. *Career Patterns in the Ch'ing Dynasty: The Office of the Governor-General,* by Raymond W. Chu and William G. Saywell.

No. 52. *Individualism and Holism: Studies in Confucian and Taoist Values,* edited by Donald J. Munro.

No. 53. *Aspects of Educational Reform in China at the Beginning of the Twentieth Century,* by Marianne Bastid, translated by Paul J. Bailey.

No. 54. *The Red Spears, 1916-49,* by Tai Hsuan-chih, translated by Ronald Suleski, with an introduction by Elizabeth Perry.

MICHIGAN ABSTRACTS OF CHINESE AND JAPANESE WORKS ON CHINESE HISTORY

No. 1. *The Ming Tribute Grain System,* by Hoshi Ayao, translated by Mark Elvin.

No. 2. *Commerce and Society in Sung China,* by Shiba Yoshinobu, translated by Mark Elvin.

No. 3. *Transport in Transition: The Evolution of Traditional Shipping In China,* translated by Andrew Watson.

No. 4. *Japanese Perspectives on China's Early Modernization: A Bibliographical Survey,* by K. M. Kim.

No. 5. *The Silk Industry in Ch'ing China,* by Shih Min-hsiung, translated by E-tu Zen Sun.

No. 6. *The Pawnshop in China,* by T. S. Whelan.

Michigan Monographs and Abstracts available from:

Center for Chinese Studies
The University of Michigan
104 Lane Hall (Publications)
Ann Arbor, Michigan 48109 USA